GETTING
OUT

By Edgar Smith

BRIEF AGAINST DEATH

A REASONABLE DOUBT

GETTING OUT

GETTING OUT

Edgar Smith

Coward, McCann & Geoghegan, Inc.

 New York

To

WILLIAM F. BUCKLEY, JR.,

for everything

Prologue

You, Edgar Smith, were indicted by the Bergen County Grand Jury under indictment No. S-276-56 for the murder of Victoria Zielinski at Mahwah, Bergen County, New Jersey, on the night of March 4, 1957, and at your trial under said indictment for murder the trial jury found you guilty of murder in the first degree without any recommendation of life imprisonment. You are therefore adjudged guilty of murder in the first degree. Do you have anything to say before the Court imposes sentence?

No, Sir.

For the reason that the statute N.J.S. 2A: 113-4 mandates that every person convicted of murder in the first degree shall suffer death unless the jury by its verdict recommends life imprisonment, you are sentenced to the judgment and punishment of death at the hand of the Principal Keeper of the New Jersey State Prison at Trenton during the week commencing Monday, July 15, 1957.

The defendant will be remanded by the Sheriff of Bergen County to the Principal Keeper of the New Jersey State Prison at Trenton, there to await execution of this sentence at that time in the place and the manner provided for by law.

AND MAY GOD HAVE MERCY ON YOUR SOUL.

How I came to be sitting on Death Row in the twenty-third year of my life is fully recounted in my first book, *Brief Against Death* (Alfred A. Knopf, Inc., New York, 1968), in which I described every facet of my case from my arrest in 1957 through what was to be my final appeal to the United States Supreme Court in 1968. For the benefit of those unfamiliar with the basic facts of the crime and my arrest, the following is a brief, concise summary taken from a document filed in the Supreme Court:

"A fifteen year old Ramsey, New Jersey girl, Victoria Zielinski, was found brutally murdered in Mahwah (an adjoining town) on the morning of March 5, 1957.

"During the evening of March 5, 1957 one of Smith's friends, Joseph Gilroy, told the Ramsey police that he had found suspicious stains on the seat and floor of his car, which he had lent to Smith the previous evening.

"After inspecting Gilroy's car at about 10:45 p.m. that evening, Detective Graber and Investigator Garabedian from the Bergen County Prosecutor's Office, along with Gilroy, went to Smith's mother-in-law's home in Ridgewood. At about 11:30 p.m. they picked up Smith there and brought him to police headquarters in Mahwah. Present at headquarters were Prosecutor Guy Calissi, First Assistant Prosecutor Fred Galda, Chief Smith of Mahwah, and numerous newspaper reporters.

"During the questioning—chiefly by First Assistant Prosecutor Galda—Captain DeMarco noticed that Smith's left hand was lacerated. Smith stated that he had hurt it while repairing an automobile tailpipe. Examination of Smith's knees revealed lacerations, contusions, and scratches which he explained had happened when he fell out of a car after becoming ill the previous evening. Petitioner stated that he had vomited over his pants and shoes which he was wearing; that he had thrown them away and would show the officers where they were. Smith accompanied Galda and three police officers to a place in Ramsey where he pointed out a garbage can where he had thrown away his shoes. After retrieving the shoes (later found to be stained with blood), the group drove to the sand pit [the scene of the crime] where Smith pointed out the area where he said he had vomited. A large light was used by the police during the search, but nothing was developed. From there the group went to Smith's trailer home to obtain some clothing he had worn the night before. While at the trailer, Smith stated that the jacket he had worn the night before was at his mother-in-law's home in Ridgewood and had been recently washed. They then drove to where Smith said he had thrown his pants after being sick on them. They searched the area until about 3:00 a.m. without success. On the return trip to Mahwah they searched another area where Smith said he had first been sick—again without success.

"After arriving at Mahwah Police Headquarters about 3:30 a.m. a detective went to Ridgewood to pick up Smith's jacket. At headquarters there was further conversation with regard to the clothing Smith wore on the previous night and there was some discussion as to the possibility of again looking for the pants. At this time Smith was seated in the back of the room with Gilroy and another person. Petitioner then advised the officers that he could explain about any blood which might have been found on his shoes previously retrieved. Coffee and buns were brought in for everyone including Smith, the police, and some of the others being questioned.

"Between 3:00 a.m. and 3:45 a.m. the officers and Smith again went to look for the place he had vomited and where he threw his pants. Smith assisted in the search by pointing out the area where he had allegedly thrown up and where he throw his pants, again without success. The group then returned to headquarters, arriving there 'quite late.'

"Around 5:00 a.m. arrangements were made to have Smith examined by Dr. Gilady [the county medical examiner] with respect to his knee injuries. Accordingly, the examination was scheduled between 7:30 a.m. and 8:00 a.m. Smith, Detective Sinatra, and Captain DeMarco then drove to the latter's home. There Captain DeMarco gave Detective Sinatra some money with the instructions that he and Smith have some breakfast prior to the visit to Dr. Gilady's office. Smith testified that he ate two eggs and a cup of coffee. After breakfast Smith and Detective Sinatra returned to Captain DeMarco's home and the three drove to Dr. Gilady's office; the examination was conducted at 7:55 a.m. The doctor found Smith to be alert and in normal health; his pulse and respiration were normal.

"After the examination the three went to the prosecutor's office [in the Bergen County Courthouse in Hackensack]. There, Captain DeMarco called a photographer to take pictures of Smith's hand and knees. About this time the Prosecutor's Office was informed that the pants had been found, stained with blood, as were a pair of socks in the pocket. Fingernail scrapings and hair samples were taken from Smith.

"After pictures of Smith were taken, Detectives DeLisle and Spahr questioned him about 10:00 a.m. as to his activities on the night of the murder. Detective DeLisle asked Smith, 'What did the girl do to you?' and he responded, 'She hit me.' He then asked Smith, 'Where did she hit you?' and he answered, 'In the face.' Thereupon Smith started crying. He asked for a drink of water and a cigarette, which he was given. Smith then asked to speak with a certain priest that he knew at Don Bosco High School; the priest was called.

"Prior to the arrival of the priest and after Smith was more composed, he told the detectives of his meeting with Victoria Zielinski. About forty-five minutes later the priest arrived and conferred with Smith for approximately a half hour. Smith then gave the Prosecutor a full statement, stenographically recorded under oath. The statement commenced at 12:50 p.m.

on March 6th and was continued in the vicinity of the crime. The statement was concluded at 3:45 p.m. and covered thirty-nine pages. Smith was then brought to Mahwah for arraignment, arriving there at about 4:05 p.m.; he was arraigned at about 7:00 p.m. that evening.

"After the written statement given by Smith had been prepared in stenographic form, Detective DeLisle visited Smith in the Bergen County jail on March 11, 1957 for the purpose of having him read and sign it. At this time Smith was under indictment and had retained counsel. After reading the statement for about 35 minutes, Smith refused to sign it on the advice of his lawyer. Detective DeLisle then asked Smith if the statement was accurate and Smith said 'Yes, it was accurate.'"

The foregoing description of the events surrounding my arrest and interrogation by the police was taken from a brief filed in the United States Supreme Court by the Bergen County prosecutor, and while it is sufficient to give the reader a general picture of those events, the reader will see, as the story unfolds in this book, how the prosecutor, through distortion of the facts, glossing over the truth, various strategic omissions, and at times outright inaccuracy, sought to present to the Court a picture quite divorced from reality.

Arrested on March 6, 1957, I was indicted March 8, arraigned on the indictment March 11, and my trial began two months later on May 14. The trial lasted two weeks, and at the end the jury, after 2 hours and 20 minutes in the jury room, including time to have lunch, found me guilty of murder in the first degree. One week later, on June 4, Bergen County Judge Arthur J. O'Dea pronounced sentence. What followed was, I believe, the longest continuous criminal litigation in American judicial history, and before it was over, I would have spent more time in a Death Row cell than any man before me—exactly 14 years and 9 months.

The sentence of death pronounced by Judge O'Dea was

stayed automatically by a mandatory appeal to the New Jersey Supreme Court. That court affirmed the conviction and sentence one year later. A few months later a petition to the United States district court for a writ of habeas corpus was denied without prejudice because of my failure to exhaust every state court remedy. Immediately thereafter my attorneys moved in the Bergen County Court for a new trial on the basis of newly discovered evidence. The motion was denied by Judge O'Dea, and his denial was upheld by the New Jersey Supreme Court in June, 1959. The following November the United States Supreme Court denied review.

A second attempt to secure a writ of habeas corpus in the United States district court was denied in January, 1962, and I was beginning to learn how slowly the courts moved once a man had been convicted and imprisoned.

My attorneys, retained by my family, withdrew from the case following the denial of a writ of habeas corpus, since my family could no longer afford to pay for their services. A few days later, having written to the chief judge of the United States court of appeals in Philadelphia, pleading for assignment of an attorney, I became the first man in New Jersey history to have a lawyer assigned by a federal court to appeal a state conviction. The appeal was denied by that court in the spring of 1963, but for the first time a judge had voted in my favor. The vote against me was 2–1. A petition for reconsideration was denied by a vote of 5–2. A few months later the United States Supreme Court for the second time refused to review the case.

Although 1962 and 1963 were years of unsuccessful appeals to the federal courts, one event took place in 1962 which was to alter irrevocably the course of my life and which would prove decisive in my fight to remain alive and regain my freedom. William F. Buckley, Jr., entered my life.

It happened almost by accident. A friend, a newspaper reporter for a small New Jersey weekly, wrote and asked me what magazines and books I had been reading. One of the magazines I mentioned in my reply was Buckley's *National Review*. The friend mentioned that in a feature story he did about my case a few weeks later, someone saw the story, clipped it out and sent it to Buckley, and a short while later Buckley wrote and asked me how I had obtained his magazine. His subscription lists indicated I was not a subscriber. When I replied that I had borrowed a copy from someone in the prison, he wrote back and offered me a free subscription.

For the next month or two Buckley and I wrote back and forth, most of my letters being in response to his questions about my case, and finally, in September, 1962, he wrote and asked me to arrange for someone, a lawyer or investigator familiar with the case, to meet with him and brief him on the background. Such a meeting was arranged, the correspondence continued, and then, suddenly, for no reason I could understand, the "Dear Mr. Smith" and "Dear Mr. Buckley" letters had changed to "Dear Edgar" and "Dear Bill," and a warm, close friendship had begun to develop.

People ask me why. Why would Bill Buckley be interested in a man on Death Row? Surely he was no bleeding-heart liberal, and just as surely he didn't need the publicity that would result from the association. What then? Truthfully, I haven't any idea. I didn't ask him when the friendship began to develop, I never asked him while he was fighting to keep me alive, and I don't intend to ask him now. It is enough to say there was never a time when he was needed that he did not make himself available, no matter that he had to get up at 5:00 A.M. to drive to the Death House to visit me, no matter that he had to rush away from a White House luncheon in a chartered helicopter to be where I needed him, no matter that it cost him many thousands of dollars out of his own pocket when I was broke and unable to pay my legal expenses. No matter what. The man literally kept me alive. He picked me up when I was down, knocked me down when I got too cocky, encouraged me, chided me, inspired me, guided me, and above all, above everything else, even above the fact that he did keep me alive, he taught me what true friendship is all about. For that, for everything, I owe him everything.

The attorney assigned by the federal court to represent me was forced to withdraw from the case early in 1964 when I had exhausted every avenue of federal appeal and the court would no longer pay his expenses. The only thing left for me to do was (a) ask Bill Buckley to put up the money to retain a lawyer for me or (b) act as my own lawyer. My pride, which often overrides my common sense, led me to select the latter course. I wrote a petition to the Bergen County Court for a new trial. That petition was denied by Judge O'Dea in March, 1964, and three months later the New Jersey Supreme Court for the third time unanimously refused to overturn the conviction and sentence. I then filed for review in the United States Supreme Court, my third petition to that court, and again the Court refused to consider the case.

In 1965 Bill Buckley and I sat down to decide what to do. We knew that my only chance lay in the federal courts, but in order to win there every possible avenue of state court review had to be exhausted and all the procedural forms had to be followed. We reached a decision: I would again file an appeal to the Bergen County Court, this time for a writ of habeas corpus, making certain that it contained every ground for a new trial that I would want later to take before the federal courts. I would take that petition through the New Jersey appellate system, step by step, and while I was doing that, Bill would write an article about my case for *Esquire*, asking the readers to contribute funds for my defense. Hopefully, the article would bring me to national attention, and by the time I had exhausted all the state avenues of appeal we would have the money to retain lawyers to fight my appeals on the federal level.

Judge O'Dea praised the legal abilities I displayed in my

petition for a writ of habeas corpus, filed before him in April, 1965, but in the same breath he denied the petition. The New Jersey Supreme Court, again unanimously, refused to permit me to appeal Judge O'Dea's ruling. A petition for reconsideration was also denied by that court. On Good Friday, 1965, Associate Justice William Brennan of the United States Supreme Court issued a stay of execution to permit me to file an appeal in the federal court. Justice Brennan's order came four days before my scheduled execution as a result of a new execution date set by Judge O'Dea.

In July, 1965, I filed in the United States District Court for the District of New Jersey the petition denied by Judge O'Dea and which the New Jersey Supreme Court refused unanimously even to consider. It would take time, a couple more years, but in the end, the United States district court, the United States court of appeals, and the United States Supreme Court each would rule unanimously that that petition set forth facts sufficient to overturn my conviction and set aside my death sentence.

As a result of Buckley's article in *Esquire*, sufficient funds were collected to enable me to retain a lawyer, and I selected Stephen F. Lichtenstein, of Trenton, who had been the lawyer assigned to me by the federal court two years earlier. Lichtenstein did a tremendous job for me, but in June, 1966, the United States district court ruled that my petition presented nothing new, and the writ of habeas corpus was denied. That ruling was affirmed by the United States court of appeals, but once again the vote was 2–1. The stage was now set for what would probably be my last appeal, my fourth attempt to convince the United States Supreme Court that my case merited review by that court.

At that same time that planning commenced for the appeal to the Supreme Court, Alfred A. Knopf, Inc., informed me that it would publish my first book, *Brief Against Death*, on September 4, 1968, just a month or two before the Supreme

Court would rule on my appeal. I was pleased, of course. Not only because I had proved to myself that I could write, but more importantly, because the publisher had paid a sizable enough advance that, for a time at least, my worries over funds to retain lawyers and pay their expenses were at an end, and I no longer had to rely on the charity and friendship of Bill Buckley.

The stage was set. What follows is the story of the climactic battle for my freedom, beginning with that fourth appeal to the United States Supreme Court and ending with a proceeding in the Bergan County Court that I can describe no other way than as "judicial theater." It is more than a story of one man's fight for freedom. It is a story about a judicial system so intent upon self-justification, so concerned with its own image, so unable to admit its own errors that in the end it must strike a bargain, make a deal so transparent, so patently outrageous and cynical as to forfeit whatever respect to which that system may have been entitled in the past.

Many readers will be shocked when they read how their judicial system really operates behind the closed doors of judges' chambers or when the public is barred from the courtroom. Others will be saddened. None will be proud of his system.

In the Prologue to *Brief Against Death*, I ended with the question: "Did Justice triumph?" Today, four years later, my fight ended and my freedom a reality, that question remains as valid as when it was first asked.

Did Justice triumph?

Each reader will have to find his own answer.

GETTING OUT

Chapter One

January, 1968

Eight months before *Brief Against Death* was to be published and just a few weeks after the rejection of my second appeal to the United States court of appeals, Bill Buckley visited me for a long heart-to-heart talk about my situation. The next step in the long fight to avoid execution would be a petition to the United States Supreme Court for a writ of certiorari. It would be my fifteenth appeal, my fourth to the Supreme Court.

The court of appeals had ruled, in a 2–1 vote, that the issues presented in my appeal had been fully decided by that court in 1963 and that a further hearing was not required because I had waived my right to a hearing during a 1959 federal court appeal. The court of appeals was wrong on both counts. I knew it was wrong, and I said so in *Brief Against Death*, scheduled for publication before the Supreme Court would hear the matter:

> To say that the majority statement is wrong is an understatement. The decision is so wrong, so contrary to fact and law, that one is led to believe that the majority based its

decision solely upon the desire to avoid taking a stand on the issues, on the merits of my claims; it is too wrong to be simply an error in judgment.

The dissenting judge in the court of appeals, whose dissent covered 14 pages of the 18-page printed opinion, said it all when he wrote: "I cannot deem the examination of this issue to have been sufficient to meet constitutional requirements."

Not only could I not have waived in 1959 the right to a hearing when that right did not exist until four years later, but moreover, the court could not have decided the issues in 1963 since the Supreme Court rulings controlling those issues did not come into existence until 1964, 1965, and 1966.

Bill Buckley and I discussed the problem at great length that January afternoon. As the court of appeals had taught me for the second time, it is never enough to be right when one goes to court, never enough to have the facts and law on one's side, for if the court will not hear the case, all tne right, all the facts, all the law are meaningless. And my problem was compounded by the fact that I had very few chances remaining. It was virtually a certainty that if the Supreme Court did not hear my appeal this time, there might never be a next time. The string was eleven years long and running out.

As I talked to Bill that morning, I was painfully aware of the fact that no type of legal action is more difficult, less often successful, or more often misunderstood than an appeal to the United States Supreme Court. You really need to win twice. First, you must convince the Court that the case merits review, that a writ of certiorari should issue—meaning simply that the Court has agreed to hear the case. Annually, only about 10 percent of all cases taken to the Supreme Court are heard. In order to have the writ issue and the case scheduled for review, the votes of four Justices are required.

It might be worthwhile here to point out that it means nothing when lawyers say, "We'll take this all the way to the Supreme Court if necessary." Many go, few are received. The

Court itself has pointed out many times, however, that the refusal to hear a case means absolutely nothing other than that the Court refused to hear the case. The reason for denying review could be almost anything: Perhaps four Justices were not convinced the time was legally or politically ripe to decide the issues presented by a given case; perhaps the Court felt the case had merit but should be decided at a lower judicial level; perhaps the issues presented were not quite ripe for determination, for almost any reason; perhaps the issues had already been accepted for review in another case . . . perhaps . . . perhaps . . . perhaps. . . .

The mere fact that my case had been to the Supreme Court three times before and a hearing had been refused each time did *not* mean, as some newspaper reporters unfamiliar with the Court seemed to think, that my appeals were without merit or that the Supreme Court agreed with the lower court rulings; nor did it mean that the Court would not hear me the fourth time. In fact, though my case had been to the Supreme Court three times, the case had never been heard by that court.

The second hurdle, after one has convinced the Court to hear a case, is to convince a majority of the Justices sitting when the issues are argued orally that the merits require the granting of the relief requested; in my case, a reversal of my conviction and the ordering of a new trial, barring which we would accept a full habeas corpus hearing in the United States district court. Even at this late stage, after the Court has accepted a case for review, briefs have been filed, and oral arguments have been heard, it is not uncommon for the Court to change its mind and dismiss the case without a ruling on the merits. And if the Court should go ahead and vote on the merits and the vote come out a tie, everything goes back to where it was before the Supreme Court heard the case. For me, having lost in the lower court, a tie vote could mean execution.

My attorney at the time of the conference with Bill Buckley was Stephen F. Lichtenstein, of Trenton. Lichtenstein had been the only lawyer ever to win votes for me on an appeal, twice losing in the court of appeals by a 2–1 vote. He had been with me five years, first as an attorney assigned by the federal court to represent me when I was without money to retain my own lawyer, later as a paid lawyer when the advance money from *Brief Against Death* enabled me to pay him a small fee—nothing near what he was worth. Steve had been the choice of all the lawyers I could have had; I considered him the best available, bar none.

By January, 1968, however, an entirely new situation had developed, and it became obvious that a good lawyer, even a great one, would not be enough. Just as someone facing open heart surgery cannot be satisfied with a "good" doctor but needs a specialist, so I needed a specialist, an attorney, a law firm, with a big name, with the prestige to attract the Supreme Court's attention, to interest the Justices enough that they would stop and read my petition a bit longer, a bit more carefully, than they might read another. I needed a lawyer with the experience, the skill, and the knowledge of the Court to convince the Justices that mine was a case meriting full review.

Steve Lichtenstein realized that bringing in a new law firm meant that, although he would remain on the case, he would no longer have absolute authority over its handling. And he knew that if we won, if the appeal were successful, he could well be lost in the shuffle of big names when the laurels were being awarded. It is to his credit as a lawyer and as a friend that he agreed without hesitation when I made my decision: We would retain the prestigious Washington law firm of Edward Bennett Williams.

The first step would be the writing of the petition upon which the Supreme Court would decide whether my case merited review. That task was delegated to Steven M. Umin, a new young member of the Edward Bennett Williams staff. Umin would also take full charge of the case.

There must be a better word than "impressive" for Umin's credentials. A 1959 graduate of Yale, *summa cum laude*, first in his class, and president of Phi Beta Kappa, Umin spent the next two years in England, at Oxford, as the Rhodes Scholar from New York, before returning to Yale Law School, where he was articles editor of the *Yale Law Journal*. From 1964 to 1965 he was law clerk to Chief Justice Roger Traynor of the California Supreme Court, followed by a year as clerk to Justice Potter Stewart of the United States Supreme Court, serving in that capacity during the term that produced the famous *Miranda* decision. After a short period of service as counsel to a committee of the United States Senate, Umin joined the Williams firm. Mine was to be his first case as a practicing lawyer. It was also to present him with a unique opportunity and challenge.

As a former clerk of a Supreme Court Justice, Umin was barred by the Court rules from practicing before the Court for a period of two years from the date of his departure from the Court. By an odd quirk of fate, his two-year waiting period would expire the day my petition was due to be filed. I crossed my fingers and hoped that was an omen of better days to come, of things finally beginning to break my way.

While Steve Umin was busy working on the petition to the Supreme Court, I was preparing the final editorial changes in *Brief Against Death*, due for publication September 4. The announcement of the forthcoming publication and later circulation of advance copies of the book began to attract widespread and favorable reaction from the news media. Suddenly people were talking about Edgar Smith, the fellow who had been under a death sentence for eleven years and had written a book about it, and within a very short time of the first publication announcement the prison authorities found themselves being questioned concerning my descriptions of life and conditions in the Death House, and rumor on the prison grapevine had it that *Brief Against Death* was going to bring about much-needed reforms.

The Newark *Star-Ledger*, in a full-page Sunday edition feature highlighting my book, reported that the warden "in an interview, confirmed much of what Smith has charged, but justified prison procedures." The same report quoted Frank McDermott, majority leader of the State Senate, who as a member of a legislative investigating commission decided to visit the prison and see for himself what things were really like. Said McDermott: "I was appalled by the way those men live. It was a real eye-opener for me." Albert C. Wagner, director of Correction and Parole, seemed mainly concerned that the Death House was an "administrative problem" for him.

To the surprise of all the men in the Death House, reforms really were instituted. On August 26, just one week before *Brief Against Death* went on sale to the public, a period of daily, one-hour recreation, the lack of which my book had spotlighted, was permitted for the condemned men. We had moved to a new Death House in December, 1966—the authorities like to call it Three Wing—and just outside was a small yard completely enclosed by walls and buildings, with a shotgun-toting guard in a tower at one end of the wall. The yard was about 200 feet long and 40 feet wide, had sidewalks, a few benches, and grassy areas within the walks. We were permitted to use only half the yard—no one ever came up with a reasonable explanation for *that* rule—and the only activities permitted were walking, jogging, and calisthenics. Previously the private yard of the honor inmates, who had been housed in the wing converted into a new Death House, it had several plots of flowers bordering the walks and a small birdbath. Before the condemned men were allowed to use the yard, the flowers were removed ("You guys might hide something in there") and the birdbath taken away ("One of you guys might pick it up and hit someone with it"). But the benches remained: Never argue against jailhouse logic.

More changes followed soon after the outside recreation period was instituted. Oil paints, previously banned, were permitted; each inmate was permitted to purchase his own transistor radio; and the entire visiting system was revamped, so that for the first time in New Jersey history condemned men were permitted visits with their children. For some men it was the first time they had seen their children in years, while others saw for the first time their children born after they had been confined.

The condemned men still did not have all the privileges given to men serving time in the general prison population, but things were getting better, a hell of a lot better, and I like to think that *Brief Against Death*, through the attention it called to the plight of men on Death Row, had some small part in bringing about the changes. Whether the book would bring about equally good changes in my legal situation remained to be seen.

My petition to the Supreme Court, the finest piece of legal writing I had ever seen—Steve Umin has since done even better—was filed on August 12, 1968, and we sat back and waited for the prosecutor's reply, due within thirty days. For Umin, making his first appearance before the Supreme Court as a lawyer, and for me, making what could be my last before any court, the summer seemed to get longer and hotter. The Court would reconvene for the new term in October, but even then we might have to wait another month or two for a decision.

The prosecutor's brief, due to be filed the same week my book was published, did not come down until one month later, and for the first time I felt we had him running scared, that we had finally wrested the initiative from the state. The reply brief was short and exceedingly shallow, and it was immediately clear that the delay had resulted from the prosecutor's having taken time to digest the impact of *Brief Against Death*. There was no doubt that the book and the tremendously favorable reception it received from the public and the news media, including the North Jersey newspapers that had previously been solidly in the prosecutor's corner but now were switching their sympathies with front-page coverage of the book, had left the prosecutor somewhat shaken. I recall commenting to one of my lawyers at the time that it seemed as if the prosecutor, prohibited by State Supreme Court rules from commenting on a pending case, had decided to use his reply brief in the Supreme Court to answer the charges made in *Brief Against Death*.

In his Introductory Statement to the reply brief, for instance, the prosecutor seemed concerned only with denying that any "substantial public doubt" existed as to my guilt, a truly remarkable denial if for no other reason than that the prosecutor must have felt that such an official denial, eleven years after my conviction, had to be made before the Supreme Court of the United States, where the issue of guilt or innocence was not in question. Moreover, the prosecutor used the remainder of his Introductory Statement to attack an article William F. Buckley, Jr., had written about my case three years earlier, in the October, 1965, *Esquire*.

Steve Umin, who apparently loves a good fight, filed a short counter-reply that completely gutted the prosecutor's arguments. Umin pointed out that attacks upon my book and the Buckley magazine article were hardly germane to the issues before the Court; that throughout the eleven years my case had been before the courts, state and federal, the prosecutor had never, anywhere, anytime, in or out of court, denied my sworn allegations of illegal and coercive police conduct during my post-arrest, incommunicado interrogation covering a period of some twenty hours; that the prosecutor had consistently refused to agree to have a court test those allegations; and that in fact the prosecutor's entire legal posture through the years consisted of fighting against having any court hear and rule upon those allegations.

Sitting in the Death House waiting for the United States Supreme Court to rule upon what may be one's final chance to escape electrocution is not a pastime I would recommend to anyone. My system of waiting it out during the years I was writing was a simple one: I usually worked all night and slept all day (I was already at work on a novel in the fall of 1968), so that on Monday, around noon, when the week's Supreme Court decisions came over the radio, I would be sound asleep. I figured that if the news were good, someone would wake me and tell me, and if the news were bad, well, waking up first thing in the morning to bad news is not my idea of fun. Better not to think about it either way.

The Supreme Court returned in October, worked a couple of weeks, then took a recess during the election day period.

A few days after the electorate blew its collective mind and elected Nixon, Agnew, and Martha Mitchell, Steve Umin wrote to me and told me to hang tight—the Court would probably rule on my petition the day it returned from recess, November 12. Sure enough, on the afternoon of November 12 a guard woke me to tell me my lawyer was waiting upstairs to see me.

"Which lawyer?" I asked.

"I'll have to call and find out," the guard replied.

By the time I had splashed cold water on my face and pulled on a pair of pants the answer came back—Steve Lichtenstein. *Oh, Christ!* I almost went back to bed. The only other times Lichtenstein had come to inform me personally of court decisions was when we had lost twice in the court of appeals. Steve is a nice guy, but a bearer of good news he ain't.

When I walked into the upstairs office where Lichtenstein was waiting, I asked: "Okay, how badly did we lose *this* time?"

He came right to the point. Sticking out his hand, he said:

"Congratulations. The Supreme Court has ordered the federal court to give you a full habeas corpus hearing on the merits."

There it was. *Zonk!* After eleven years, eight months, and six days of coming up a loser every time, Smith was a winner. Other victories would be needed, other hands had to be dealt, but I was back in the game with a fistful of brand-new money and a new deck.

Deal the cards! Deal, dammit, deal!

The Supreme Court, Lichtenstein explained, had accepted my case for review—granted the writ of certiorari—summarily reversed the court of appeals, and remanded the case to the federal court for a full habeas corpus hearing on the merits of my claims of illegal police conduct. And surprisingly, for it is extremely rare in summary reversals, the Court issued a five-page opinion pointing out where and why the court of appeals had been wrong. No controversial 5–4 vote in this criminal case. None of those squeaker votes that bring down the wrath of the National Association of District Attorneys. Not this time. The vote was 8–1 in my favor, and the vote of the lone dissenter, Justice Byron White, was a negative vote only insofar as he thought the Court should have heard the case on its merits and disposed of it right then and there, without a remand, so in fact all nine Justices were agreed that my case merited full review. And that, I suggest, is as complete an answer as one could want to those few cynical newspaper reporters who had been writing for so many years that if my case had any real merit, the courts would have listened to me.

I had written in *Brief Against Death* that one of the difficult truths about my case was that "if the merits of my appeal are considered, there is no way under the facts and law that an appeals court can avoid reversing my conviction." Many people scoffed at that statement, including the editor of the New Jersey Bar Association *Journal*, who noted how often the courts had refused to hear my appeals and who cited my statement as proof that I was refusing to face the truth. But I meant what I wrote, and finally the Supreme Court gave me the opportunity to prove I knew what I was talking about.

Lichtenstein and I talked for a few minutes about the remand procedure, then he asked: "Tell me, Edgar, how do you feel right now?"

The question surprised me because until then I hadn't stopped to think about how I felt or how I should feel having finally won a point.

"I haven't thought about it," I told Lichtenstein. "It's over, done, we won, and now there's still a lot of work ahead of us. I guess as soon as you told me we won, my mind shifted gears and started thinking about the next step. If you spend too much time thinking about the home run you just hit, you're liable to strike out the next time. When does the hearing start?"

"We have to wait for the mandate to come down from the Supreme Court to the court of appeals, then for an order to go down to the district court. I'd guess the hearing could begin sometime in the spring, April or May."

"You figure a one-week hearing?"

"At a minimum."

I must say I was surprised by the media coverage of my victory in the Supreme Court. I was front-page news in the New York *Times*, and it was immediately apparent that the impact of *Brief Against Death*, including the exceptionally favorable public reception of the book, had produced a subtle but significant shift in the media's treatment of my story. Where once the newspapers might have headlined my victory something like NEW JERSEY CON WINS HEARING, suddenly they all read EDGAR SMITH WINS. Unquestionably, much of the credit for bringing me to the public's attention must go to Bill Buckley and the article he wrote for *Esquire* in 1965. That article, plus the fact that an acknowledged law-and-order Conservative had stated his belief in the innocence of a convicted murderer, had made it certain that henceforth whatever happened in my legal struggle would not go unnoticed by the media and the public.

Even more significantly, newspapers that for eleven years had labeled me a "sex killer" or "sex murderer" and had published scathing editorials about my "seemingly endless frivolous appeals" suddenly dropped the "sex killer" routine (I had shown in *Brief Against Death* that the trial court had specifically ruled that there was no evidence of a sexual attack, actual or attempted), and they have not since suggested that any of my appeals had been "frivolous." In fact, several newspapers published quite favorable editorials praising my book and noting my "indomitable courage" in refusing to give up. I suppose that newspapers, like the guys in the bleachers, love winners. The bandwagon was beginning to fill up.

Steve Umin came to visit me in January, 1969, and with him was Vincent Fuller, one of the top trial practitioners on Edward Bennett Williams' staff. If Fuller's schedule permitted, he would assist Umin at the habeas corpus hearing. I looked forward with great glee to seeing a pro like Fuller going to work on the prosecutor's witnesses.

Again I asked: "When will the hearing be held?"

"The court of appeals' mandate will come down next month," Umin told me. "The prosecutor has written a letter to the court of appeals, agreeing that a full hearing must be held as a result of the Supreme Court opinion. We figure we ought to be ready to go in May. We need a couple of months to clear our schedules and prepare. There are witnesses we will have to interview and depositions to be taken."

"What are we going to do about my ex-wife? She's remarried and settled down in Colorado with a couple more kids, and the people out there don't know who she is. I doubt whether you'll get her back here without a subpoena. She doesn't want any part of the past."

"We can take a sealed deposition from her out there. Her married name and present whereabouts needn't be used."

"You say we can get going in May, right?"

"Probably."

"Okay, let's go get 'em."

Chapter

Two

All sorts of fascinating and important things were happening while I was awaiting the scheduling of my habeas corpus hearing. Perhaps the most important single event was the election in the fall of 1969 of a Republican governor—William Cahill.

In the state of New Jersey, the county prosecutors are the primary agents for enforcement of state laws. All violations, including homicide cases, are investigated and prosecuted by the prosecutor of the county in which the violations take place, and for this function he is provided with a staff of assistant prosecutors, investigators, and county detectives. All twenty-one county prosecutors are appointed to their jobs by the governor for a five-year term.

With the election of Governor Cahill ending sixteen years of Democratic Party rule in New Jersey, it became only a matter of time before each of the twenty-one county prosecutors, all Democrats, were replaced by Republicans. That meant that Guy W. Calissi, fifteen years the prosecutor of Bergen County and the man who had put me in the Death House and fought my appeals for more than eleven years, would be on his way out and with him most of his staff, which served only as long as he held his office.

My feelings about Calissi's departure were mixed. While I was glad to see him go for one reason—any change had to be a change for the better, since the new people coming into office would not have *their* records, *their* reputations at stake in my case—I regretted seeing him leave for another reason: I *knew* I was going to win my appeal, that my conviction would be reversed, and that Calissi's handling of my case, particularly during the period of my arrest and interrogation, would be condemned by the federal court when the full story came out at the habeas corpus hearing. I would have preferred having that condemnation put on record while he was still in office. But I didn't shed any tears when the day he stepped down finally came.

One thing I'll have to say for Prosecutor Calissi: He went out of office fighting—literally!

Just a few weeks before Calissi stepped down, the federal government made public what came to be known as the DeCarlo tapes, a series of tape recordings of bugged phone conversations involving Anthony "Gyp" DeCarlo, an alleged "Mafia" figure, and several of his associates, including one Frank "Tippy" Bellizzie, of Bergen County. In the course of the taped conversations between DeCarlo and Bellizzie, reference was made to Chief of Bergen County Detectives Walter Spahr, Calissi's top investigator, whom Calissi had appointed to that post. The conversation indicated that Spahr was a man the mob had to "protect," that he was their man in some way, and that they had known for some time before Spahr got his job that he would be made chief of detectives.

When newspaper reporters went to question Spahr about the tapes, they found he was on "sick leave" and staying in Florida. The trouble for Prosecutor Calissi started when he held a press conference and the Spahr subject came up. One reporter wanted to know what sort of "sickness" Spahr had contracted. Calissi didn't know. The reporter wanted to know if Spahr would be back. Calissi and his son, an investigator in the office, grabbed the reporter, apparently threatened to throw him out a window, and finally settled for throwing him out of the office. A bad scene. Bad publicity. Suits and counter-suits. Shortly thereafter Guy Calissi was out of office for good.

The new prosecutor was Robert Dilts, formerly Calissi's first assistant prosecutor and the only Republican on his staff. Immediately a new staff was brought in, but within a month most of them had resigned. (Within eighteen months the new prosecutor would be under arrest.)

Under New Jersey law, prosecutors and their assistants were permitted to maintain private law practices on the one condition that they not handle criminal matters, so as to avoid con-flicts of interest. One of the first acts of the new legislature under Governor Cahill was to change the law and bar prose-cutors and their assistants from *any* outside practice, and as a result most of the new prosecutor's staff resigned within a month of taking office. Few could, or would, give up lucrative outside law practices, practices built up over a period of years, just for a minor title and a salary ten times less than most of them made in their own offices.

Unfortunately, while the new law was good in one respect, in that it eliminated conflicts of interest between private prac-tices and official duties, it had the immediate bad effect of reducing the quality of law enforcement and prosecution in the counties. Most men willing to take an assistant prosecutor's job under the new law were lawyers of lesser abilities, lawyers whose private practices didn't amount to much, who could afford to give them up for a small salary, or younger, less experienced lawyers who had not yet had time to build profit-able private practices. The law also had the effect of bringing into the prosecutor's office men whose political ambitions were such that they did not mind giving up private practices or taking a low-salaried job, because they saw the job as a step-ping-stone and defendants as bodies to be stepped over on the way up. The latter seems to be what I wound up with.

The new prosecutor's staff was appointed shortly after the

law was passed, and my mother, who clips newspapers the way Howard Hughes clips bond coupons—*constantly*—sent me a clipping listing the names of the new staff members. Only one name was important to me—the name of the man whose job it would be to handle appeals. Yep! There it was— Edward N. Fitzpatrick, Esq., of Allendale, New Jersey.

FITZPATRICK??? LITTLE FITZ??? OHMIGAWD!!! I'VE KNOWN THIS GUY SINCE HE WAS IN SHORT PANTS!!!

When my family moved to Ramsey, New Jersey, in the latter part of 1949 and lived on Elm Avenue, the Fitzpatrick family had lived just around the corner on Oak Street. Ed Fitzpatrick was then about ten or eleven years old, and his older brother, Jimmy, about my own age, soon became my drinking and partying buddy as well as a schoolmate. We used to call the brothers Big Fitz and Little Fitz, which was something like calling a bald man Curly. Little Fitz was already three feet wide and destined to grow up to be a gorilla, twice the size of his brother.

I couldn't believe it. The loudmouth (he still is!) little kid we used to tell to get lost and stop bothering us, who used to whine and beg to be taken with us to Ebbets Field to watch the Dodgers play when Stan Musial and the Cards were in town (their father owned a religious goods store in Brooklyn and still does), who finally grew up, became a lawyer, married, moved to Allendale, New Jersey, and there became *my* older brother's occasional drinking partner and Sunday afternoon basketball game teammate—now the kid was a prosecutor who would handle the state's fight against my appeal and try to put me in the electric chair. *Jesus Christ! What next in this screwball case?*

"Hey, Tommy," I yelled to a Death House buddy who also had been convicted in Bergen County. "Guess who our new prosecutor for appeals is?"

"Eichmann?"

"Not quite, but you might be close."

Tommy "lived" in the cell beneath mine—I was on the second tier—so after he came to the air vent that ran up through the wall between our cells to a ventilator on the roof (we called it the telephone) and I told him the story about Little Fitz, he laughed for about seven years, then said: "Igor, you've got it made."

"Made?" I screamed. "Made? I'd have it made better if I were a dumb Jew like you and did get Eichmann. My spies tell me this guy is one hungry dude who wants to be a politician. The bastard will probably break my balls just to show he isn't playing favorites."

Another fellow hearing my conversation with Tommy joined us on the vent. "Don't you know anything rotten about the dude?" he asked. "You know, like he used to sleep with a twelve-year-old chick or something like that?"

"Man, I don't even know if he likes chicks. All I know for sure is that the dude drinks, plays basketball on Sunday afternoons, and wears Bermuda shorts."

"Hey, man, he sounds cool!"

My lawyers apparently had the same misgivings I had. When I wrote and told them the news, Steve Lichtenstein replied: "Let's wait and see."

We waited, that's for damn sure. I watched 1969 go past like a bowl of potato salad at a Weight Watchers picnic. All through the year my lawyers told me over and over and over that they thought the hearing would be held "soon," but nothing ever seemed to happen toward that desired end. The case had been assigned on a tentative basis to Federal Judge Lawrence Whipple, who normally sat in the federal court in Newark but who occasionally sat in Trenton, where my petition had been filed in 1965. My lawyers were at one point so sure that Judge Whipple would act that they spent two days observing a hearing he held in another case, just to see how he handled himself. They liked what they saw, but still we waited.

It was a tough year for me, perhaps the toughest of all, a year of waiting, waiting, waiting some more, writing bitchy letters to my lawyers, mostly to Steve Umin, wanting to know why the delay, why didn't he *do* something, insisting that the court was playing games with me, forcing me to do more time, wanting me to do a life sentence on appeal. The excuse given was that the court had a shortage of judges and that when Nixon appointed new judges to fill the federal court vacancies in New Jersey, my hearing would have top priority on one of the new judges' calendars. That wasn't a good enough excuse to me.

Near the end of 1969, the court of appeals ruled that one of the Supreme Court cases upon which I had been relying would not be applied retroactively. When Umin wrote and told me about that case, *Allison v. New Jersey,* I wrote another of my impatient letters:

> You don't have any more bad news lying around your office, do you? If so, now would be a good time to get rid of it by dropping it on me. I am having other problems, non-legal, so I might as well take all the bad news at once. Perhaps I had the right idea when I suggested to Bill [Buckley] that the answer would be for someone to give me a rope for Christmas.
>
> So, all right . . . what the hell do we do? Sit and wait? I have been sitting and waiting for a long time, and it has cost me a great deal aside from the money, and thus far it hasn't done me a damn bit of good. Because of *Allison* we are in a much more difficult position than we were a year ago. Perhaps we should wait another year. By that time [other cases] may be lost to us, and another year after that, something else, and then all we have to do is keep waiting until before long we have nothing left because all the issues were settled through other cases, for all of which, it seems, the courts are able to find plenty of time, and then just a tiny bit more waiting and (a) I will have died of old age or (b) the state will finally

pass the bill abolishing capital punishment and substituting a life sentence with a thirty-year minimum for parole. Beautiful! (I'll bet that will be retroactive!)

There is only one problem with all this waiting: I am slowly running out of excuses for my mother and brother and aunt and uncle and Bill and Sophie and Juliette and all the readers [of my books] who write in, all asking me why it is that everyone else seems to be able to have his case heard but me. You know, people like Allison. If you have any suggestions for new excuses I can give the folks, let me know. Most folks, like Bill, for instance, can't seem to understand that the rules require me to crawl around on my knees so that we don't antagonize the court by being so presumptuous as to demand something I have a right to demand.

What a stupid son of a bitch I am! I could have pleaded guilty thirteen years ago, been out of here by now, and nobody would have given a damn whether I really was guilty or not. And then I could have written a book telling the world I was guilty, instead of innocent, and made twice as much money. Yes, sir, a little more brains and a bit less principle and belief in what is right, and I would have been a hell of a lot better off.

Well, this will be my thirteenth Christmas in here. Merry Christmas, everybody!

The record of delay is incredible. The court of appeals order requiring the federal court to hold my hearing was dated February 14, 1969. Umin waited until April 9, and when nothing seemed about to happen, he wrote to Judge Whipple, with the prosecutor's approval, and suggested that the hearing be held May 19, a date agreed to by the state. A week later Judge Whipple wrote back that he would talk to the chief judge about it. A week after that Judge Whipple wrote to Umin: "*If and when* my schedule permits . . . I shall contact you immediately."

Umin wrote to Whipple again on April 29, saying that he would keep in touch with the judge's clerk.

On July 15 Umin wrote again, this time to Chief Judge Anthony Augelli, pointing out that the case had been dragging along without action since February and suggesting, again with the prosecutor's approval, that the hearing be scheduled for November, exactly one year after the Supreme Court had sent the case back down to be heard. Umin also stated that if necessary, for the court's convenience, we would agree to have the hearing held in Newark instead of Trenton and that it could be broken up into segments, heard over a period of time. Umin ended his letter by saying: "I understand that a Trenton appointment [of a new federal judge] is long overdue. But likewise is a hearing for this twelve year old case that has been pending on habeas corpus for four years."

A week after Umin's letter to the chief judge we received a reply stating that Judge Whipple had agreed to "assist in every possible way to expedite a disposition of this case."

Another month went by, still not a word from Judge Whipple, so Umin wrote again, and again with the prosecutor's approval, this time requesting a show cause order, a simple thing, a mere formality that required the prosecutor to reply formally to the petition I had filed in 1965 and never before answered by the state. (!!!) All that was required of Judge Whipple was that he sign the paper and have his clerk mail it back to us, nothing more, and then the lawyers could begin making their preparations and plans for the hearing. Again Judge Whipple stalled, and again I wrote Steve Umin a bitchy letter:

> I have, as you will note, taken my time considering your letter of September 18, and I might as well tell you right off that I cannot and will not buy your "month or so" further delay. I cannot buy it because I do not believe it. I have been hearing these optimistic predictions and promises for ten months now, but for all of it, the plain and simple fact is that we are today, if we are lucky, exactly where we were one minute after the Supreme Court ruled in my favor. I say "if we are lucky" because all my instincts tell me that we have blown it, let the situation deteriorate, losing all the forward

momentum that had been provided by the fortunate combination of a favorable court ruling and equally favorable public and press reaction to my book. That was the time to zap them, but instead we threw them a daisy.

Look, try to see this from my point of view. First I was told that there was a good chance of a February hearing, and when that passed, I was told it would probably be in the spring. Spring came and went and I was told it would be May. When that went by, I blew my cool, you asked me to be patient until July something-or-other, which turned out to be one of history's least noted and remarked days. Finally you told me the hearing would be in November, and now that is a lost cause, so you tell me a "month or so" longer. Let's face it, Steve, you do not have the slightest notion in the world when the hearing will be at the rate we are going. If you have some bread you would like to lose, I am willing to bet you that your "month or so" will prove to be less accurate than the *Times* announcement of Dewey's victory in '48. You see, there is one basic difference between us: I have been through all this before and I *know* how the courts handle my case. I know, for instance, that as of now I have spent a total of four and a half years doing absolutely nothing but waiting for the federal court to decide whether to hear my case. You obviously did not believe me months ago when I told you exactly what was going to happen with this case, when I told you that we would not set one foot inside that court until after the prosecutor Calissi retired in January of '70, when I told you that we were going to face delay upon delay upon delay upon delay and that the only way we were going to be heard was to push for it as hard as we could, and in every way we could.

I very much fear that our patience has had the deleterious effect of leading the court to think we are content to wait for just as long as the court wishes to shove us aside. In other words, that we have passed the point whereat continued silence and patience can only be self-defeating.

You will recall telling me that we had no cause for mandamus because we could not show that the court was delaying unreasonably. That was several months ago, and I think now we have a different situation. It may be argued that the federal court does have a shortage of judges which prevents the holding of my hearing, and a reasonable case for that could probably be made, but unless Judge Whipple has had an unpublicized accident in which he broke both arms, there is not one goddamn reason in the world why he cannot sign that show-cause order. All he has to do is pick up his pen and sign his name. If he cannot and will not do that, then the question arises: Just why in hell was he assigned to my case? To shut us up.

I was telling Bill the other day that there are quite a few arguments we could use on mandamus.* One is that continued delay will have the effect of denying me the right to private counsel, because it is not going to be very much longer before I can no longer afford to pay anyone anything, and it would be an unfair disadvantage for the court to stall until I have no choice but to ask for assignment of counsel who is not familiar with my case. I would also make the point that continued delay is evidence in itself of the federal court's incapacity to perform its functions within the framework of fundamental fairness to the petitioner before the court, and on this basis I would petition the Supreme Court to reassume jurisdiction over the case, removing it from the federal court. There are other arguments which I will not go into here.

I could go on with this for another ten pages and still not say everything that is bugging me. I have been through this mill for twelve years, and you might as well understand right now that I am not about to go through twelve more. I cannot sit here with a Supreme Court decision granting me a hearing and a passel of expensive lawyers sitting in their offices waiting patiently while the months and years slip away from me. I cannot afford it financially or in terms of my own time. I really hate like hell to put you on the spot because you are not responsible for the court's reluctance to hear me, but on the other hand, I have a responsibility not only to myself but to a lot of other people who have been waiting as long as I have and who continue to wait. It is unfortunate that we sometimes forget my successes and failures do affect a great many others, some of whom are taking this last delay very badly. I cannot and will not let this go on. Promises are no longer enough.

* For an explanation of mandamus, see page 43.

And so, with that long and perhaps unnecessary preamble out of the way, let me tell you how it is going to be: I will wait until November 12, one year to the day from the Supreme Court ruling, and by that date I will expect to have seen the federal court take some concrete action toward holding the hearing. Nothing less than the issuance of the show-cause order and the commencement of the prehearing activities will suffice. I want no more promises or predictions. If by the twelfth of November I do not see movement, real movement, not promised or imagined, toward the hearing, I will write to you that date and request that you move immediately in the Supreme Court for mandamus ordering the federal court to implement the Supreme Court ruling or, upon a finding that the federal court is incapable of acting promptly because of the shortage of judges and the crowded docket, for an order bringing the petition back to the Supreme Court for hearing there. Sure, that may be a novel approach, but I *am* a novelist, remember? My letter to you will contain a complete summary of all the federal court delays in my case beginning in 1958. A copy of that letter will go to Chief Judge Augelli, a copy to Judge Whipple, and copies will go to a couple of newspaper people who were especially nice to me on my book.

As I have said, I hate to put you on the spot like this, but the time for patience is over. Naturally, I will leave you a way out. If upon receipt of my letter you feel you cannot take the action I request, you will be free to withdraw. I will then make the application myself. I would rather have you remain with me, but not against your wishes in such a situation. And that is how it will be.

I await your outrage.

I must give Umin credit: I was breaking his back with my letters demanding action, but through it all he remained a damn good friend, patient even when I seemed to be blaming him for the delay, always trying to explain, each time with less and less conviction, that the court was short of judges and my case might have to wait until Nixon got around to filling vacancies on the bench.

But even Umin was losing his temper. On October 1 he

wrote to Judge Whipple again, this time asking why the letter of August 20 requesting the signing of the show cause order had not been answered, why the order had not been signed. Umin also reminded the judge of the chief judge's promise that Judge Whipple would "assist in every possible way to expedite the disposition of this case," adding that signing the order was "virtually a ministerial act" that would not disrupt the court's schedule. Hell, he could sign the damn thing with one hand while standing in the men's room.

For the first time Umin added to his letter of October 1 something that no judge with hopes of furthering his career could ignore. He wrote: *"I respectfully submit that* [this action] *should be taken now so that necessary delay does not become undue delay."* Translated from lawyerese to English, that was a plain warning: "Get off your ass or we're going over your head." A few days later the show cause order was signed, sealed, and delivered.

For several months, while the court's delay was becoming more and more intolerable for me, I had been pressing Umin to do what he had threatened to do in his October 1 letter to Judge Whipple: file in the court of appeals for a writ of mandamus, an extraordinary writ, one rarely issued, that was in fact an order from one court to a lower court or judge directly ordering compliance with a previous order, which in my case was the February 14 order that a hearing be held.

Umin agreed that we were entitled to such an order, that the delay had reached the unreasonable stage, but he begged me to be patient just a bit longer, saying the time wasn't quite ripe for mandamus, that when you go for *that*, you'd damned well better have an airtight case or you'll thereafter be dead with the court you attacked. "If you strike at a king, you must slay him." We were not quite ready to slay a federal judge—but the time was coming.

On October 22 Umin again wrote to Judge Whipple, again

with the prosecutor's approval, suggesting a hearing date be set at once, with a minimum of forty days for preparation. Nothing happened, and 1969 passed into history with me still sitting on Death Row.

January, 1970, began with two new federal judges appointed and sitting. Again Umin wrote to the chief judge, this time asking that my case be assigned to one of the new judges for action. Amazing! Three days later my case was assigned to Judge George Barlow, a former county judge appointed to the federal court by Nixon and now sitting in Trenton.

On February 6, not having heard anything from the new judge, Umin wrote to him, once more with the prosecutor's approval, and suggested April 20 as the date to begin the hearing.

Judge Barlow replied promptly, agreed to a prehearing conference in his chambers sometime in March, and added: "*If circumstances permit*, we will be able to establish a hearing date at the time of the pre-hearing conference."

That did not satisfy Umin. He wrote back to Judge Barlow and made it clear that leaving me subject to "other commitments" and promising me an early hearing only "if circumstances permit" were not good enough. "As a matter of professional responsibility," Umin wrote, "I can no longer agree to such uncertainty." Umin went on:

I have become increasingly sympathetic with my client's view. He has asked for no more than the effectuation of the Supreme Court order. And he urged that, ironically, his status as an imprisoned man may have been leading the courts to a lesser, rather than a greater, sense of urgency. Nevertheless, I was able to forestall a proposed application for mandamus upon the promise, implied in letters to me, that Smith's case would stand first in line when new judges are appointed.

It may be that I have already done Smith a disservice by urging patience upon him. In any event, I cannot honorably go back to him now with anything other than a hearing date.

I cannot responsibly advise him that he must wait again upon "other commitments" or more convenient "circumstances." I must tell him that some court, *even if not the New Jersey* [federal] *District Court,* will reward his restraint and fulfill the Supreme Court's mandate, nearly a year and a half old.

Again Umin's warning that he would apply for mandamus if the court did not act was plain. Judge Barlow may not have been a federal judge very long, but he got the message and quickly summoned my attorneys to his chambers. He agreed to accept prehearing briefs in April, but no date was set for the start of the hearing itself. Newark's Mayor Hugh Addonizio had been arrested, charged with extortion, and the case given to Judge Barlow for trial. That case, the judge told us, had to take precedence over mine, notwithstanding the fact that Addonizio had been charged only a couple of months before and was free on bail. The federal prosecutor wanted an early trial of the Addonizio case, and more often than not, what federal prosecutors want is what federal judges give them.

Now it was my turn to lose patience, and on February 25 I decided to sit down at my typewriter and welcome Judge Barlow to the federal bench my own way. The letter I wrote was a long one, at times intemperate (for a defendant to write to a federal judge is in itself considered intemperate!), but I reproduce that letter here in its entirety to give the reader some sense of the frustration I felt after sitting on Death Row for more than a year, watching the federal court ignore a United States Supreme Court mandate to give me the hearing I was entitled to have.

DEAR JUDGE BARLOW:

You probably will not appreciate this letter and unquestionably it will give my attorneys a few more gray hairs, but if I let either of these reasons deter me, I might not like myself so much tomorrow. (Some might suggest that in itself is reason enough not to write.)

My chief counsel, Steven M. Umin, of the law firm of Williams and Connolly, has written and advised me of the results of his conference with you on the nineteenth. He told me that briefs are to be filed by March 20, and that a pretrial hearing is to be held April 10, but counsel suggested that the hearing might be held in June, but he did not indicate that this court had made any specific commitment to a hearing at that time. If I understand this correctly, the court rates my habeas action as second on the list of the court's priorities, the first priority going to the Addonizio matter, the reason being, apparently, that the government has found itself unable to guarantee that its principal informer will live long enough to testify against Mayor Addonizio.

I am aware, Your Honor, that my attorney has advised the court of my position in this matter, and that the court is aware that counsel has repeatedly resisted my requests that an application for mandamus be made. Counsel has been very sincere in this matter, advising me that such an application could prove counterproductive and taking the court's side in seeking to convince me that the court has been shorthanded and unable to keep up with matters crowding the docket. To put it bluntly, I have not believed a word of it. Virtually every morning during the past year I have picked up the New York *Times* and read where this court had found the time and the judges and the courtroom space to satisfy the government's desire for speedy hearings and trials in cases in which arrests had not even been made at the time my matter was already pending on the docket as the result of an order from the Supreme Court. I have seen other men in this same wing of the prison in which I am confined file habeas actions in this court months after the Supreme Court had remanded my case for hearing, and in these cases this court was able to find time and judges to act in a matter of days to issue show-cause orders and ask for the filing of briefs, actions delayed in my matter for more than a year.

Notwithstanding the above, and while I have strongly disagreed with counsel as to how we should proceed, I have honored the ancient notion that counsel knows more than his client, and I have accepted counsel's assurances—in lieu of an application for mandamus—that my matter would be the first order of business when the Senate finally got around to confirming new judicial nominations for this district. Now, however, I find that is not to be. Now I find that counsel and apparently the court ask me to accept the theory that my right to have the court determine whether I have been illegally arrested, convicted, and confined under sentence of death for more than one-third of my life is a right inferior to a government prosecutor's desire to enhance his conviction record, to convict a man arrested barely two months ago and presently free on bail and not substantially limited in the exercise of his rights. Now I am asked to accept the theory that the desires of the government supersede my rights as an individual, rights unanimously affirmed by the Supreme Court of the United States. Now I am asked to accept the theory that convictions, not individual rights, are the highest concern of the federal court.

I realize, Your Honor, that the popular notion is that men in prison are not overly principled, but some of us *do* have principles, and mine tell me that I cannot accept status as a second-class petitioner, that I cannot accept this altogether novel concept that habeas corpus is a second-class writ. I must ask this court to reconsider its priorities. I do not ask this court to believe I am innocent simply because I said so in a book, or to believe I was illegally convicted and confined simply because my petition makes this claim, but I *do* believe that when a petitioner comes before a federal court and claims that he has been illegally convicted and confined under sentence of death for more than thirteen years, more than one-third of his life, then this court has no greater priority, no higher duty, than to determine promptly and effectively whether those claims are true.

Perhaps, as counsel has suggested, it would take longer for me to obtain a hearing via the mandamus route than if I waited for the court to call me, but I have the feeling that a few extra months in prison are not too high a price to pay for my beliefs, not too high a price to pay to reestablish my rights as a human being, and certainly not too high a price to pay if the result is the Supreme Court's restatement of the preeminence of the writ of habeas corpus. Perhaps, also, that in order to reestablish my rights it will be necessary to seek new counsel, perhaps an activist attorney more aggressive in fighting for my rights as opposed to the rights and desires of the prosecutor in the Addonizio matter. I would deeply regret having to do that, since my present counsel is as good a friend as he is an attorney, but to put it candidly: In order to protect my rights in this matter, I would resurrect Attila the Hun if I thought I could get him past the bar exams.

I would suppose that the court is surprised by my attitude in this matter. What the court does not realize, I am certain, is that there is far more involved for me than the simple fact that I do not take kindly to being caged like an animal for a crime that I did not commit, far more than the real possibility that continued delay, every day of which costs me money, will almost certainly leave me in a position in which I will find myself unable to afford to retain counsel of my own choosing, and will have to rely on second-rate assigned counsel unfamiliar with the complexities of my case.

Among the many other considerations are the many friends who write to my publisher week after week and to whom I find myself unable to give a reasonable explanation as to why the court refuses to act in my matter. I feel a personal obligation to reply to each and every one of these people, to give them an explanation, but I find myself unable to do so. What exactly do I tell the soldier in Korea, the sailor on a destroyer in the South China Sea, the group of Air Force men in Brazil, the entire high school class in North Carolina, the farmers in Idaho, the Mexican girl in Houston, or the hundreds of others, including even the clerk of a federal court in South Carolina? What do I tell the schoolteacher in California when she asks me how she should explain my case to her students? Should she tell them, as the Attorney General tells the public: "Don't believe what you hear. Just believe what you see done." But above all others, what do I tell the paratrooper in Vietnam who, upon returning from a combat patrol and reading my book, asks: "What the hell am I fighting for over here when a guy like you at home can't even get a court to listen to him?" I wish to God I could think of an answer for *that* one. What I try to tell these people is the sad truth, that "As matters now stand, I will in all likelihood have spent more time in the Death House fighting for my rights than I would have spent in prison had I pleaded guilty and received a life sentence." But I add to this that "I resist the obvious implication" that under our system of justice "it is better in the long run to be guilty than innocent." I continue to resist that notion, but resisting becomes more difficult as this court comes closer and closer to forcing me to serve a life sentence on appeal.

One thing should be understood: I *do* know that this court is busy, and consequently I do not ask the court to set tomorrow, or next week, or even next month as the time for my hearing, but I do ask this court to make a commitment to hear my matter at a specific time in the reasonably near future. As matters now stand, more than fifteen months after the Supreme Court held that I am entitled to be heard, the only commitment this court has made is a commitment to talk in April about talking some more at some unspecified time sometime thereafter. Counsel suggests that I will be heard in June, but the matter could be put over until the fall. That would be intolerable. I have advised counsel that I cannot accept that, and that unless the court will reconsider its priorities, I must insist that an application for mandamus, or for some other relief, be made, and if such action prejudices the court against me, I will accept that burden. I have further advised counsel that I will not require him to act against his better judgment, and that if he feels his agreement with the court precludes his making the application for mandamus, I shall seek other counsel. I mention this only so that the court will not feel Mr. Umin has gone back on any agreements he may have reached with the court during the February 19 conference.

I trust the court will have no difficulty understanding the reason I felt compelled to write this letter. One need only review the history of my efforts over the past ten years to obtain a hearing in the United States District Court for New Jersey to find that it has not been a history of litigation, but rather a history of frustration.

Judge Barlow did not answer me. Instead, he wrote to Umin and said, in part: "I appreciate Mr. Smith's concern. . . . As you know, I regard the setting of a [hearing] date now as impractical and premature. . . . Please advise Mr. Smith that any further communication to the Court should be made through counsel."

The old bullshit! I'm a federal judge! I'm God! Don't talk to me! I talk only to lawyers, not to criminal vermin!

I checked the signature on the letter just to be certain it wasn't signed by Julius Hoffman.

And so the wait went on. Waiting. Always waiting. They don't waste any time getting you inside, but when you want out, and you insist you have a right to be out, that they are wrong to keep you in, then suddenly they aren't in a hurry: they have all the time in the world. I don't know what their logic is on that. Perhaps they figure that if a man has been wrongfully confined for thirteen years, then a few more weeks or months aren't going to hurt any. At least not too much.

That's how long it was for me at that point. I wrote to Judge Barlow just a week before my thirteenth anniversary in prison, just three months before my thirteenth anniversary on Death Row. A long time. A goddamn long time. I had turned thirty-seven just a few weeks earlier and had spent more than a third of my life on the Row. That first day, the day they brought me down to Trenton, is one of those days in my life I'll never forget.

Chapter Three

June 6, 1957. Hot. Humid. Just three months after my arrest, two days after being sentenced to death. Only three days before my first wedding anniversary. I was brought in handcuffs from Hackensack to Trenton by two deputy sheriffs. The reality of it still had not penetrated, and over and over through my mind ran my attorney's assurances that my conviction would swiftly be reversed and I would be returned to Hackensack for a new trial. Had I known that day that I would not again see the sky for nine and a half years, that I would spend the next nine and one half years in a small, sparsely furnished solitary confinement cell, getting out only fifteen minutes each Friday for a quick cold-water shower, and that I would never again see my daughter, then only six months old, I think I would have taken the rope—jail parlance for hanging oneself.

Check in. Take off your clothes. Hands over your head. Open your mouth. Turn around. Bend over. Spread your cheeks. Lift your feet and let the cop see the soles. No contraband concealed on your body. Put on the "fish suit"—a pair of white hospital-type pajamas that new men, known as fish, wear when they are being processed and until prison uniforms can be supplied.

"Can I keep this photo of my wife?" I ask naïvely.

"No pictures."

"How about my eyeglasses?"

"We'll give you new ones."

"Okay, I'll just keep the smokes."

"No outside cigarettes allowed in the prison. You'll be able to buy some later. Follow me. We'll get you a regulation haircut."

A regulation haircut. Death House regulations. Shave it all off. Shave it all off the day you come in the prison. Shave your head every Friday morning when you get out of your cell for a shower. No hair. No beards. No mustaches. No individuality. From the moment I walked into the jail I was #34837, and everyone knows numbers don't have hair. Or feelings.

A few more regulations are explained while the barber is shaving my head. My wife could write to me five times each month. I could write a *total* of ten letters each month. Visiting, immediate family only, was permitted for thirty minutes per month. I would not be permitted to see my daughter at all. No one under eighteen is allowed to visit in the Death House.

The lieutenant explaining the rules while the barber worked put it down tough. No bullshit.

"You're gonna be in your cell all the time, Smith. If you get sick, we'll bring the doctor down to you. You get a toothache, the dentist will come down and pull it in your cell. We don't fix teeth for men who are under a death sentence. And we don't give yard time or recreation for guys in the Death House. All you have to do to get along around here is mind your own business and don't think you're smarter than we are. You're not. When you talk to an officer, you call him mister, and you do what you're told. If you don't like it, do it anyhow. You don't argue with officers. Any complaints, you tell the officer you want to talk to me. One more thing—every guy that comes in here sooner or later thinks about escaping. Don't try it.

Try anything like that and we'll kill you. If you don't believe
me, when you get in the Death House you can ask the other
guys what happened to the last man that tried to escape."

Jerry Vazorich was the man the lieutenant was talking
about. Jerry broke out of the Death House in the early fifties
and made it as far as the roof of the prison laundry. They
knew he was up there. They knew he was unarmed. They
knew he couldn't go anywhere because by that time local and
state police had surrounded the prison. The guard who went
up after him carried a submachine gun. When they brought
Jerry down, he had enough lead in him that the guard could
have staked a mining claim on the body. Jerry got buried and
the guard got promoted to sergeant.

The cell. Brick walls painted vomit green—the standard
color in jails all over the country—about 8 feet by 8 feet,
concrete floor, and three locks on the door—one huge Yale-
type lock that required a key nearly six inches long and weigh-
ing more than the average prison meal, a monster padlock
that looked as if it had come from a vault at Fort Knox, and
finally a brake lock. A brake lock is a device consisting of a
4-foot lever at the end of each tier of cells, to which is welded
a one-inch steel bar running the length of the tier just above
the bars of each cell. When the lever is pulled down, it rotates
the bar, to which is welded pieces of steel one inch wide, half
an inch thick, and approximately five inches long—one piece
directly in front of each cell door. These steel fingers—for lack
of a better term—fit between the bars of the cell doors when
the lever is pulled and the bar rotated, making it impossible to
open the sliding door. (And if that explanation is complicated or difficult to understand, don't worry about it. What is
important is that the damn thing works, not so much *how* it
works.)

More about the cell. I look around me while the lieutenant
and the guard on duty go through the routine of locking me in.

There is a bed, a white enamel frame single bed, the hospital type, standing along one wall, its torn mattress dirty and sweat-stained. No pillow. Opposite the bed is the sink, a small porcelain bowl with one water tap. Cold water only. (The authorities regard hot water as a weapon that can be used to disable the guard in the event of an escape attempt. For the same reason, I learn later, pepper is not allowed in the Death House.) The toilet, also porcelain, stands in the corner next to the sink. There is no lid or seat on the toilet. Again, the authorities are taking no chances. A toilet seat or lid is a potential weapon.

There is nothing else in the cell. As time goes by, I will learn to add little conveniences like homemade shelves made of pieces of cardboard or a seat made from a cardboard carton filled with magazines. I will also learn that every now and then the guards will come into the cell and tear the shelves off the wall and throw out the box of magazines, all done under the guise of "security," the excuse for everything that makes a prisoner's life a bit more difficult or uncomfortable.

The lieutenant has gone and now the guard comes over to brief me on a few more rules. No newspapers or magazines more than a month old are allowed in the cell. I ask why and receive an answer I will hear thousands of times over the next fifteen years: "Because that's the rule." The guard goes on: No paperback books in excess of six are permitted in each cell; there is a prison commissary from which Death Row prisoners may order once a week cigarettes, candy, cookies, and a limited variety of food, but nothing in cans or jars. Again, the reason is "security." Mail is delivered each night at 10:30 P.M. We have a refrigerator to store foods bought from the prison commissary, as well as anything we want to save from the prison meals. We will eat in our cell, the food served by the guards. Breakfast is at 7:00 A.M., lunch at 11:00 A.M., supper at 4:00. We can eat if we want, skip meals when we aren't hungry, sleep when we want, get up when we want. The lights will be on twenty-four hours a day.

The guard explains a few more rules, then tells me who the other men on the Row are and what each did. Three black fellows are in as a team. A killing during an armed robbery. Another black fellow is in for killing his wife. Two white guys are in for killing a cop during a supermarket holdup. Weird. The cop's name was John Law! Then the guard warns me. Watch out for Larry, the black kid in the cell next to mine, the one who killed his wife. The guard tells me Larry is a wise son of a bitch.

It is 2:20 in the afternoon. The guard goes off duty, another guard comes on. Larry, the black kid in the next cell, throws a piece of paper on the floor in front of my cell. I pick it up and discover it is a note:

SMITTY:
    You're new here so I'd better warn you. Watch out for the guard who just went off duty. He's a wise son of a bitch.
                                                LARRY

I spend the rest of the afternoon sitting on my bed, trying to figure out if I am on Death Row or in an asylum. Probably both. And just one year before, exactly one year before, I was busily preparing for my wedding, renting a limousine, picking up a tuxedo, double-checking the list to make sure all the invitations had been sent out. Now it was the warden who was double-checking a list of invitations—a list of people to be invited to watch me die.

For the first few days I did nothing. My wife came to visit me June 9 for a tearful celebration of our first wedding anniversary, the only break in the monotony of eating, sleeping, and feeling sorry for myself. Most of the time I paced the cell, three and a half steps from back to front, three and a half from one side to the other, or sat on the edge of the bed, sorting out my thoughts, listening to the other guys rapping about sports or politics or whatever subject one of them brought up. It took time for my mind to make the transition from freedom to a death cell, for me to realize that I was no longer a free, screw-the-world twenty-three-year-old hanging around gas stations, drinking with other guys like myself, doing what I wanted when I wanted whether anyone liked it or not. The whole thing—the arrest, trial, jury verdict, and that insane "May God have mercy on your soul"—had left my mind numb.

It can't *really* be happening to me.

But gradually I began to accept it, to believe it, and then I got down to the facts of life, or at least that would be the fact of my life for the next fifteen years—surviving.

Surviving. That's what its all about on Death Row. Keeping alive. Physically alive. Not letting the state kill you. And keeping your mind alive. Keeping sane.

The first battle, finding legal means to prevent your own death in the electric chair or gas chamber or at the end of a rope, is the most obvious and in some ways the easiest task confronting a man when he arrives on Death Row. One has many allies in the battle to stay alive, physically alive—your own lawyer, automatic stays of execution when an appeal is filed, judges who lean over backward to find sufficient cause to halt or delay an execution, and a society which has shown itself increasingly reluctant to accept and countenance the legal murder of others for some supposed, but unproved, "public good."

The first date set for my execution, July 15, 1957, was automatically canceled when my trial attorney filed an appeal with the New Jersey Supreme Court, and over the years whenever a court would set a new date for my death, it would be forestalled by another appeal, although there would be times when I would come within hours of having the sentence carried out. There was also the period, during 1964–65, when I was without a lawyer, because of my family's inability to continue to carry the financial burden and when I had to school myself in the law to act as my own attorney. It was during that period when, without the aid of an attorney and laboriously handprinting with a ball-point pen, I wrote the petition to the federal court in New Jersey that would eventually result in my regaining my freedom. But that was later, much later, and in the meantime I had to keep myself mentally alive in the hellhole known as Death Row. That is the second battle one must fight.

The second battle, the one to remain sane, is the tough one, the one you have to fight alone, your only weapons being the mind and spirit you were born with. If there is a secret to my success, to my own mental survival while spending nearly one-third of my life in a Death Row solitary confinement cell, it is that while allowing the state of New Jersey to confine me physically, to incarcerate my body, I refused to allow the state to confine my mind, to put my head in a cell.

Not every prisoner can do that. Not every prisoner can go on year after year believing, absolutely certain in his own mind that tomorrow, next week, next month, soon, any day now, something is going to happen, anything, perhaps a new landmark decision from the United States Supreme Court, that is going to permit him to walk out the same door he came in, rather than being carried out in a box through the execution chamber. I did believe. And because I believed, I survived. Never, not for a single instant in my nearly fifteen years on Death Row, longer than any man in American penal history, not even on the two occasions when I came within hours of being executed, did I doubt that the day would come when I would walk out the front door.

The survivors, those who are able to retain their sanity and the freedom of their minds, whether for a year or two in a prison's general population or for many years in a Death Row solitary confinement cell, must always struggle to avoid boredom and "keep their heads over the wall." To allow boredom to set in, to vegetate, or to accept confinement as the natural course of events is to become institutionalized, and to become institutionalized is to become a prisoner in the truest sense of the word.

I fought boredom over the years by every means, the variety of techniques limited only by my imagination—and *that*, on Death Row, where distractions are few and far between, can run to extremes. For the first few years in the Death House I kept myself busy and my mind free by reading dozens and hundreds (perhaps thousands) of paperback novels, including, I think, everything ever written by Erle Stanley Gardner. And then there was baseball. . . .

The Death House was equipped with an internal radio system operated from a central control room in another part of the prison. Each cell was supplied with a set of headphones plugged into a terminal box with a three-way switch. From six in the morning until midnight the radio would be on, and by switching from station to station (there were only three) each man could listen to the programming of his choice—music, sports, or news and talk shows. I found very quickly that baseball—a game I normally avoid listening to or watching as avidly as I avoid, say, the *Al Capp Show*—provided as much relief from boredom as anything.

Any self-respecting statistician would have cried over the records I kept through the late fifties and early sixties. Day after day, season after season, I listened to three, four, sometimes five ball games a day, meticulously recording each pitch, each hit, even the foul balls. It all seemed terribly important at the time, and in a sense it was. When I was keeping track of, say, how many foul balls Mickey Mantle hit down the right field foul line in the third inning of the first game of a doubleheader in Detroit's Tiger Stadium on a Thursday afternoon, I was not fully aware that I was sitting in a death cell, not paying attention to whether it was my 71st or 471st day on Death Row.

Then there was the jigsaw puzzle phase. The prison's Protestant chaplain, a truly nice man, got permission from the authorities sometime in the early sixties to bring the puzzles into the Death House, something not previously allowed, and for a while they were the principal boredom chaser. I used to work on two or three at a time, doing two on the cell floor and one on my bed, staying awake until the one on the bed was finished, and when I had the three of them done, I would take them apart and do them over again. More than once, to make a puzzle more difficult, and therefore occupy my mind for a longer period of time, I would turn the pieces facedown and put it together without seeing the picture. Once, in a mad moment that brought out the masochist in me, I mixed two one-thousand-piece puzzles together and worked on both at the same time. I think it took me three days to finish them.

Men in confinement spend a great deal of time seeking ways to make their existence more comfortable, and if doing so gives them a feeling of putting something over on the authorities, so much the better. That's a key component of the prison game.

Shortly after the condemned men were moved to a new and larger Death House at the end of 1966 and following repeated complaints that the lighting in the cells was inadequate, the authorities equipped each cell with new ceiling fixtures—the square kitchen-type fixture with a hinged bottom for access to the bulb.* A special type of screw was installed in the bottom of each fixture to prevent the men from opening the flap and getting at the bulb or wiring. It took us about fifteen minutes to figure out how to remove the screws and perhaps another day to discover that, in addition to having new lights in our cells, we had convenient little 100-watt ovens for cooking.

---

* The 1966 move to a new Death House also resulted in our being given small desks and chairs for our cells, and later we were allowed to purchase our own transistor radios. Television sets were installed not long after.

A small stainless-steel bowl from the prison mess hall, slipped in through the bottom of the light fixture, made a perfect cooking dish. Water for instant coffee, purchased from the prison's inmate commissary, could be boiled in five minutes. A couple of eggs—they were also sold in the commissary—could be fried in ten minutes in an aluminum pie plate or a dish made of Reynolds wrap supplied by a friendly guard. So much cooking was done at night, with men preparing everything from eggs to concoctions made from dinner leftovers, that the Row sometimes smelled like an all-night eatery—and a real greasy spoon joint at that. The night-shift guards, when they were awake (they used to take turns sleeping), ignored it, often in return for a fried egg sandwich.

My first attempt to cook eggs in the light turned out about as successfully as John Lindsay's Presidential campaign. I put three eggs in a pie tin, along with a great gob of butter, popped the whole works in the light, waited ten minutes, then took the pan down and prepared to feast. Something seemed wrong about the way the eggs looked sitting there waiting to be eaten, and "something" turned out to be the fact that there were only two yolks showing. I knew damn well I had put three eggs in the pan, but just to be sure, I checked the carton. Sure enough, there were nine eggs left of the dozen. Then, looking up at the light, I saw it, my missing yolk, hanging from the bulb like an elongated golden teardrop, looking as if any second it would burst and decorate my bed and floor. I just managed to grab a bowl and spoon and scrape it off the bulb before falling on the bed and laughing like an insane jackass.

(The guard on duty that night must have thought I really was an insane jackass. When he made his rounds an hour later, I was standing over the sink in my cell, scrubbing the bulb with steel wool and scouring powder. Let Josephine the Plumber try *that* someday!)

The most common method of fighting boredom on Death

Row is to talk. The Row is never quiet. At any given hour of day or night some of the men are awake and rapping, always discussing, usually loudly, this or that subject none of them really knows anything about. The subject matter varies. Sports is a favorite subject, with hours spent arguing whether, for instance, the New York Jets were really *that* much better than Baltimore in the 1969 Super Bowl. And of course there are unending legal arguments.

The men on Death Row, perhaps more than any prisoners anywhere, are keenly alert to any changes in the legal scene. Let any court, in any state or in any of the federal judicial circuits, render a decision that could in any way affect the men on Death Row, and the men there are the first to know it. During the middle sixties, when I was doing much of my own legal work, representing myself in the federal courts, I spent the greater part of each day reading and rereading the decisions in the *Federal Supplement* (U.S. district court rulings), the *Federal Reporter* (U.S. circuit court of appeals rulings), the *United States Reports* (U.S. Supreme Court rulings), and the various publications which reported the rulings of the state supreme courts. Most of the other men did the same, and when there appeared to be a ruling of importance to us, we would shout back and forth between cells, dissecting and interpreting and analyzing the wording of the decisions, seeking to make sense of them, trying to figure out what exactly the courts meant, and then looking for some way the rulings could be applied to our own individual cases. There was always hope, always confidence that this, that, or some other decision was the one that would unlock the door. Not surprisingly, a superficially insignificant United States Supreme Court ruling on a procedural question, which went by virtually unnoticed by me in 1961, proved to be the key to my cell door, for it was on the basis of that decision that in 1968 the Supreme Court would order the federal court to grant me the habeas corpus hearing I had long sought.

Not all Death Row conversations were shouted from cell to cell. Although in New Jersey the statutes governing Death Row required that the condemned men be kept in solitary confinement, conversations could also be held on the "telephone"—the system of ventilator shafts connecting the cells and enabling men in cells close together to talk without being overheard by the guards, a considerable advantage when the talk is of escape.

It was not uncommon for the men on Death Row to discuss generally the possibility of escape, planning escapes on a theoretical level. All men in all prisons do that from the day they arrive to the day they leave. Only once in my fourteen-plus years did such a discussion continue over an extended period of time, going beyond the theoretical and evolving into a genuinely serious consideration of methods and details.

Five men were involved, including myself, and as the planning continued over two weeks or so, there emerged in my mind what I considered a truly creative plan, one that took into consideration and depended on the predictability of the prison authorities' response to a common emergency situation —which we tested and found to be exactly what we expected it to be. (Prison authorities plan for every conceivable emergency, and their response to a given situation is identical each time—predictably identical.) Only two things were needed for our plan to be successful: a snowstorm, preferably a roaring blizzard, and white outer garments made of bed sheets.

Although I took part in the planning of the escape attempt for lack of anything better to do at the time, I never would have gone along with it; I was too certain of eventually winning my freedom by legitimate means. But it would have worked, of that I am certain, and unless there have been some basic changes in the operating procedures at the New Jersey prison, as well as basic physical changes in the prison's architecture, it would still work.

Every particularly memorable event in the Death House had some sort of name, and the story of the typewriters was known as the story of J. Edgar Hoover's Magic Spring. Late at night, when the condemned men were reminiscing, telling new men about things that had happened over the years, someone sooner or later would yell out to me: "Hey, Smitty, tell 'em about J. Edgar Hoover's Magic Spring."

"Well, yeah, I'll tell ya, it was this way. . . ."

For what seemed most of my life—actually it was only about one-third of my life!—I had been asking and asking and asking for permission to have a typewriter, a privilege always extended to men serving time in the prison's general population but never to men under sentence of death. There were hundreds of typewriters in the institution. Any inmate in the general population who had twenty-five bucks to pick up a used machine from a hock shop could have one, and it was one of the first things new men bought when they arrived in the prison. They were indispensible for doing legal work, and with personal mail (outgoing) limited to one-page letters written on both sides of the paper, typewriters enabled one to get a hell of a lot more on a page.

(If anyone is wondering why it was permitted to write on two sides of one sheet of paper but not on one side of two sheets, which adds up to the same amount of writing but is much easier to read, both for the addressee and the mailroom censor, the curious will have to make up their own explanations. Prison logic has about as much to do with real logic as the bombing of Laotian villages has to do with the national security of the United States. And if one were to ask a responsible official about either, the answer would probably be the same: "Oh, you wouldn't understand." Yeah! Right on!)

At one point in my long string of requests, written and oral, for permission to have a typewriter, a senior prison official, well, in fact, the chief deputy warden, came to my cell to discuss the request, apparently hopeful that he could convince

chaplains, the reading material available to me was quite varied. Each day I would read four or five newspapers, including the New York *Times*, the Philadelphia *Bulletin*, the Philadelphia *Inquirer*, the New York *Daily News*, and one or two of the local New Jersey newspapers. Every week, without exception, I read the major newsmagazines—*Time*, *Newsweek*, *U.S. News & World Report*, *The Nation*, and *National Review*. I also would read, on a more or less regular basis, *Life*, *Look*, *Saturday Evening Post*, *Ebony*, *Playboy*, *Esquire*, and a number of ethnic and religious magazines. In addition to this reading of American publications concerned with national and world affairs, I subscribed to a service which provided me each week with a different foreign newspaper published in the English language.

Most of the books I read, as noted earlier, dealt with current events and the world situation. A sample of my reading in the few months before writing *Brief Against Death* includes: Santo Mazzarino's *The End of the Ancient World*, John King Fairbank's *The United States and China*, Edgar Snow's *The Battle for Asia*, Senator J. William Fulbright's *The Arrogance of Power*, Anthony Eden's *Foreign Affairs*, and Herman Kahn's *On Thermonuclear War*.

Not only did reading make it easier to get from hour to hour and help keep my head outside the prison walls, but before long I found myself realizing how little I knew, how much more about myself and the world I needed to learn.

I suppose it seems odd to some people that men under sentence of death are concerned with what is going on in the world from which they have been separated, that they keep abreast of the news and even follow closely the changes in such things as fashions, morals and mores, but again, this all is part of the continuing struggle to keep from being institutionalized. Every man I met on Death Row believed that someday, somehow, he would be a free man again—none ever believed that *he* would be one of the unlucky few actually executed—and each sought with varying degrees of success to prepare himself for the big day, to be ready to make the transition back into the free world with as little difficulty as possible, so as not to feel out of place or as if time and the world had passed him by.

Not everything happening outside interested every man. Some of the men on Death Row with me were deeply upset by the Kennedy assassinations, most were excited by the launching of the first Sputnik, but only a few felt any sense of drama or fear during the Cuban missile crisis. Oddly, unanimity of feeling seemed to come only with the moon landings. If ever there was a major event which to the men on Death Row was a major nonevent, it had to be the first landing on the moon. At best it prompted a protracted yawn while we waited for regular television programming to be resumed.

As might be expected, it was only when their own problems were involved that the men on Death Row evidenced any passionate interest, not because they cared less than others when the President was assassinated, but rather because with their own lives on the line every day, with death never more than one unfavorable court ruling away, they simply did not have time to think about anything but keeping themselves alive. That is, after all, what Death Row is all about. It is not a place where men wait to die; it is a place where they wage a daily struggle to stay alive and remain sane. It is also a place where some men change.

There are those—the majority, I suppose—who are embittered by the prison experience, who grow more rebellious and resentful of authority. Others, like myself, discover in prison a unique opportunity for self-examination and evaluation and, not liking what they see in themselves, are able, through education and hard work, to effect a genuine and lasting change for the better.

Much has been said and written, mostly by others, regarding my own rehabilitation—or transformation, a word I much prefer. *What* I did for myself is much better known than how and why I did it.

It is impossible for me to pinpoint any single event that caused me to look at myself, realize that I had done nothing but waste my life, and resolve to make myself better than I had been. Obviously, being in the Death House, having so little to do—or so much time to think introspectively—gave me the opportunity to see myself as I had never done before, to realize that all my life I had been a half-educated wise guy who had blamed all his troubles and all his failures on others or on "bad luck." Perhaps the triggering event, the one thing that really made me stop and think and take a good look at myself, was my divorce while on Death Row.

For five years, from 1957 to 1962, my wife remained at my side, writing me as often as possible (five times a month) and never once missing a visiting day. I suppose that her faithfulness throughout the ordeal of my arrest and trial and loss of appeal after appeal led me to believe that she would always be there, that I could take her for granted, and so it was an absolutely shattering moment when, in late February, 1962, she visited me in the Death House and told me that she would not be coming back, that for the sake of our daughter, then five years old, she was going to divorce me, remarry, and try to begin a new life as far from New Jersey as she could get. It took her five months to go through with it, to fly to Reno and set herself free, but when she finally did it, I wrote to Bill Buckley that I had reached the bottom of the ladder, that I had lost everything there was to lose, and that from then on there was no way to go but up.

Getting straight after twenty-eight years of being a slob wasn't easy. Education had to come first, if not simply to learn, to know more, at least to develop a habit of discipline such as I had lacked all my life. I had decided as far back as 1960 that I wanted to write a book about myself and my experiences with the judicial and penal systems, and to do that I had to learn both the English language—something of a mystery to me all my life—and how to discipline myself to forego the things I would rather be doing in favor of what I had to do for my own good. Even then I understood how terribly important that first book would be to me in my legal battle with the state of New Jersey.

It took me six months to earn my high school diploma, and then for the next two years I worked at college correspondence courses, acquiring and polishing the skills I needed. My educational efforts were interrupted during the 1964–65 period when I was without a lawyer and found it necessary to set aside everything else while I learned enough about the law to act as my own lawyer. My trial lawyer, paid by my family, had remained with me all through the appeals to the State Supreme Court, and then another lawyer, recommended to my family as a specialist in such matters, had been with me during the first unsuccessful round in the federal courts, but he had left me soon after my family could no longer pay the bills. A third lawyer, appointed by the federal court, went beyond the stage required by his appointment, even though he was not being paid for his efforts, until finally he, too, had to step out of the picture for financial reasons, leaving me facing a new death sentence and having to represent myself.

It is incredible what one can do when one's life is at stake. Within two weeks I had read and absorbed a complete volume on United States Supreme Court practice, sufficient knowledge to enable me to file a reasonably competent and professional-looking petition in that court. The petition was denied a few weeks later, but by that time I had learned enough about habeas corpus procedures that when I filed a petition in the Bergen County Court, the judge, the same judge who had sat at my trial and sentenced me to death in 1957, remarked in denying the petition that it had been prepared with the "consummate skill of a seasoned practitioner."

I was losing, but I was learning. More petitions. Several to the New Jersey Supreme Court, another to the United States Supreme Court, and finally, a huge petition for a writ of habeas corpus in the United States District Court for New Jersey. That was July, 1965. I did not realize it at the time, but that petition, after several more years of legal struggle to force the federal courts to render a decision on its merits, would prove to be the winner.

Learning the law and representing myself with my life at stake was a self-satisfying experience, but I must confess that at the start I was scared stiff. No one knew better than I what one mistake could cost me, what one failure to file a petition or application for a stay of execution in the allotted time could do to me. I don't think that in my entire life I had ever put so much time and effort into anything, that I had ever so disciplined myself, not because I wanted to or because it was any fun, but simply because I *had* to do it, because I was not going to give in and allow the state of New Jersey to kill me. The editor of the *Journal* of the New Jersey Bar Association once described me as "the best jailhouse lawyer in the country." Whether or not that was an accurate assessment I do not know; what I do know is that I managed to keep myself alive long enough to write *Brief Against Death*, earn the money that was needed to retain top-rated lawyers, and finally, after eleven years of frustration and defeat, set the stage for one of the most unusual and controversial courtroom proceedings in American legal history, a proceeding that would allow me to step from a Death Row cell to freedom.

It is not without reason that I have so often mentioned *Brief Against Death* in the course of this narrative. There is no way, surely, that I could understate, or underestimate, what that book and my published writings as a whole have done for me. *Brief Against Death* proved to be the beginning of the end of my legal struggles, the point at which Edgar Smith emerged from the shadows of Death Row and the legal tide began to turn in my favor, and my second book, *A Reasonable Doubt*, proved to the critics and publishers, and more importantly to myself, that I was not a "one-shot" writer.

Where once I was a name familiar only in the local press, *Brief Against Death* boosted me into a nationally and internationally known figure, a Death Row *author*, not merely a Death Row inmate; where once the known side of my legal struggle was the state of New Jersey's side of the story, *Brief Against Death* told my side and showed the reading public that the case against me was not so cut and dried as the prosecutor would have had the world go on believing, that there were an awful lot of unresolved doubts for which the state had no answers; where once the courts could dismiss my appeals without concern for public reaction, certain that the news would be reported, if at all, back among the classified ads in the local press, *Brief Against Death* moved me to the front pages of the New York *Times*, where the media and public could watch and question every move the courts made; where once the prosecutor could do or say as he liked, certain that I had no means to reply, *Brief Against Death* put him on notice that I had both a forum and a following; where once I had no money for lawyers and had to handwrite many of my own appeals or rely on second-rate state-appointed lawyers, my writings enabled me to retain the best lawyers available, lawyers who would not roll over and die when the going got tough; and where once the prosecutor had the media in his pocket, *Brief Against Death* and my subsequent writings won me friends and supporters in the news media who would prove invaluable as my legal fight drew to a close.

Ultimately, I suppose, *Brief Against Death* can be equated with a graduating thesis, the end product of years of working to educate myself, to grow up, to prove that I could do something other than hang out in gas stations and drink beer, to show that I could contribute to society, to be a worthwhile member of society, and to raise in the public consciousness the question: Who benefits from keeping Edgar Smith in prison?

That question would haunt the state of New Jersey throughout the closing stages of my fight to regain my freedom, and in the end the state would have to concede that whatever reasons there might have been for putting me in prison in 1957, those reasons no longer existed in 1971, for in fact the Edgar Smith of 1957 no longer existed.

Chapter

Four

Along toward the end of February, 1970, as we continued to wait for Judge Barlow to act to set a date for my hearing in the federal court, Steve Umin flew up from Washington to visit me at the prison. With him were Steve Lichtenstein and David Webster, another trial lawyer on Edward Bennett Williams' staff, who would work with Umin on the hearing.

During the course of our conversation that February afternoon the old question of a "deal" arose. For more than a year my lawyers and I had been discussing in general terms the possibility that at some point in the proceedings, if not as the date for the start of the hearing approached, then surely when the hearing began and it became obvious the state was losing, the prosecutor might make it known that he would be willing to make some sort of an "arrangement" with me, that the new prosecutors might be willing to give up something I wanted in return for not being saddled with my case for a dozen or so years, as their predecessors had been. I was not *their* case. *They* hadn't arrested and charged and convicted me. *Their* records, *their* reputations were not at stake. I was an unwanted inheritance. All the new people could do was lose. If the state won, if my conviction were not reversed, the old people would get the credit for having been right to begin with. If the state lost, the new people would get the blame for losing what the others had managed to win.

Nothing was proposed during the February meeting, but it was pointed out to me, as only lawyers can "point out" things they don't wish to come right out and say, that the new man on the case, Ed Fitzpatrick, had given some slight indication during the previous week's conference with Judge Barlow that the new county prosecutor might be amenable to some sort of "arrangement" that would permit the state to maintain the conviction record while giving me what I wanted —my freedom! Umin promised to keep his ears open.

At first it seemed that my letter to Judge Barlow had been a complete waste of time and paper, and I again pressed Umin to file for mandamus, to have Barlow *ordered* to hear my case. Much to my surprise, however, Barlow reacted a short while later by scheduling a prehearing conference for April 10 and agreeing to have me present to observe and personally ratify the proceedings. It would be my first trip outside the walls of the prison in thirteen years, and I looked forward to it with great anticipation. The world had changed greatly during those thirteen years, I knew that for sure, and I anxiously awaited the opportunity to see for myself what changes there had been.

On April 10, handcuffs on my wrists, the cuffs attached to a thick leather belt around my waist and buckled in back, so that I couldn't even raise my hands to light a cigarette, I was taken by two prison guards to the Federal Courthouse in the center of Trenton, only a ten-minute ride from the prison. There, in the office of the United States marshal, I was placed in a large detention cell to await the hearing scheduled for 10:00 A.M.

It was a day of impressions I'll never forget. As I looked out the courthouse window and watched the people walk by on the sidewalks below, saw cars coming and going from the parking lot across the street, and looked over the rooftops of the city, no impression burned itself more deeply in my mind than that of the world being so much dirtier, shabbier, more run-down and depressing than I had last seen it thirteen years before. Compared with what I saw out there, the prison was cleaner inside than a hospital operating room. The streets, the air, the buildings, all seemed to grow dirtier as I watched, and the people in the streets, hurrying along, their clothes of green and purple and chartreuse and orange and lavender and hot pink, their bell-bottoms and mini-skirts and maxi-coats flapping and bouncing as they rushed along, all seemed to be unsmiling, preoccupied with problems, looking neither right nor left, ignoring each other, their brightly colored clothing in stark contrast to the hard, sober faces.

I had heard and read much about the New Morality, the new life-style, the greater freedom, the ever-increasing leisure time people "on the street" were enjoying—but wow! *Enjoying?* No one seemed to be enjoying a goddamn thing out there. All of a sudden I wondered about the worth of my thirteen years of struggle. Is *that* what I was fighting to get back into? Later that day I wrote to Bill Buckley about what I had seen and felt:

IMPRESSIONS: The outside world is filthy, the air stinks, the new buildings look like cheeseboxes, and the new cars look like toys made in Japan. The dirt is what amazed me. I cannot remember the world being so dirty, and I wonder if I notice it only because I was seeing it—almost—for the first time. I wonder if others, who are out there every day, realize how filthy the buildings and streets are and how rotten the air smells. Believe it or not, in the big parking lot across the street from the courthouse, the most astonishing thing was not the designs or the bright colors of the new cars lined up in rows, but the fact that I did not see one clean car in the entire lot. Every one was filthy, the colors muted by a film of dirt. The streets are the same way, dirty, littered, and filled with bumps and holes and cracks. The people were clean, all dressed in the wildest, brightest colors one could imagine, and the girls were wearing skirts that almost weren't, but they weren't smiling. Everyone was walking around looking as if he had just flunked algebra. And the car I went over to court in was small, cramped, and put together like a plastic scale model of the *Titanic*. It was a '70 Plymouth. Keep it. I don't want it.

The girls were a surprise. It is impossible to tell how old a girl is these days. They could be fifteen, twenty, or twenty-five; they all look alike, dress alike, walk alike, and when they smile, smile alike, one of those "I'll smile but I don't really want to" smiles. But the dirt—that really got me. Doesn't *anyone* clean *anything* anymore? The only clean things I saw all day were a new Cadillac and the courtroom. The Cadillac probably belonged to the judge. Jesus! How do people live out there? Either they have lived with it for so long they have stopped noticing, or they have stopped caring. As I told Sophie,* Trenton you can almost forgive because this town doesn't have enough class to be a first-rate slum. "Effete snobs" hell! What this world is full of is effete *slobs!*

Two hours and several cups of U.S. marshal-supplied coffee after my arrival at the courthouse, Mark Segal, one of Steve Lichtenstein's partners, came to the detention room to advise me that there would be several more hours' delay. Umin, Webster, and Lichtenstein had gone "somewhere" to meet with Assistant Prosecutor Fitzpatrick.

"What's it all about?" I asked.

"I'm just a message bearer," Mark replied unconvincingly.

"Come off it, Mark. It doesn't make sense. Fitzpatrick is coming to Trenton for this conference, so why couldn't everyone just wait here until he arrived if they wanted to meet with him? Why did they have to go somewhere else to meet? What's brewing?"

"I guess they'll tell you when they get here, around one o'clock," Mark answered, saying nothing I hadn't already taken for granted.

---

* Sophie Wilkins, a friend and the editor of *Brief Against Death*.

Poor Mark! Lichtenstein is forever sending him with messages like that, and always he has to go along with the game and pretend he doesn't know what anything is about. He knew, and after a few minutes thinking about it, I had a good idea myself what was going on.

Umin, Webster, and Lichtenstein arrived at 1:40 that afternoon, and we promptly got together in the rear of the detention cell for a conference, out of hearing of the marshals and prison guards. Umin told me they had just come from a secret meeting with Fitzpatrick in the chambers of a prominent New Jersey judge who had agreed to mediate the discussions.

Fitzpatrick had stated at the outset of the meeting that the Bergen County Prosecutor's Office and the state of New Jersey thought it would be to everyone's benefit if my case were terminated. It was felt by certain public offiicals that my first book, *Brief Against Death*, had cast serious doubts upon the fairness and integrity of the judicial system (exactly what I had intended); that I had been using my position as a man under a death sentence, therefore a man able to command wide attention in the public media, to wage war against the judicial system in general and the county prosecutor's office in particular; and that the publication of my book in Europe was resulting in a bad image for the American system of law. Also of significant concern was the fact that some European law schools were using my book in courses in comparative law, showing the American system's weaknesses and inability to admit error; and the fact that some police science schools in this country were using the book to teach future police officers how *not* to handle a criminal case.

For these reasons and others, including the enormous cost to the taxpayers in defending the state's case against my appeals, the state would be willing to reach a settlement which would (a) grant me my freedom in the shortest possible time while (b) preserving the state's conviction record, so that the state could, in effect, tell the world: "You see? Smith *was* guilty, therefore the system *does* work."

Wheeeeeeee! Long live the system! Let's all pin on our little American flag pins and cheer.

One of the first possibilities discussed between my lawyers and Fitzpatrick had been that I file a postconviction relief application citing *Witherspoon v. Illinois*, the United States Supreme Court ruling that persons opposed to capital punishment could not be excluded from first-degree murder case juries. *Witherspoon* was fully retroactive, and the state was willing to concede that there had been violations of the rule in the selection of my trial jury.

One of the problems with *Witherspoon*, however, was that the Supreme Court had ruled only that in cases in which the rule had been violated in jury selection, the death penalty could not stand. The court did not say what penalty should be imposed in place of the death penalty, how the new penalty should be decided, or even if a new trial had to be ordered. Most states have decided against giving a new trial, instead giving a life sentence in place of the death penalty. My lawyers argued during the conference with Fitzpatrick and the judge that nothing prevented a judge from modifying *my* death penalty to a second-degree penalty, under which I would be eligible for immediate parole. Fitzpatrick indicated the state would be willing to accept second-degree sentencing, but the judge mediating the conference stated that while the death penalty could easily be voided in my case, since violations had surely occurred, it would be impossible to modify to a second-degree sentence. The State Supreme Court, though it had not yet spoken on the subject, probably would not allow such a precedent to stand. The judge felt that only a life sentence would be permitted.

A life sentence was totally unacceptable to me. It was too uncertain. While parole eligibility begins at fourteen years and eight months under a life sentence, the parole board has absolute discretion to deny parole for as long as it wants and without giving anyone a reason. I could never have accepted anything as uncertain as that, not even with more than thirteen years already served, and my lawyers so informed the judge. Further discussions were held.

Finally, after the judge stated that he would be willing to write a personal letter to the parole board, recommending parole at first eligibility on the grounds that he felt I was fully rehabilitated and the state should use me as an example of the success of the rehabilitory process, Fitzpatrick consulted with his superior, Prosecutor Robert Dilts. Dilts agreed that if I accepted a life sentence and the judge wrote his letter as promised, the prosecutor's office not only would agree *not* to oppose parole for me, but in fact would make known to the parole board certain confidential information, in the form of investigation reports, that would clearly indicate to the parole board that my case never should have been a first-degree murder case to begin with, and therefore I should not be serving a life sentence. The information, my attorneys were told, was such that would indicate the crime might have had some basis of provocation and/or justification.

In return for the arrangement and the representations to the parole board by the judge and prosecutor, I was to agree to withdraw my appeal in the federal court and agree to forego all further challenges to my conviction.

The formula for settlement was still unacceptable to me because of the uncertainty of parole from a life sentence. Neither the prosecutor nor the judge could guarantee parole. My attorneys advised the judge I would not accept such a "deal," and a new formula was devised.

Under the new formula, the prosecutor and my attorneys would go to Federal Judge Barlow, who knew of the conference taking place and was awaiting its outcome, and advise him that they wanted a continuance until May 8. At that time, by agreement, both sides would argue whether my conviction was legal under the *Greenwald v. Wisconsin* standard. *Greenwald* was a 1968 case in which the Supreme Court had voided a conviction and ordered a new trial due to the use of a confession obtained in circumstances remarkably similar to those in which the police had extracted statements from me in the period immediately after my arrest. No habeas corpus hearing would be required prior to the proposed arguments; the case would be decided strictly upon the record compiled in the state court. The state would oppose me on the issue, argue against applying the *Greenwald* standard to my case, but Judge Barlow would be informed in advance of the arguments that a ruling favorable to me would result in the termination of my case through agreement.

The reversal of my conviction and the ordering of a new trial were crucial to the effectuation of an agreement, for only if the conviction were voided could it be arranged for me to be given less than a life sentence. As long as I remained under a first-degree conviction, second-degree sentencing was impossible. Once Judge Barlow voided my conviction, however, and ordered a new trial, the prosecutor agreed that he would not appeal the ruling and drag the case out if I would immediately return to Bergen County, waive my right to a new trial, and plead *non vult* to the indictment.

In the state of New Jersey, all murder indictments are so-called open indictments. They do not specify any degree of murder, rather only a general charge of murder, with the specification of the degree left to the trial jury to decide after hearing the evidence. The prosecutor may ask the jury to return a first-degree conviction, but it is left to the jury to decide whether the crime had been first or second degree. As a result of this "open indictment" situation, the New Jersey statutes permit the *non vult*, or "no defense," plea to the indictment, and it is left to the judge accepting the plea to determine whether to impose a life sentence or a sentence not exceeding the maximum sentence permitted for second-degree murder. The maximum is thirty years, and a minimum must also be set.

Generally speaking, parole eligibility in New Jersey occurs when one has served one-third of the minimum sentence less credits for work time and "good time," days taken off the sentence for good behavior in confinement. The maximum anyone serves, again generally, is two-thirds of the maximum sentence less work time and "good time." Thus, if one were sentenced to, say, 21–30 years for second-degree murder, one would become eligible for parole in one-third of 21 years less work and "good" time, or somewhere around 5–6 years. One would "max out"—have done the maximum time and be able to walk out the front door without parole—at roughly two-thirds of 30 years less work and "good" time, or somewhere around 16 years.

My understanding of the deal being offered by the state, at the time I was told of it, was that if Judge Barlow voided my conviction and ordered a new trial, and if in return for the prosecutor's waiving his right to appeal I would waive my right to the new trial and would plead *non vult* to the indictment, the prosecutor would recommend and the judge would accept second-degree sentencing. Assuming I were given the maximum sentence, I would be long overdue for parole and in any case could not be required to serve more than another year or two. If the judge gave me the more "usual" sort of second-degree sentence, which runs somewhere in the neighborhood of 20–25 years, I would "max out"—be able to go free without parole—within a couple of months.

My attorneys explained to me that it would be made clear to Judge Barlow, a new federal judge handling his first major case, that the formula for settlement would work as much to his benefit as to mine, since with the state agreeing not to appeal his decision, if he ruled in my favor, there would be no possibility that an appeals court could overrule his first important decision from the federal bench. Moreover, should he not go along with the arrangement, not rule in my favor, then the Supreme Court mandate would compel him to hold a long, expensive habeas corpus hearing, at the end of which he would have a much more difficult decision to make and one that was certain to be appealed by the losing side.

Steve Lichtenstein told me during the detention cell meeting that he had already checked with the prison authorities regarding my parole eligibility on a second-degree sentence. He had been told that the authorities regarded me as an "exemplary prisoner" and that even if I were to receive the maximum sentence, I would be immediately eligible for parole. Steve also pointed out—he didn't need to—that if I refused the deal, my thirteen years already served guaranteed that I would spend more time in prison on appeal than had I received a life sentence back in 1957. I was, in fact, keeping myself in jail by not giving up, by continuing my appeals.

Steve Umin was doing most of the talking during the conference, and after he told me that Judge Barlow would be fully advised of the arrangement, fully advised that the state desired an end to my case, he said it was probable that we would have a decision by the first of June, since that was the date Judge Barlow had set to begin the trial of Newark's Mayor Addonizio. It looked, Umin said, as if the deal could be concluded in time to have me resentenced and eligible for parole by the end of the year.

For some reason the deal seemed to stink. I was doing some quick on-my-feet thinking, and however I cut it, the story about the prosecutor's concern for the image of the judicial system sounded awfully weak. It was going to take a hell of a lot more than convicting Edgar Smith to restore the image of *this* judicial system. More likely, I thought, it went something like this: The habeas corpus hearing was due to begin soon, the prosecutor knew damn well we were going to whip him, that after losing and having a fair-sized portion of his evidence ruled inadmissible, he wouldn't have a prayer in hell of getting a conviction if he retried me, so now he was running scared and trying to avoid all those problems by making like a good Samaritan. Losing a murder conviction is always a bad scene for a prosecutor; losing *my* conviction would be a disaster for Fitzpatrick and his political ambitions. No way he could hide that on the back page of the Oshkosh *Daily Snort*. If Fitzpatrick lost me, he would lose me on page one of the New York *Times*. Nothing cool about that.

Umin did not agree with my thinking—or so he said. He said he believed the prosecutor was sincere in wanting the case closed in the best possible way for all concerned, and the best possible way at that moment seemed to be to give me my freedom in the shortest possible time in return for my letting the state keep its conviction. Lawyers always ascribe pure motives to their brothers at the bar. They have a great club.

I still didn't like the deal, or even the idea of a deal. Many people who believed in me, who trusted me, would be let down, would feel betrayed, if I copped a plea. My closest friends would know what the deal had been, would understand that after spending more than a third of my life in a Death Row cell I wanted nothing but *out*, and to get that while I still had some life left to enjoy it I had to give up something. Sure, I could go on fighting, go on protesting my innocence, and perhaps in another four or five or six years I would win, I would prove that everything I had said was true, and no doubt many people would say that is what I should have done, but unfortunately those who took that attitude were not going to volunteer to come down and wait in the cell for me, were not going to go broke paying my legal expenses for me. It is awfully easy to say, as one woman said to me, "I wouldn't plead guilty to something I didn't do if they tore out my fingernails with hot pincers." It is easy to say because she will never have to prove it. Anyway, they don't do that to you. Hot pincers? I should be so lucky. *That* doesn't last thirteen or fourteen years.

Umin was pressing me for an answer. I stalled, asked as many questions as I could think of, looking for more time to consider the arrangement. I knew immediately that I didn't have to worry about my friends, that they would stand by me and would understand that a plea was the price I was paying for my freedom, that it was just a technical plea, the sort of thing done a thousand times every day in our courts, meaningless except to those in the prosecutor's offices who keep score of their convictions and worry about their images and batting averages, as if justice were some kind of grand ball game.

As for the others, those who were never on my side, who always believed I was guilty—I took a hardheaded attitude toward those people years ago. I knew they wouldn't believe any differently even if I won a new trial and were acquitted by a jury in thirty seconds flat, with the prosecutor then being arrested and indicted for malicious prosecution and misuse of his office. People like that always have excuses for their beloved system, always blame things on technicalities or slick lawyers, always refuse to believe that, well, maybe the good old American system of law *does* sometimes get screwed up, *does* make mistakes, *does* put the wrong guy behind bars or in the electric chair every now and then. Those people, many of them the same ones who will cheer Nixon and idolize Agnew, thinking the latter is some great intellectual because he can pass the *Reader's Digest* vocabulary test, and who think we really *are* defending something called the free world when we send our best young kids to get zapped in Vietnam, they really mean nothing to me—I'd rather leave 'em than take 'em, even if they do occasionally happen to buy my books.

My pride was another roadblock that April afternoon as the lawyers pressed me for an answer. I just hate to give up anything, anytime, to anyone. There is a crazy sort of joy, a sense of accomplishment, in doing what I had done to the state of New Jersey for thirteen years prior to the offer of the deal. Everything the state had—unlimited money and manpower, the best legal talent available—had been put into the effort to kill me, and they had failed, failed, even though for a period of a couple years I had no lawyer and was doing my own legal work. Now, to give all that up by pleading, by accepting the deal, seemed to be nothing more than letting the state off the hook, wasting all those years of effort, saying to others who were in conflict with the power of the state: "You can't win."

I had to make a decision. No getting around it, no putting it off until later, no passing the buck to my lawyers.

"Okay, Steve, let's go to court," I told Umin. "I don't like it, but Fitzpatrick just bought himself a deal."

"Good. We'll talk to Judge Barlow first, brief him on this, then go to court and move for a continuance until May eighth for the purpose of arguing *Greenwald*. It will take two minutes."

"I'm ready," I said, standing and reaching for my suit jacket.

"There's just one more thing, Edgar."

"Yeah—like what?" I asked cautiously, my hand halfway to the jacket. I had learned to be leery of lawyers. They always like to add "buts" and "howevers" to things. Every lawyer seems to have been born with a big "but."

The things Steve Umin proceeded to tell me, the conditions he outlined, are so revealing of how the justice game is played in this country (many reviewers of my second book, *A Reasonable Doubt*, questioned whether backroom defense lawyer-prosecutor dealing *really* works as I depicted it in the book) that even while Umin was speaking, I resolved to record it in an affidavit as soon as I returned to prison that afternoon. I felt it was imperative to make a contemporary record of what I was told that day, so that a year or two or three years later, if questions arose or if I decided to write another book about my case, I would not have to rely on my memory. Therefore, when I returned to the prison that day I summoned Sergeant William Dean, the prison mail room supervisor and a notary public, and with him as a witness I executed an affidavit recording the complete details of how and when and why the deal with the state had been consummated and who had said what to whom. The following, quoted from pages 5–6 of that affidavit, is how I recorded the conditions Umin told me the prosecutor wanted agreed to in return for the deal:

(10) That in addition to my commitment to plead guilty to second-degree murder if and when Judge Barlow ordered a new trial, counsel advised me that the state required one more thing of me. I was to agree that at no time, under no circumstances, would I reveal that Assistant Prosecutor Fitzpatrick was a friend and neighbor of mine before my arrest; that I have known him and his older brother, with whom I went to school, for many years; and that today Fitzpatrick is a neighbor and friend of my older brother. Counsel stated that I was not to mention Fitzpatrick in correspondence, or at any other time, or make public the fact that we are old friends, since the prosecutor fears the public will not understand the situation and may feel I am being given some sort of special deal because Fitzpatrick and I are old friends.*

Isn't it wonderful the way our system works so honestly and aboveboard? *Yippee!*

Even after agreeing to everything, when I returned to my cell that afternoon, I was already having doubts about the arrangement, doubts that the deal was as airtight as my attorneys had led me to believe (inadvertently, I suspect), doubts that I was doing the right and honest thing in pleading guilty just to buy my freedom. Those doubts were reflected in the affidavit:

(11) That following all the foregoing, I did commit myself to a plea of guilty to second-degree murder and did agree to conceal the fact of my relationship to the assistant prosecutor. I made these agreements even though I have always denied,

---

* I do not regard it as a violation of the agreement with my attorneys to reveal the association with Fitzpatrick since that matter has become one of public knowledge and has been reported by the news media.

and still deny, that I killed Victoria Zielinski. It is my belief that a plea to second-degree murder is the only way I can be released from prison in the foreseeable future. . . .

(12) That the purpose of this affidavit is to establish the truth of what I have stated herein. I realize that if, after the deal with the state is concluded, I were to tell this story, few people would believe that I pleaded guilty because it was part of a deal to effect my freedom. Therefore, well in advance of the implementation of such a deal, I have prepared this affidavit to establish that such a deal will take place. It is my hope that when the public sees that the things I have stated here come to pass, the public will begin to understand why respect for the system is declining, why so many people no longer believe their public officials. Only by making this deal with the prosecutor and the judge, only by participating in this sham, then making it public, can I show why so many, particularly the blacks and the poor, those who are not as fortunate as I am to have friends, money, and the high-class lawyers who can make under-the-table deals, no longer believe they can receive justice under this system. If I am to be given a deal resulting in my freedom, it is not because I am innocent, not because of the merits of my case, not because the state of New Jersey wants to see justice done in my case. If I receive such a deal, it will be because I was smart enough to write a book about my case, fortunate enough to have friends to get it published and highly publicized, and as a result of that book, financially able to retain the best lawyers available, lawyers who could, simply put, pull the strings that the poor and the black cannot even reach.

Not a well-worded affidavit, nor as complete an account of the deal as I would have liked to have written at the time, but it says what I felt then and still feel now. I'll take the sort of deal for myself that other men on other death rows can only dream about, because there is nothing I want more than my freedom, but I don't have to like dealing. And I damn sure won't keep quiet about it.

By an odd quirk of fate, just as my attorneys and I were discussing the possibility of concluding the deal with the assistant prosecutor, my second book, *A Reasonable Doubt,* was going to the printer, and in that book is a passage, a bit of dialogue between a defense attorney and an assistant prosecutor who are trying to work out a deal in a murder case. Speaking of his client, the defense attorney says at one point:

". . . Fellows like Bender are difficult to see into. They're born and raised in a cynical world whose cynicism rubs off on them, a world in which they are surrounded on all sides by hypocrisy—the two of us sitting here as we are, bargaining over justice, is just the sort of thing Bender's generation has come to hate about us, about the establishment we represent."

When I had agreed to everything my attorneys had put before me and to the prosecutor's conditions, I was led by two prison officers and a U.S. marshal across the corridor into the courtroom, a very large room, walnut-paneled, huge slabs of variegated black marble rising up behind the judge's bench, thick red carpets and red upholstered reclining-back swivel chairs neatly aligned behind the walnut counsel tables, their tops polished like mirrors. It was most impressive, awesome, a display of wealth and power that said: "This is it, Charlie. This is a FEDERAL courtroom and you'd bloody well better believe it."

I recall that after I was seated at the counsel table on our side of the courtroom, I turned to David Webster and said: "The whole joint was probably a WPA project. Look at that marble up there. Some poor Italian *paesano* back in Vicenza or somewhere during the thirties probably got paid six cents an hour to carve and polish that."

David just grinned and looked at the ceiling, also paneled with richly carved wood.

Several newspaper reporters came in and sat in the jury box off to my left, all of them young, in their early twenties, not much older, the new breed, long-haired and mod, wearing clothes that made them look like walking rainbows, one a tall redheaded girl who reminded me of someone in the dim past, a now-shadowy figure I had come close to marrying eighteen years before. You can lose 'em but you can't forget 'em.

In came Edward N. Fitzpatrick, assistant prosecutor of the County of Bergen, counsel for the state of New Jersey, before the federal bar of justice. I almost fell out of the chair laughing.

Little Fitz had grown tremendously since I had last seen him—*out*, not up! He looked as if he weighed 250, at least, walked with a waddle on short stubby legs, had a face like an English bulldog, and wore thick black-framed eyeglasses that kept sliding down, causing him constantly to wrinkle up his nose in an attempt to hold them, thus adding to the bulldog impression. Now and then, the nose wrinkling unsuccessful, he would jab at the bridge of the glasses with his middle finger, thrusting them back against his forehead, as if perhaps if he pushed them back hard enough, they might stay in place.

In came God. Well, almost. United States District Judge George Barlow, a small, gray-haired, baby-faced man entered from his chambers to the right of the courtroom, and while his clerk mumbled out the formula about how if you were real nice and paid attention and had business before the court the judge might just decide to let you speak, Barlow ascended, not quite into heaven, only up carpeted steps to his bench several feet above the clerk's desk and the witness stand. And there he sat, totally at ease, in all his power and glory, looking down at the common folks, then nodding to Umin to begin.

There were no microphones in the courtroom, and I have great difficulty hearing, so when Umin walked up to the speaking rostrum, spoke for about a minute, then returned to sit beside me while Fitzpatrick waddled up and growled out his say before returning to his seat, I was surprised to see Judge Barlow nod again, say a few words I couldn't understand, then leave the room.

"Congratulations," Steve Lichtenstein said, sticking out his hand. "You won."

"Swell. What did I win?" I asked, puzzled by the whole affair.

"You moved for a continuance and it was granted."

"I knew that was going to happen when you told me about the arrangement with Fitzpatrick. So what's the big deal?"

"No one else knows," David Webster replied with a conspiratorial wink.

Chapter Five

Several times between April 10 and May 8 I met with Steve Lichtenstein and discussed the deal we had made with the prosecutor, and each time I liked it less. What I had thought would be a plea to second-degree murder, as reflected in my affidavit, where I mention such a plea, would in fact be a *non vult* plea to the open murder indictment. That sort of plea, as I have explained, would give the judge the option of imposing either a life sentence or a sentence in years not to exceed the maximum sentence for second degree. I had questions: How did I know that once I had made the plea and it was too late for me to back out, the judge wouldn't double-cross us and zap me with a life sentence? How did we know the prosecutor wouldn't double-cross us and refuse to recommend second-degree sentencing? How did we know that even if the judge went along with the deal and gave me second-degree sentencing, he wouldn't give me the max, then both he and the prosecutor oppose parole for me?

Lichtenstein sought to assure me that everything had been agreed upon, that although it was always possible there could be a dirty deal pulled, although it was possible I might not be paroled right away, he felt the prosecutor and judge would keep their side of the bargain.

"What assurance do we have?" I asked.

"We have their word," Lichtenstein replied confidently.

"But nothing *guaranteed*."

"No, of course not. These deals don't work that way. There's nothing in writing, no guarantee that you won't receive a maximum sentence, and you have to be prepared for that possibility. You have to be prepared for the possibility that you'll do more time, but your record in prison indicates you won't have to do much more, and certainly there is no way in the world they could make you do more than the max. At the very worst, even without work and commutation time credits, you would only have to do another five years."

Only five years! The way lawyers talk about years you'd think they were talking about golfing weekends.

Then Lichtenstein said something I was to hear several more times over the next year or so.

"I think the state will want you to do just a little more time," he told me, "before you are released. It is bad for the public image if a man is released from the Death House to the street too quickly. They might want you to do a few months in minimum security status. It looks better for the public that way."

By the time we were ready to return to court May 8 I had written several times to Steve Umin to tell him I thought he had bought me a lousy deal, that in fact it was worse than a bad deal—it was no deal. As I saw it, I gave the state everything the prosecutor wanted—the plea, the conviction, the withdrawal of my appeals, the restoration of the judicial system's "image," the whole damn works—and all I got in return, as best I could see, was a nebulous promise that *after* I had sold myself out, *after* it was too late for me to change my mind, the state would come through with *something*, that something specified but not guaranteed. The very people whom my federal appeals charged with illegal, unconstitutional, coercive conduct in the investigation of my case, with having held me sleepless and incommunicado through more than twenty hours of interrogation, who had refused to allow me contact with my attorney or my wife, who had taken my wife into custody so that she couldn't contact my attorney, who had admittedly used illegal search and seizure methods against me, and who for thirteen years had made every effort to kill me, even going so far as to lie deliberately to the appeals court (as documented in my first book and never denied by the authorities)—now these same people were asking me to take their word, to trust them. Why should I?

The prison authorities got me to court late the morning of May 8. Umin and Webster had been in the courtroom waiting, having asked the authorities to get me to court early enough for a conference before the arguments began. They wanted to go over the deal and resolve my doubts, but there was no time.

Sitting in the courtroom, waiting for the judge to enter, David Webster said I had to make a quick decision right then, and it had to be a final decision. If I wanted to back out of the deal, there was still time, but he would have to inform the judge before the arguments began.

"What do you think, David?" I asked. "Is it a good deal?"

"I think so, but you're the one who has to decide."

"Do you trust them?"

"I wouldn't put it quite that way," David replied. "I'd say that all things considered, it would be to the state's advantage to keep its word on this thing. They would have nothing to gain by double-crossing you at this stage. The state wants this case closed as much as anyone does."

"You really think it's the best we can do?"

"I think so."

"Okay, David, go."

The oral arguments before Judge Barlow that morning were dull, as legal arguments on technical issues, as the *Greenwald* argument was, tend to be. Umin, as always, was prepared beyond belief. Had Judge Barlow asked, I think Umin could have told him which Supreme Court Justice had heartburn the morning the *Greenwald* decision was handed down. Slowly, calmly, methodically, he dissected the *Greenwald* decision, took the pieces of that case apart, then took apart the manner in which the police had arrested and interrogated me, laid the pieces of the two cases side by side, then put them back together again, demonstrating how they matched, how the parts were interchangeable, making it clear that what the Supreme Court had done in *Greenwald* Judge Barlow had to do with my case—reverse the conviction and order a new trial. Even one of the prison guards sitting behind me leaned forward when Umin finished his presentation and whispered: "He's great!"

Fitzpatrick has one tone of voice—loud. Booming out his objections to Umin's arguments, wrinkling up his nose, jabbing at his glasses when the nose wrinkling was unsuccessful, Little Fitz used the old argument that the Supreme Court had rejected in sending my case back down for a hearing; he argued that the issues had been decided by the court of appeals in 1963. It was a good move. To the newspaper reporters sitting in the jury box, making notes, it sounded like a strong argument, as if the prosecutor were really fighting me tooth and nail, and that would look good to the public later when the deal was made.

An hour after they had begun, the arguments ended and Judge Barlow had taken the matter under advisement. I had a short visit in the back of the courtroom with my mother, brother, and some friends—Fitzpatrick had pretended all morning not to see my brother, walking past him after court as if he did not exist—then I was on the way back to the Death House with Umin's estimate of how things had gone for us.

"It looks fifty-fifty," he had told me.

Lawyers being basically conservative dudes when it came to making predictions, I figured those were good odds.

The wait for Judge Barlow's ruling seemed to take forever. Friends and relatives and certain people connected with my publishers knew of the pending deal and wrote cheerfully to me, offering suggestions for the future. Reunions were planned, new books and magazine articles were proposed, TV appearances to discuss my case and its meaning within the context of the American system of justice were arranged. Finally, after thirteen long years, the end seemed to be in sight. Not a glorious end, not a "victory" in the sense I would have liked, but an end nonetheless, and I looked forward to the day when freedom would again be mine. Umin may have said the odds were only 50–50, but I knew he thought they were a lot better than that. And why not? The state wanted the case closed as badly as I did.

June 1 came and went, the trial of Mayor Addonizio began before Judge Barlow, and still we waited for the ruling on our *Greenwald* arguments. Perhaps, I thought, Barlow was playing it cool, waiting for a dramatic moment in the Addonizio trial, when the headlines would be taken up with that matter; then he could come down with a ruling in my favor and hope to have it slip by relatively unnoticed. Umin and Lichtenstein seemed less confident as the weeks went by, but I still believed we had it made. No judge, not even one newly appointed, could be so stupid as to pass up the opportunity to settle a major criminal case by mutual agreement, with no danger of having his ruling appealed and starting off his federal career with an appellate court reversal. Surely Judge Barlow did not want my case dragged out, did not want to find himself compelled to hold a long habeas corpus hearing that would leave him at the end with an infinitely more difficult decision to make. Surely he knew that if he didn't go along with us on the *Greenwald* issue, we would appeal.

July went by, then on August 4 Judge Barlow surprised me by rejecting the *Greenwald* arguments, in effect refusing to allow the case to be settled out of court, thereby forcing us into the habeas corpus hearing. Somehow Judge Barlow had bought Fitzpatrick's cockamamie argument that the issues the United States Supreme Court had ruled were not fully decided in 1963 *had* been decided in 1963. As I read through Barlow's opinion, two things seemed clear: (1) During his time as a county judge he had quite obviously failed to study and appreciate the meanings of certain Supreme Court rulings, and (2) he was, for some reason, prepared to see my case dragged out on appeal for a few more years, since that would be the necessary result of his ruling.

Immediately after reading the Barlow decision I wrote to Umin and told him what I thought of it, pointing out that Barlow seemed totally ignorant of *Johnson v. New Jersey*, the Supreme Court ruling that held that even where issues had been decided previously, as Barlow said they had been in my case, an appellant is entitled to have them reconsidered in light of later Supreme Court rulings.

Umin replied that he would "submit another memorandum to [Barlow] restating our view of *Johnson v. New Jersey*. As you have noted, he totally misunderstands the case."

We decided to file an interlocutory appeal of Judge Barlow's August 4 ruling, an appeal that would be heard in the United States court of appeals, while at the same time my lawyers would continue planning for the Supreme Court-ordered habeas corpus hearing. Interlocutory appeals do not delay other pending proceedings, so no time would be lost. If the court of appeals overruled Barlow on the *Greenwald* ruling, no hearing would be necessary; a new trial would be ordered. If the court upheld Barlow, things would go forward as if there had been no appeal.

Barlow agreed to the appeal of his ruling and agreed to sign the "certificate of probable cause" noting his own "substantial doubt" as to the correctness of his decision. Without this certificate, which is a procedural requirement, an interlocutory appeal would not be permitted.

On the day Judge Barlow was to sign the certificate of

probable cause, he backed down, obviously having second thoughts about signing a document that, for all practical purposes, was an invitation to the court of appeals to look over his shoulder. Then came an unusual and highly irregular phone call from Barlow to Steve Umin. A "resolution" had been achieved.

In return for our agreement to postpone the interlocutory appeal for three weeks, while he took a vacation and thought about his *Greenwald* ruling, Judge Barlow would schedule a conference for immediately after his return from vacation, and at that time he would give us an opportunity to restate our view of *Greenwald* and *Johnson v. New Jersey* in an attempt to persuade him that he was in error.

Umin wrote to me: "[Judge Barlow] might see fit to certify the questions [for appeal] or, more unlikely, he may even change his mind on the merits."

The judge also agreed during the phone call to meet our proposed schedule for the habeas corpus hearing if he decided against certification and did not change his mind on *Greenwald*.

"The phone call and these consequences are highly irregular," Umin wrote me, "but such are the ways of the federal judiciary."

Judge Barlow returned from his vacation shortly after Labor Day, and we waited for the scheduling of the conference. Finally, after several phone calls from Umin pressing him to act, the conference was set up for October 2. Motions for reconsideration of the *Greenwald* issue were filed September 25, but by the time the conference was held a week later Umin realized we were going to get nowhere with Barlow. The motion for reconsideration was withdrawn and with it our effort to file an interlocutory appeal. Instead, with the prosecutor's consent, we proposed January 15, 1971, as the date to begin the habeas corpus hearing.

Judge Barlow agreed to accept January 15 but only as a

"target date" (his own description). There was no commitment to begin the hearing on that date, and in fact nearly a year after the case had first been assigned to him, Barlow had still not completed certain necessary formalities, by ruling, for instance, that the Supreme Court order required a hearing. The judge denied that any such ruling was necessary, since the intent of the Supreme Court's order was obvious, but nonetheless without such a ruling and the answering of certain questions, such as which side had the burden of proof at the hearing, it was impossible for either side to begin planning strategy. Also yet to be determined was the scope of the hearing, what issues the judge would permit raised, what evidentiary rules would be followed, what prehearing discovery would be permitted, and what degree of proof would be required. Would we be bound by federal rules of criminal procedure, since mine was a criminal case, or by the rules of civil procedure, since habeas corpus is a civil proceeding? Until Barlow answered these questions, neither my attorneys nor Fitzpatrick could proceed to get ready for January 15.

Almost two years to the day after the Supreme Court had sent my case back down to be heard, Umin lost patience and decided it was time to strike. We would finally go for mandamus, seeking to have Judge Barlow *ordered* to act without further delay, barring which we sought his removal from the case. It was a tough decision for Umin to make, to ask for the removal of a federal judge only one year on the bench, since that removal would forever be reflected in the judge's record should he be considered for promotion, but we had given him every chance to avoid our taking such a drastic step and still he sat in his chambers and refused to act.

The arguments in Edward Bennett Williams' office went both ways, some of the staff thinking it was time for mandamus, others arguing that it was too soon, that we didn't yet have a strong enough case, and that failure would forever prejudice me with Judge Barlow. It was Umin's decision to make, and he decided the time had come. Many months later he would write to me of that decision:

> I'm sure I will think for the rest of my life about the decision, finally, to attack the New Jersey [Federal] District Court and seek a new judge. That decision was reached over some dissent in this office since it is not a step to be taken unless you are absolutely invulnerable. . . . But after two years, though not before, I felt we were invulnerable, so I went ahead. Plainly, that . . . was the turning point.

And attack he did. In a scathing denunciation of the tactics of Judge Barlow and the judges who had preceded him, Umin laid bare the record of frustration, inaction, delay, equivocation, and outright refusal to comply with the mandate of the United States Supreme Court. The petition for the writ of mandamus was filed in the United States Court of Appeals for the Third Circuit, in Philadelphia. Meanwhile, back at the ranch, Judge Barlow was rushing to shore up his defenses, issuing the orders and making the rulings that he had for more than a year refused to make, declaring that the burden of proof would be on the state, defining the issues to be heard during the habeas corpus hearing, agreeing to permit full discovery under the civil rules of procedure, and setting the hearing date for January 15, 1971—in each instance ruling as we had asked him to rule. Then, in a letter to Umin, a copy of which he sent to the court of appeals, the judge sought to defend himself, to deny that the delay was his fault, blaming Umin for the delays and pointing out that he *had* acted as we had asked.

Give Steve Umin a good legal fight and he is happier than a fat man in a cream puff factory. After one look at Judge Barlow's letter he filed a supplement to our petition for mandamus, this time attacking the judge personally, directly, and without reservation. The covering letter sent me with a copy of that supplemental petition was short and to the point. "We are," Umin wrote, "at war!"

All wars should end so quickly and bloodlessly. Clearly

torn between sympathy for a brother judge under attack and the obvious strength of my position, the court of appeals compromised. Mandamus was denied on December 3, 1970, but in its denial the court stated that the denial was "without prejudice in the appellant's right to renew the motion if the hearing in the District Court for the District of New Jersey is further delayed." The warning to Judge Barlow was clear: "Get off your butt. We can't protect you forever."

Steve Umin was not satisfied. A week later, unopposed by the prosecutor, who was as unhappy as we were with Judge Barlow's refusal to act promptly, Umin took the matter to Associate Justice Brennan of the Supreme Court, the circuit judge who supervised the New Jersey federal court and the Third Circuit Court of Appeals. Again Umin blasted away at Judge Barlow, and again the petition was denied, but this time the denial was window dressing. A few days after Justice Brennan denied my petition, Judge Barlow quietly disappeared from my case, removed by the court of appeals, and in his stead appeared a member of the court of appeals, Circuit Judge John Gibbons.

Judge Gibbons, whose offices were in Newark, was specially designated to sit as a district court judge for the sole purpose of hearing my case, and he immediately ruled that he would begin the hearing January 18, 1971.

We had slain a king! Long live the king!

It is impossible to say too much about the effort Steve Umin and David Webster put into preparing for the hearing. With only a couple of weeks to prepare, rather than the forty days they would have liked, Umin was working eighteen hours a day by the end of December, seven days a week, sifting through the records of the case, reading transcripts and petitions and briefs from earlier appeals, interviewing prospective witnesses, flying to Colorado to take a deposition from my former wife, flying to Florida to take another deposition from

one of the detectives who had conducted my post-arrest interrogation, spending days in Bergen County interviewing past
and present members of the prosecutor's office, going through
the prosecutor's files made available to us under the rules of
civil discovery, and with meticulous care compiling several
thick loose-leaf binders with notes, breakdowns of testimony,
statements and depositions, everything and anything that
could in any way bear upon the issues to be heard. By the
second weekend in January, with well over one thousand hours
of preparation already put into the case, Umin was ready to
begin working on me, to prepare me for my testimony.

There was no doubt about it: Steve Umin had learned that
the key to success in the legal business was preparation, preparation, and then still more preparation. The difference
between Umin's efforts and Fitzpatrick's would show up in
the hearing.

Arrangements were made with the prison authorities to provide a private room for my lawyers to meet with me and stay
as long as might be necessary, a place where, if we required
it, our meals could be served. Then, for two successive weekends, from early morning until long after dark, Umin, David
Webster, Steve Lichtenstein, and at times Lichtenstein's partner, Mark Segal, took my testimony apart, put it together
again, then took it apart and started all over again. Most days
we worked without eating, sending out for coffee but not
stopping work to drink it, smoking up my cigars and cigarettes as fast as I could open them.

At the end of each day we left the room a mess, the table
and floor littered with scraps of notepaper, coffee cups all over
the place, ashtrays overflowing with butts and empty cigarette
packs, ashes from Umin's pipe all over everything. But if we
left the room a mess each day, our case for the hearing grew
more tidy.

Right at the outset it was decided that I would not be
permitted to read any of the dozens of police reports compiled

at the time of the original investigation fourteen years before. There were stacks of them, one written by each policeman, detective, investigator, and prosecutor's official who had had any contact whatsoever with the investigation, each describing in detail what its writer had seen and heard and done. Umin felt that the story I told on the witness stand at the hearing had to be *my* story, just exactly as I remembered it fourteen years later, uncolored by anything I might read in the police reports, for only in that way would I be able to stand up under cross-examination. The lawyers could prepare me for my testimony by taking my story and going over it, distilling it down to the essentials, weeding out unnecessary detail, teaching me to answer the questions asked and *only* the questions asked, knocking out things I was not dead-sure of, excess language that added nothing but could provide a lever for tripping me up on cross-examination, but beyond that they could give me but one piece of advice: Just tell what you remember as you remember it, nothing more or less.

The strategy we developed was a simple one: When Umin called me to testify, we would begin with the moment of my arrest and take the story from there through the time I was finally arraigned on the murder charge, bringing out the story just as it happened, in chronological order, no jumping around and risking forgetting something or getting the judge confused. We would just keep it neat and simple.

The second weekend of preparation was even tougher than the first. Mark Segal arrived the last day, Sunday, early in the morning before the others, and under his arm was a tape recorder.

"Well, I've got a surprise for you," he told me, putting the recorder on the table in the conference room and looking around for a place to plug it in. "Do you know what this is?"

"I don't think I want to know," I replied, an idea of what the recording might be shaping up in my mind.

"This is a tape made in the prosecutor's office while you were being questioned and giving a statement," Mark told me, referring to the so-called confession the legality of which would be the key issue at the hearing. "They had a dummy phone on the desk, with a mike inside it."

"Lovely. That sounds like the prosecutor's way of working. Oh, well, it can't hurt any. If the judge finds the statement coerced, the tape isn't worth a damn."

"Right, but still we want you to listen to it," Mark told me. "Steve and David will be a little late this morning, so we want you to listen to this while you wait."

"Okay, let's do it."

It was an eerie sensation, hearing my voice on a recording for the first time, the voice of the twenty-three-year-old I was when the recording was made. I was intrigued. Nothing else could have brought back more clearly, with greater impact, the memory of that cold March day in 1957 than this few hundred feet or so of dry, brittle acetate tape. Other voices, those of prosecutors, detectives, even the court stenographer called to record my statement, voices I had not heard since that day fourteen years before, all came back and were familiar, instantly recognizable. It was weird.

Only five minutes or so of the tape had run when a guard entered the room and informed me that Bill Buckley was waiting downstairs to see me. Bill was preparing to leave for Switzerland for his annual skiing holiday and wanted to see me one last time before the hearing, to be certain everything necessary was being taken care of.

"Go ahead," Mark told me. "We'll have time to finish listening to this when you get back."

Bill stayed for about an hour, listened carefully as I told him how the lawyers were preparing me, looked surprised but unworried when I told him about the tape recording and assured him that it wouldn't hurt me if Fitzpatrick were foolish enough to put it in evidence at the hearing; then with a few words wishing me luck, he left just in time to meet Umin and Webster arriving for our final day's session.

The last day was a picnic compared with the others. Umin

changed his mind and said he didn't want me listening to the tape recording, for the same reason he didn't want me reading the police investigation reports. Over and over he repeated: "It's *your* story we want, just as you remember it, no more, no less, not something you think you remember just because you heard or read it. If you don't have your own independent recollection, we don't want to talk about it."

David was his usual relaxed, mod self that day, wearing red plaid slacks, sort-of-yellow suede chukkah boots, a blue sports shirt open at the throat, and a nondescript kerchief tied around his neck. He looked better prepared for a casual garden party in Chevy Chase than a knock-down, drag-out habeas corpus hearing in Newark, a city an editor at *Playboy* recently described to me as "the Lake Erie of cities."

"We're making custody arrangements for you," Umin told me at the end of that day. "We're having you transferred to federal custody while the hearing is in progress. You'll be kept either in the Somerset County Jail, here in Jersey, or at the Federal Detention Center in New York City. We're also making arrangements with the judge and the United States marshal to have you kept in Newark each night after court, and for a private room to be available to us."

"Why?"

"We're not done with you, Mr. Smith. Every night after court I want to go over that day's events, check the transcripts, prepare for the next day, and work more on your testimony. We'll probably keep you pretty late each night, and you won't get much sleep—but neither will we."

"How does it look right now?" I asked. "What do you think the odds are?"

"Let's wait until we hear a couple of days' testimony," Webster replied. "When we see how honest the police witnesses are going to be, then we'll be in a better position to judge."

That sounded reasonable to me. "There's just one other thing," I told Umin. "Take a look at this."

I handed Umin a copy of my book, *Brief Against Death*, and pointed out the photo on the jacket. "Take a good look at that," I told him. "That was taken a week or two after my arrest."

Umin looked, handed the book to Webster, then asked: "So what about it?"

"Now look at this one," I said, handing him a copy of the New York *Times* review of *Brief Against Death*. "Look at this photo. This one was taken while the police were interrogating me."

It wasn't necessary to say more than that. The photo on the jacket of my book showed me smiling and alert and physically sound, in an obviously "normal" condition. The photo taken during my interrogation was of another person entirely. It showed me being assisted into a police car, supported by each arm by a detective, a cigarette dangling limply from my lips, my face puffy, eyes half-shut, hair hanging down in my face, my whole attitude being that of a man beat, worn-down, worn-out, tired, detached from the reality of his surroundings.

"*That*," I told Umin when he had handed the second photo to Webster, "is what happens to you when the police interrogate you all night and all the next day."

David slipped the photo into his briefcase and told Umin: "Make a note to subpoena the original of this from UPI."

I had made my contribution.

Chapter Six

January 18, 1971, the first day of the habeas corpus hearing on the petition I had laboriously handwritten and filed five and a half years earlier, at a time when I was without a typewriter, lawyers, or money—but not without hope—dawned clear and bitter cold, one of the coldest days of the year, but even as I stood shivering in a lukewarm shower at 6:30 in the morning, contemplating the long ride to Newark, it seemed like a hell of a fine day.

Once again I was dressed in a shoddy prison suit, called court clothes because they are used over and over and over again by men going to court, pressed but not cleaned after each use, most of them several years old, with buttons missing and cracked, the material shiny from use, smelling of sweat and dirt, the fit unbelievable. They simply pick out a size that is somewhere near what you wear, then do a five-minute alteration job, and that's it, however it looks. The pants of the suit I was given came to my ankles, and I had to leave the top button unbuttoned for fear of splitting them open when I sat down. And once again we had to go through the asinine routine of handcuffs attached to a leather belt around my waist. Fourteen years and umpteen thousands of bucks fighting for this day and "they" think I might escape.

Escape? Baby, I'm going out there to WIN, not run.
The hour and a half drive to Newark was both depressing
and exhilarating. It was great to be out again, not to have bars
or walls surrounding me, not to see blue uniforms everywhere
I looked—the two prison guards with me wore civilian clothes
—and to relax in the back seat of the new Plymouth sedan (I
still say I think they are made in Japan!) while my chauffeur
did the driving. But how the world had changed in those
fourteen years.

U.S. Highway 1, through central Jersey, a road once bor-
dered for a great part of its length by farms and woodlands
and open fields, running over clean rivers like the Raritan, was
now like a detour through a junkyard. Both sides of the road,
mile after mile, seemed to consist of nothing but factories,
hamburger joints, motels, gas stations, more motels, more gas
stations, more hamburger joints, more gas stations, and still
more motels and hamburger joints and gas stations, the dreary
procession of dreary motels and dreary gas stations and dreary
hamburger joints broken only occasionally by the appearance
of a dreary discount store. What a stinkin' mess!

Gino's . . . Burger Chef . . . BP . . . Esso . . . Burger Chef . . .
Esso . . . Roy Roger's Something-or-Other Bar B-Q . . .
Gulf . . . Dunkin' Donuts . . . BP . . . Gino's . . . Esso . . .
Holiday Inn . . . Burger Chef . . . McDonald's ("Over One
Billion Served") *. . . Esso . . . Burger Chef . . . Holiday Inn . . .*
The Edison Diner . . . Burger Chef . . . Gulf . . . Harry's
Junkyard and Auto Wreckers . . . The Happy Stop Motel . . .
Gino's . . . Burger Chef . . . Two Guys from Somewhere . . .
Esso . . . BP . . . Bill and Mary's Motel ("Sleep with Us. You
Won't Be Sorry") *. . . Burger Chef . . . Howard Johnson's*
(98 Zillion Flavors) *. . . Esso . . . BP . . . McDonald's* ("Over
Two Billion served") *. . . Gino's . . . Burger Chef . . . Holiday*
Inn . . . Esso . . . Dunkin' Donuts . . . and on . . . and on . . .
and on . . . and on . . . and Ohmigawd! The Raritan River
looks thick enough to walk across! And look at the sky over
Newark Airport from those stinking, smoking jets taking off,

the black trail of a 727 just hanging there waiting for the next plane to fly through! All right now, everybody at once, let's have a big cheer for America, the industrial and technological leader of the free world! Eeeeeeeeeech!

Off Route 1 and into Newark—an underpass littered with newspapers and empty coffee containers hubcap deep, beer cans dotting the grassy slope down from the road above—some clown in a battered Mustang with a huge I SERVED IN THE UNITED STATES NAVY AND I'M PROUD OF IT sticker in the back window (he probably spent twelve months in the Tonkin Gulf lobbing five-inchers into NV fishing villages) and an American Legion decal on each side window (nothing in front?) . . . the huge Breyer's Ice Cream factory, abandoned, windows stoned out, the paint-peeling sign on the roof leaning precariously, the whole place looking bombed out ("Breyer's Costs More But Tastes Better") . . . houses, stores, gas stations abandoned, vandalized, some of them burned out . . . high-class shops on Broad Street with their windows covered with sheets of plywood ("You never know when those niggers might start up again.") . . . abandoned autos, wheels missing, windshields spiderwebbed by rocks, hoods up or torn off and lying in the street, doors askew, upholstery ripped out, some of the cars burned out like the buildings . . . and everywhere, again, as before, the people expressionless, humorless, looking neither right nor left, hurrying along the street with pocketbooks and packages clutched tightly, others standing as if comatose at bus stops, only the very young seeming alive, but even they standing around looking bored, occasionally coming to life as a pretty girl walks by. . . .

Do I want to win? Do I want to be set free to become a part of this? Is this freedom?

We park in front of a long row of abandoned tenements and stores a block from the Federal Courthouse. As we walk along, a few photographers are backing along the sidewalk ahead of us, urging me to smile, asking how I feel.

"That dude there is carrying about fifteen hundred bucks' worth of Hasselblad," I tell one of the guards. "Let's mug him!"

The guard grins and we keep walking. Across the street, reaching above everything else around it, is the new Federal Office Building, an aluminum and glass monument to bureaucracy. I try to estimate how many low-cost housing units for the Newark ghetto they could have built with the money they spent on that catastrophe.

My mother is coming across the street from the coffee shop. We wave, my wave from the waist, just a fluttering of my captured hands, and then I am inside, waiting by the elevator.

A voice behind me asks: "Can we ride up with you?"

It is Little Fitz, Assistant Prosecutor Ed Fitzpatrick, wrapped in a very official-looking black overcoat large enough to mothball a battleship, attaché case in hand, a plump, pleasant-looking woman with him. His secretary. I grin. He looks the other way. The guard nods. We get in together. *Up! Up! And Awaaaaaaaay!* Little Fitz is cool. He looks at the floor counter dial. The guards and I get off on the third floor, head for the U.S. Marshal's Office, go through some paper work, pick up a couple of marshals, and head for the court-room on the fourth floor. The cuffs come off at the door. The leather belt stays on.

We're late! United States Circuit Court Judge John J. Gibbons is already on the bench, talking with Little Fitz and David Webster.

The courtroom, actually a bankruptcy hearing room, the only thing available for the next two weeks, is tiny, with space for perhaps fifty spectators in the pewlike seats, and only eight feet or so from the first row to the judge's bench, the area between crowded, filled with the two counsel tables standing end to end. The clerk sits off to the right at a tiny table that looks like a typist's stand borrowed for the occasion, and off to the left, the court stenographer and his machine.

As I squeeze into the upholstered chair that barely fits between the counsel table and the railing separating the spectator area, sitting with Steve Lichtenstein on my left, Umin and Webster to my right—there is so little room David is sitting half at our table, half at the prosecutor's—a dozen or so newspaper reporters stretch their necks to get a look at the so-called Dean of Death Row. I recognize a few, smile, grin at my mother sitting directly behind me, then settle down to listen to what is going on.

One look and I like Judge Gibbons. A small man, slender, graying black hair all curls, his eyes betraying a sense of amusement with what David is saying, a gorgeous yellow shirt with broad red stripes sticking up out of his black robe —I liked him even more when I saw that—he reminded me of a leprechaun escaped from the cast of *Brigadoon*.

The first order of business is over quickly. The judge orders my custody changed from state to federal, the prison guards leave with their handcuffs and the leather belt I am glad to return to them, and after a short discussion it is decided that I will be kept nights at West Street—the Federal Detention Center in New York City.

Now formalities. The burden of proof is on the state, the judge rules, and the degree of proof that will be required, a tricky legal question, is deferred. Then Little Fitz blows his first argument. He argues that the issue of the voluntariness of my statements to the police will, of course, be determined by the 1957 voluntariness standards, the law at the time of my arrest. Coerced statements in 1957 were as inadmissible as they are in 1971, but while the principle is the same, the test of coercion has become more meticulous, more sophisticated, through the years.

Judge Gibbons looks at Fitz as if he doesn't believe what he has just heard. He doesn't even wait to hear our counter-arguments.

". . . The general developing law on what constitutes coercion under federal standards is fully retroactive," he rules.

It is 1–0 our side, and Little Fitz has discovered that this is a federal court, not a state or county court where the judge says "Yassuh, Boss" when the prosecutor burps.

We all watch Fitzpatrick to see how he will react to his first setback. The palms of his hands go up as if to plead, drop to his side, the eyeglasses are shoved back up his nose as he turns and walks partway up a side aisle, puzzlement on his face— "I'm a prosecutor! How could he rule against *me?*"—trying to cool off, then he comes back, unconvinced, wanting to argue more. The judge and Webster have gone on to another issue.

The "housekeeping chores," various technical points of procedure that set the tone and direction of the hearing, are completed. Fitzpatrick calls his first witness—Joe Gilroy.

Formerly my best friend and an usher at my wedding, Gilroy has put on about 30 pounds since I last saw him in 1957. His testimony was essentially the same as it was at my trial. He said that he had let me borrow his car on the night of March 4, 1957, that I had returned it the same night, and that the next day he had noticed spots on the seat covers which he thought might have been blood, so he had gone to the police. At 11:30 P.M. on the night of the fifth, he had taken the police to my mother-in-law's home, where I was staying with my wife and daughter, and at that time I was taken into custody.

The first hint that Fitzpatrick had not done as thorough a job as he should have done in preparing for the hearing came when David Webster began cross-examining Gilroy and asked the assistant prosecutor for a copy of Gilroy's March 8, 1957, statement to the police. Fitzpatrick looked as if he had never seen or heard of the statement.

"We do not have it here in court," he told the judge. "I did not go over it with this witness. I do not have it here."

The judge, not exactly pleased to do so, agreed that the state could let Gilroy off the witness stand and call another witness while a detective was sent to Bergen County to get a copy of Gilroy's statement. Fitzpatrick called Detective Vahe

Garabedian, a short, jowly, hard-eyed man who had been a member of the police team that had taken me into custody and had interrogated me on the night of March 5.

Garabedian had just taken the stand and identified himself as a prosecutor's detective since 1955 when Webster interrupted and asked for a ruling that all prospective witnesses be barred from the courtroom until after they had testified. The judge agreed, and later in the hearing he would take note of the prosecutor's attempt to circumvent the ruling.

On his direct testimony, using his original investigation reports to refresh his memory, Garabedian stated that on the night of March 5, 1957, he had examined Gilroy's automobile and had found spots on the seat covers which "may or may not have been blood." Then, at the order of First Assistant Prosecutor Fred Galda, he had gone with Gilroy and Detective Gordon Graber to take me into custody.

After Garabedian had described some of his activities on the night of the fifth, after taking me into custody, he was asked:

"Now, would you describe for the court, please, Mr. Smith's demeanor . . . the morning of March 5th."

"I would say for the most part he was quiet, cooperative, he appeared sure of himself. Yeah, I'd say cocky, cooperative, maybe, a little bit."

Garabedian also testified that at 8:00 A.M. on March 6 he went to the Ramsey, New Jersey, police station to pick up a pair of trousers and take them to the prosecutor's office. "Would you describe those pants, please?" Fitzpatrick asked.

"They were brown khaki trousers. They were dirty. On the bottom parts of the pants there was quite a bit of blood."

"Do you recall what Mr. Calissi [the prosecutor] or Mr. Galda did with those pants when you brought them in?"

"He [Mr. Galda] had them on the desk in his office and he asked Mr. Smith if they were his trousers."

"Would you recall, as best you can, the response of Mr. Smith when he was asked that?"

"Yes, sir. He denied they were his."

Later in the morning, Garabedian recounted, he and another detective clipped and scraped my fingernails because the police felt "possibly there might be underneath the fingernails hair, blood, or fibers of the victim."

Little realizing it, I'm sure, Fitzpatrick and Garabedian were making the first really important points for my side. It was being established that by 9:10 A.M. on the sixth, when the fingernail scrapings and clippings were being taken, I had passed from being a general suspect for investigation to at least a specific suspect, if not the prime suspect, and that by that time the police were seeking evidence, not information.

On cross-examination, Umin went right to that point.

"Did you ever take fingernail scrapings from Joe Gilroy?"

"No."

"To your knowledge, were fingernail scrapings taken from Joe Gilroy at any time?"

"Not to my knowledge."

"Do you know about fingernail scrapings being taken from any other person apart from Edgar Smith?"

"On that evening, no."

Umin had driven home the point, establishing that I was *the* suspect, not merely *a* suspect. The importance of this cannot be overstressed, for once the police have fixed upon a prime suspect, once they begin seeking evidence to convict that suspect, rather than seeking general information to help solve the crime, that suspect becomes *in fact* a criminal defendant and a whole new ball game begins; all sorts of legal protections come into the game, including prompt arraignment before a magistrate and warnings as to the suspect's rights. Throughout the hearing Umin and Webster would seek to draw out from the prosecutor's witnesses the fact that the police had a good enough case against me to arraign me long before they did so, long before they allowed a magistrate to advise me of my rights, and that that delay resulted not from an attempt to solve the crime, but rather from an effort to build a *better* case by continuing my interrogation until I made incriminating statements. If we proved that, we would win.

Fortunately, we would be aided throughout the hearing by the detectives and police officials, who really had little understanding of what the hearing was all about. In almost every instance, these witnesses would display a common police mentality, a concern for nothing more than guilt or innocence, thinking that the guilt or innocence issue meant something in the hearing in progress, and so they would bend over backward to insist to my lawyers that "Sure, we had a damn good case against Smith. We knew he was lying. We knew he was guilty. All we needed was to get him to make some kind of statement we could give to a trial jury." And in taking that attitude, the state witnesses would be doing our job for us, proving exactly what we wanted proved.

I do not mean to belittle the issue of guilt or innocence, to give the impression that it doesn't make any difference whether I committed the crime or didn't. It is simply a fact that every person, guilty or innocent, is entitled to certain protections, certain constitutional privileges, and the hearing underway was intended solely to determine whether the police had denied me those rights and privileges. No other issue was before the court, so when I write that my guilt or innocence "did not mean anything" at the hearing, I intend that only in the strictest legal sense, in the sense that I was not on trial for the crime.

Umin wanted more from Garabedian and with a few more questions elicited again for the record the fact that even before taking me into custody, the police knew from Gilroy that I had used his car on the night of the murder, that the next day he found stains in the car, and that the police assumed they

were bloodstains. Garabedian admitted that he was so concerned about the stains that he had the car immediately
"secured" for protection and that immediately after that the
order went out to take me into custody.

UMIN: "When you took [Smith] back to the Mahwah
Police Headquarters, did anyone at the Mahwah Police Headquarters tell Mr. Smith that he was free to leave at any time?"

GARABEDIAN: "I don't know. Not while I was there."

JUDGE GIBBONS: "Did you have any instructions to inform
[suspects] they had an option [to refuse to go with the pol-
ice]?"

GARABEDIAN: "I would have to say no, sir, no specific
instructions as to that."

JUDGE GIBBONS: "You didn't so inform Smith?"

GARABEDIAN: "That's right. We did not."

UMIN: "Did you tell Edgar Smith that he was being picked
up because the First Assistant Prosecutor had told you to pick
him up after receiving information about the blood spots in
Gilroy's car?"

GARABEDIAN: "No, sir."

The cross-examination of the detective lasted through the
morning until the lunch break, most of the questioning bringing out restatements and refinements of the previous testimony. Umin and Webster looked satisfied with the morning's
work, and I certainly was feeling better, but for a different
reason: During the midmorning recess I had discovered the
relative joys of federal custody.

Being in police custody is never fun, never good, but anyone who has ever experienced both state and federal custody
knows that if one has to be in someone's custody, then the
place to be is with United States marshals, a thoroughly
decent, understanding, professional group of men. And that's
the difference, I think—professionalism. Federal officers do
not need to hide, as state officers seem to do, behind petty and

restrictive rules designed, it seems, to cover the lack of training and self-confidence of the latter. Moreover, unlike state officers, and particularly prison guards, who tend to treat prisoners like some piece of state-owned property, federal officers will normally do everything within reason to treat their prisoners as human beings.

The difference for me was apparent as soon as court recessed for lunch the first day of my hearing. Where state officers would have immediately handcuffed my wrists to the leather belt around my waist and hustled me out of the courtroom to a detention cell, not allowing me to speak with anyone, including my family, the federal marshals permitted me to remain in the courtroom for a while, talking with friends and family. And afterward, when we walked down the corridor to the detention room, where we would have lunch, they allowed me to go without handcuffs and to stop to speak with friends. They were with me every second, of course, but it is not likely that anyone seeing us in the corridors would have suspected that I was a prisoner. As one of the marshals put it: "As long as a man acts like a human being with us, we treat him like one."

I am certain Ed Fitzpatrick would have wished it were otherwise, for the first person to come over to say hello to me after recess was called was his father! And with him was Big Fitz, the older brother with whom I had gone to school.

It was a crazy scene. I had just turned to walk out of the courtroom when I was confronted by an elderly man whose face was vaguely familiar but impossible for the moment to place. Then I saw Big Fitz, who had not changed appreciably over the years. And there we stood, laughing and shaking hands and looking like old friends meeting at a cocktail party —except that the "old friends" were the father and brother of the man who was trying to keep me on Death Row, who wanted to see me executed. In a case filled with curious twists and coincidences, this was one of the strangest, and the sight of his father and brother standing there rapping with me was a bit too much for the assistant prosecutor. He must have had a lot to say afterward because it was the last time his father, who attended every day of the hearing, let on that he knew me. For the next two weeks he sat there and pretended he didn't see me. And Big Fitz never came back.

Fitzpatrick got in trouble as soon as court resumed after lunch. He had apparently realized (Assistant Prosecutor Springstead may have brought it to his attention) the importance of the fact that the police *thought* the stains on the seat cover of Gilroy's car were blood, therefore making me a suspect in the eyes of the detectives, since I had used the car the night of the crime. Fitz recalled Detective Garabedian to the stand and asked if the lab tests had later proved the stains actually *were* blood. David Webster was waiting in ambush.

Objecting, properly so, that anything the detectives learned later was irrelevant, David pointed out that all that mattered was the state of the officer's mind at the time he first saw the stains. Did he *think* they were blood?

Fitz argued, tried to convince the judge that what was learned later was important, but Judge Gibbons cut him off in midargument.

THE COURT: "I can't see the relevance of it at the moment."

Fitz tried to save face, asked a few more questions of little importance, sat down, changed his mind, got up, then put his foot in it.

"Did you know at 3:00 A.M. on March 6 whether or not Edgar Smith had been in the company of Victoria Zielinski on the night of March 4?" he asked.

Some lawyers ask too many questions. Some ask too few. Fitz and Springstead would prove to be the sort who ask too many. Fitz just had.

Garabedian checked his report, thought about it for a few moments, then replied: "I would say possibly at 4:00 A.M. I probably may have known. Yeah. I—there would be more of a reason for me to know at 4:00 A.M. than 3:00 A.M."

David smiled happily. Fitz was doing a good job—for us.

The detective who had been sent for Gilroy's 1957 statement returned at 2:00 P.M. and Gilroy was recalled for David's cross-examination.

Briefly, Gilroy testified that I had used his car on the night of March 4, 1957; that he had found what he thought was a bloodstain on the seat cover the next day; that he and another young man, Donald Hommell, had picked me up with my wife and daughter at my mother-in-law's house in Ridgewood on the afternoon of March 5; that Hommell had told me the police were looking for a Mercury (Gilroy's car was a Mercury) in connection with the death of the Zielinski girl; that I had had a startled look on my face when Hommell said that about the Mercury; that the previous night I had told him I had thrown away a pair of pants I had stained when I had got sick to my stomach; that on the afternoon of March 5 I had had a pair of shoes with me that to him seemed suspicious; that when he had reported to the police that he had found stains on the seat cover of his car, the police had asked if his tires had recently been changed (they had not); that on the night of March 6 at Mahwah police headquarters the prosecutor had chased reporters away who had tried to question me; that he had never told me what he had told the police; that I seemed "cocky" at police headquarters; that he had been released by the police at about 3:00 A.M.; that he had been very tired when he was released; that he had never been fingerprinted, never had his fingernails clipped or scraped; and that the police had impounded his car, taking the keys from him.

Webster was satisfied with Gilroy's testimony. Again, he had shown that the information given the police by Gilroy, prior to my arrest, was sufficient to lead a reasonable man to conclude that there was more than a passing reason to suspect me of some complicity in the crime.

Gilroy was followed to the witness stand by Mahwah Police Chief Russo, who testified that at 6:30 A.M. on the morning of March 7 he had been called to an area on Oak Street, in the town of Ramsey, adjoining Mahwah, where the Ramsey police had found a pair of bloodstained khaki pants.

Detective Lieutenant Brennan of the Mahwah police was the next witness, testifying that at 11:45 P.M. on the night of March 6 he saw me at the Mahwah headquarters, that I had my feet up on a desk and looked "cool, calm, and collected."

Gordon Graber, an elderly, puffy-faced, red-nosed detective lieutenant from the prosecutor's office, followed Brennan to the stand. He was questioned by Assistant Prosecutor Springstead. Fitz sat quietly, looking quite unhappy with the course of the proceedings.

Graber testified that on the night of March 5 he and Detective Garabedian had examined Gilroy's car "to see if there was any evidence of bloodstains in the car" and that he had found "what appeared to be blood" on the seats. A short while later, having reported the suspicious stains to the prosecutor, Graber was detailed to pick me up at my mother-in-law's home and bring me to Mahwah for questioning.

For the remainder of the afternoon Graber recounted the course of the investigation on the night of March 5 and early morning of March 6, at one point recalling that I had been taken to the scene of the crime by a number of detectives, and that while there I had complained about being cold.

Court recessed for the day at 4:30, and after a few minutes visiting with my mother and a few friends, the marshals and I walked down to a third floor jury room to await the arrival of my lawyers. Judge Gibbons had agreed that I would be kept in Newark each night until at least 8:00 and that a room would be made available where my lawyers could confer with me, continue to work on my testimony, and await the delivery of the typed transcript. We had arranged for the two court reporters to type the daily transcript immediately after each day's session, to give the lawyers time to review it overnight and be ready for the next day.

Ron Arp, a United States marshal and a very nice guy, and I were sitting at a conference table in the room, reading a couple of newspapers left by a jury who had used the room earlier in the day, when another marshal arrived with goodies —coffee, pastry, and pepper/egg/sausage on hard rolls. I was stuffing my face when Umin, Webster, and Lichtenstein walked in, asked the marshals to leave us alone, then told me that we were going to do the same thing we had done both weekends at the prison.

"We'll start right from the beginning," Umin told me, "and go over your testimony as you will give it."

"Again?"

"Again. You'd better get used to going over it, and you'd better have it straight, the same way every time. Fitzpatrick is going to do a job on you. If there are any contradictions or inconsistencies, we'd better find them before he does."

And so we went over it, and over it, and over it. Now and then David or Steve Lichtenstein would break in with a question, trying to trip me up, asking me to explain this or that or some other thing, but mostly it was Umin. By the time 8:00 rolled around I was dead tired and sick of looking at them.

"Don't feel badly," Umin told me. "You're going to West Street to sleep. We're going back to the hotel to sit up most of the night reading today's testimony and preparing for tomorrow."

What a fantastic sensation it was to walk outside the courthouse that night. I had forgotten that it was night, and my first thought when I stepped out the door onto the sidewalk was that something was wrong, something I had not experienced before. IT WAS DARK OUTSIDE! The first time I had been outside at night in fourteen years, the first time in that period I had seen the moon or the stars. What a night! Bad enough I was half in shock from the rediscovery of night, but then halfway to New York City, on the Pulaski Skyway, my eyeballs almost fell out as we drove past a drive-in theater. Right where you could see it from every car driving by was a twenty-foot, fang-toothed vampire eating the neck of a twenty-foot naked chick!!!

Slow down, dammit! Slow down! This I gotta see!

Ron and the other marshal were laughing like hell as I all but unhinged my neck twisting around to look out the back window.

I'll take two of those. And I don't care how many holes she has in her neck.

"That's a tame one," Ron told me. "I'd rate that one GP. Just wait'll you see one of those X jobs."

"Spare me. Jail has weakened my heart."

At the midpoint of the Holland Tunnel, built into the tile wall, is a line indicating the boundary between New Jersey and New York. When we were kids, taking the bus to New York, my brother and I used to play a game, competing to see who would be the first to spot the boundary marker. It's curious how memories like that come back. I hadn't been through that tunnel for maybe twenty-five years, yet as we rode along, wisecracking about the vampire and the chick, I found myself leaning forward, looking out the front window, watching for the boundary marker.

There it is! I saw it first!

West Street. The Federal Detention Center for the New York metropolitan area. An aging, dingy, red brick building that might once have been a warehouse or some sort of garage, it is located on Manhattan's Lower West Side, across Twelfth Avenue from that great, wide sewer known as the Hudson River. (I have been in three jails, and each has been within sight or smell of a polluted river—more a comment on America than on the penal system.) West Street would be my "home" for as long as it took to complete my court hearing in Newark.

The U.S. marshals left me with the officer on duty at the door, telling me they would be back to pick me up at 8:30 the following morning to return me to court, and then it was time to go through the checking-in process. Beautiful! West Street, it turned out, is one of those curious jails that is easier to get out of than to get into—and not only because of that jail's long record of successful escapes. Checking out to go to court, or to be released, takes about ten minutes, only as long as it takes to exchange one's jail-issued clothing for one's own. But checking in gives one the impression that one is not wanted. Two hours after the marshals dropped me off, and fitted out in khaki pants and shirt, carrying sheets and a blanket under my arm, and leaving behind in the administrative offices a stack of forms and a couple of dozen mug shots of myself, I was taken to the third floor and locked in a large holding cell with seven other men—three black dudes from the Bronx, two whites from Brooklyn, a Filipino, and a young kid from Venezuela.

All jails are dirty, and West Street was no exception; the floors were littered with cigarette butts and empty packs, paper coffee cups, old newspapers and magazines, candy wrappers, a few squashed cockroaches, and one little old dead mouse—which may have committed suicide to get away from the noise.

The noise. The place is Bedlam West. From early morning until midnight a radio connected to a PA system blares rock 'n' roll throughout the living quarters, and everywhere men are shouting. They shout from cell to cell, from the cells to the dormitory areas, from one end of a corridor to the other, up and down staircases, from and to wherever at least two men want to rap, conversations on top of conversations, each group shouting louder to be heard, often in several different languages, and it goes on all day and into the early morning hours. I've been in some noisy places—the Death House in

Trenton was one of them—but the federal jail on West Street has to be the prizewinner. I can't blame that mouse if it killed itself. It was probably the only way it could get some sleep.

Federal jails have a reputation for being places where men are treated far more humanely than in any state prison (that's true), where rules and regulations are much more lax and rational (that's also true), and where the food is usually pretty decent (I won't argue with that). There is, however, another distinction federal jails have—you meet a much better class of criminal in the federal slammer. That's for sure. In the cell with me were five bank robbers and two narcotics smugglers, not one of them with less than $250,000 bail on him. And a few days later we got a couple of new men, one who had stolen the Napoleonic sterling collection from a Florida museum ($500,000 bail), the other a hijacker who had lifted a trailer truck load of mink coats (also $500,000 bail). And in the cell next to us was a dirty old man who looked like a Bowery bum, but who was in fact an international narcotics dealer with $1,500,000 bail on him.

The first of several fights I would see began ten minutes after I settled down in the cell and began rapping with the other guys, several of whom had read my first book and knew about me. Looking from our cell we could see a dozen men or so brawling in a dormitory area across the corridor from us. A lot of punches were being thrown, and a few wooden chair legs were flying around, but no one seemed to be getting hurt too badly. Damn sure the guards weren't getting hurt. They play it cool. As soon as the fight started, they cleared out of the area and locked the doors, then stood and watched. For what Uncle Sam is paying them, they aren't about to get their heads cracked with a chair leg or shivved with a sharpened spoon handle.

The fight was over in a short while, broken up by some of the other prisoners, no one hurt seriously, and along about midnight the place began to quiet down enough for me to crawl up onto a top bunk and get some sleep. I had been awake for nearly eighteen hours, and the next day was going to be another long one in court, not to mention after court, when my lawyers and I would again meet to go over my testimony.

Chapter Seven

When court reconvened Tuesday morning, Detective Graber returned to the witness stand and resumed his testimony by describing how, on the morning of March 6, after I had been transferred from Mahwah police headquarters to the prosecutor's office in Hackensack, he had been detailed to take my wife into custody and bring her to the prosecutor's office by a back stairway, so she would not be seen by reporters covering the case. He returned my wife to her mother's home once during the day, he said, to pick up one of my shirts but had brought her back to the prosecutor's office, where she remained in custody.

Asked to describe my attitude at the various times he had seen me, Graber said something that was to come back to haunt the state. I had been cool, calm, and collected at 2:00 A.M., Graber testified, but by 2:00 P.M. the following day, after twelve continuous hours of interrogation, I was subdued, hanging my head—"which he had not done previously"—and very quiet.

Steve Umin took over for cross-examination and very carefully continued the line of questioning we had established. After first establishing that my wife was not free to come and go once she had been taken into custody, Umin got Graber to admit that he knew plaster casts of tire tracks had been made at the scene of the crime; that he regarded the stains on the seat covers in Gilroy's car as "suspicious"; that he regarded debris on the car's floor—small stones and sand similar to that in the sandpit—as "suspicious"; that he told First Assistant Prosecutor Galda it was a "suspicious car"; that immediately thereafter Galda had ordered me taken into custody; and that my mother-in-law had been told by police that I was being held for questioning.

Umin knew he was doing well with Graber, and it was no time to let up.

"Did you tell Smith he didn't have to say anything to you?" Umin asked.

"No, I did not tell him that."

"Did you tell him anything he said might be used against him?"

"I did not tell him that."

"Did you give him any information about his legal rights?"

"No, sir, I did not."

Further questioning revealed that I had told the police I had taken a pair of shoes to a shoe repair shop, found out they were not worth repairing, and that I had thrown them in a nearby garbage can. In the early morning hours of March 6, I had taken the police to the place where I had thrown the shoes.

"Can you tell us what your observations of the shoes were?" Umin asked.

"There appeared to be some stains on the shoes that could be blood," Graber replied, "and there was a red fiber adhered to the sole of one of the shoes that appeared similar to the texture of the sweater that the Zielinski girl was wearing."

"On the 2:00 A.M. trip [to locate the shoes] was Edgar Smith a suspect in the investigation of the murder of Victoria Zielinski?"

"Yes, I would classify him so."

"Would you say he was the *prime* suspect at the time?"

"I would say he was the only one who had been with the victim the evening before."

Umin concluded his cross-examination by having Graber establish that by 9:00 A.M. the morning of March 6, while I was being interrogated in the county courthouse, judges were available in the building before whom I could have been charged and arraigned.

When Umin was finished, Judge Gibbons held the witness for a moment to ask if during the time I was being questioned in the prosecutor's office I had been dressed in a "uniform from the jail."

Graber admitted that I had been dressed in such a uniform after my own clothing was taken from me.

Walter Spahr, former chief of Bergen County detectives, previously mentioned in this story as the man who had retired after his name came up in some tapes of bugged telephone conversations of so-called "Mafia" leaders, would be one of the most important witnesses to testify at my hearing. Tall, blond, slender, tanned from his year in Florida, Spahr is the Bob Cummings type who never seems to age, looking as young, if not younger than he had when he was a detective in the prosecutor's office, assigned on March 6, 1957, to play a key role in extracting a statement from me.

Fitzpatrick opened Spahr's testimony by taking the witness through his initial activities concerned with the investigation of the murder, then turned to the time the detective actually came in contact with me. That time was on the morning of March 6, 1957, Spahr testified, at about 9:15 A.M., in the Bergen County Prosecutor's Office. He had seen fingernail clippings being taken from me, he said, and when that was done, he had suggested to the captain in charge that a county jail coverall be obtained so that my own clothing could be taken from me. Shortly thereafter, the captain, a man named DeMarco, now deceased, directed Spahr and Detective Charles DeLisle to interrogate me and obtain some kind of statement.

"As normal investigative technique I formally introduced myself and Detective DeLisle to Mr. Smith," Spahr explained. "We then started explaining the reason why we were there, that we were there to ascertain the truth of what had occurred relative to the death of Victoria Zielinski, and whether or not Mr. Smith had any part in this matter."

The detective explained further that he had discussed with me my educational background, family, where I lived and worked, and "generalities," and that following these "generalities" he had told me of the "tremendous strides" law enforcement had made in scientific detection, and pointed out that if I had been at the murder scene, it would be scientifically proved, as it would be possible to prove that the pants the police had found were mine.

As a result of the interrogation and discussion of the "generalities," certain oral statements had been elicited from me, Spahr concluded.

FITZPATRICK: "Was there any physical contact between you and Edgar Smith that morning?"

SPAHR: "Yes, sir . . . it was at a point between the time the fingernail scrapings were being taken and—this is my recollection—the taking of his clothes. Mr. Smith was seated in a swivel-type chair, wooden structure, and he said: 'I am getting out,' and he started getting up. I guess with reflex action I put my hand out and caught him. I must have caught him off balance—this is my opinion—*I just touched him with the edge of my fingers.* I don't know whether he fell down and spun out of the chair when he sat down, or else fell back out of the chair. . . ."

I was amazed that Spahr had admitted that much about the incident, though not surprised that once having opened that can of worms, he would try to make it seem as if I had fallen because I was off balance, not as a result of his "touch" with the edge of his fingers.

Even Fitzpatrick seemed surprised by Spahr's relative honesty and quickly changed the subject.

"At any time on the 6th of March did Mr. Smith ask you whether he could make a telephone call or get a lawyer or ask you to get a lawyer or request a lawyer?"

"He never asked that of me, sir, nor in my presence."

That made me feel better. Too much honesty from one detective might have been more than I could have endured.

Fitzpatrick's direct questioning of Spahr lasted through the morning session until the 1:00 P.M. lunch recess. One hour, two bacon, lettuce and tomato on toast, a French cruller, and two cups of coffee later we were back in the courtroom for Umin's cross-examination of Detective Spahr. It was to be, I learned some months later, Steve Umin's first extensive cross-examination of a witness in a criminal matter, and he was to tell me later that he believed it was Spahr's relative honesty that proved to be the key to the hearing.

My impression, from having discussed Spahr during pre-trial preparations, was that Umin was rather fond of the former detective. They had met in Florida, during the taking of his deposition, and by the time of the hearing they were on a first-name basis. Umin was certain that Spahr would be a cooperative witness, and I was anxious to see how accurate that assessment would be.

The initial portion of the cross-examination dealt with my attitude during interrogation, precisely what had taken place during the time I was being interrogated by Spahr and DeLisle, and the precise time Spahr reported to his superiors that I had made oral statements of importance.

Umin was still trying to establish the state of mind of the prosecutor's office, the fact that in the minds of the people in charge of the investigation I was the key suspect, and that therefore I was entitled to certain legal warnings and protections, when he asked the detective what time he had come to work that morning—"About 9:00 A.M."—whether he had gone into Prosecutor Calissi's private office—"Yes, sir"—and what Prosecutor Calissi had told him about the status of the investigation—"He said: 'We have a pair of pants with blood on them.'"

UMIN: "Did he say whose he thought those pants to be?"

SPAHR: "He said: 'We think we may have the man to whom the pants belong.'"

UMIN: "Did he tell you where that man was now?"

SPAHR: "Yes, he said he was in the office."

UMIN: "Did he tell you the man was free to leave?"

SPAHR: "I don't believe he mentioned whether he was free to leave or not, no."

Under continued questioning Spahr conceded that prior to interrogating me with DeLisle he knew that I had been in police custody all night, that he knew the pants in the prosecutor's office were assumed to be mine, and that, as soon as he had seen me in the office with other detectives, he had suggested that my fingernails be scraped and clipped.

All the questioning of Spahr thus far seemed petty and overly detailed to most of the people in the courtroom—some of whom later commented to me that Umin didn't seem to know where he was going with the witness—but it was obvious that Judge Gibbons was listening carefully and being impressed by it. Gradually Umin was unfolding for the judge a clear picture of me as the prime suspect, a man the police probably could have charged with the crime early on the morning of the sixth, but whom they continued to interrogate not to solve the crime, but for the sole purpose of extracting *more* evidence, evidence in the form of my own words. If we could convince Judge Gibbons of that, then the prospects of victory were indeed bright.

Umin turned to the incident when Spahr "touched" me with the edge of his fingers and I fell to the floor.

"Was it your impression that Edgar Smith was trying to escape from that room?"

"I think—my impression was that he was trying to leave that office, that was my impression, yes."

I saw the U.S. marshal across the courtroom break into a wide grin. Later, in a corridor during the afternoon recess, he would tell me: "As soon as that guy put his hand on you and stopped you from leaving that room, you were under arrest no matter what he wants to call it."

Umin wanted to hear more about the incident and asked Spahr to describe what happened to me when he had "touched" me.

"He ended up on the floor between—well, between the chair and the wall. . . ."

"Why did you do that?"

"Well, the—that man was there under greater authority than mine. . . ."

"What did Edgar Smith say when he ended up on the floor?"

"Nothing that I can remember."

"What did you say to him?"

"I can't remember."

"Were you told by Captain DeMarco at that point to interrogate Edgar Smith?"

"I think he used the word 'talk,' go talk to that fellow."

"Did you use that word when you wrote your report?"

"Yes, I did."

"Which word?"

"Interrogate."

Spahr then testified that Captain DeMarco told everyone to leave the room so that Spahr and DeLisle could be alone with me. Thereafter, while explaining that he and DeLisle had agreed in advance on a technique to be used on me, Spahr said: ". . . in my opinion, from looking at and hearing about the crime, what had occurred, *this was no deliberate and pre-meditated thing.*"

"Did you know at this point [on the morning of the sixth] that Edgar Smith had been with Victoria Zielinski the night of the murder?"

"I think I did at that point, yes, sir."

A few moments later Spahr reiterated his feelings on this issue when he said, ". . . that was and still is my contention, that this was not a well-planned, laid-out thing. It happened on the spur of the moment."

Beautiful! The cops think it's not first degree, so what am I doing sitting in the Death House for fourteen years?

"Do your notes contain any indication that you told Edgar Smith that the act must have been done with great provocation?"

"No, they don't, sir."

"But you did tell him that?"

"Yes, sir."

Ask him why he didn't tell the jury that, dammit!

"At any time during this period did you show Edgar Smith a legal file?"

"Yes, sir."

"Can you tell me what that legal file was?"

"I believe the name was Ledwin or Ludwin, Ludon, State versus—it was a homicide case."

"What did you tell Edgar Smith about it, if anything, when you showed him the file?"

"Yes—I explained that it was my impression, and I think it was correct, that all murders are presumed to be second degree, and that the prosecutor would ask for degrees of murder at the opening of his trial, and I said: 'Now, here's a case where this man killed his brother and look what he got,' or something to that effect."

Right on! Although a layman might have missed it, Judge Gibbons did not. By inference, by suggestion, by reference to his belief that this had not been a first-degree murder case and that the degree would be set by the prosecutor at trial, Umin had drawn from Spahr a clear picture of the detective trying to implant in my mind the rewards, the promises of leniency that would come from my cooperating with the police. Not even the most hardheaded law and order supporters in the legal profession or the staunchest advocates of unlimited police interrogation are in favor of making promises, direct or implied, in return for cooperation. We were halfway home.

When Umin finished with his cross-examination, Fitzpatrick, knowing his case had been hurt badly, jumped up and began a redirect examination, hoping to salvage or neutralize something. His first question was a dumb one.

"Did anybody in the prosecutor's office say to you: 'Go in and talk to this guy and get a confession'?"

"No—*and he never made a confession.*"

I half-expected Fitzpatrick to ask that his question be withdrawn. There we were after nearly fourteen continuous years of litigation over a disputed confession, and the detective who extracted the statement in question is saying he doesn't believe the thing *is* a confession.

"Did you and DeLisle get out in the hallway and say: 'Listen, Charlie, we have to go in there and get this guy to talk'?"

David Webster objected, but only as to the form of the question.

JUDGE GIBBONS: "Let's hear the answer anyway."

SPAHR: "I think that's the underlying point, was to see if he had any knowledge, he'd respond in the way he did."

WEBSTER (with a big grin): "I will withdraw the objection."

Fitzpatrick tried desperately to recover ground but got nowhere. After a few minutes more and some questions by Judge Gibbons, Spahr was dismissed and a short recess called.

I was standing in the corridor with the marshals, having a cigarette, when Walter Spahr came along and stopped to chat.

He surprised me. I had been as tough on Spahr in *Brief Against Death* as I had on anyone, yet the man stood there chatting as if we were lifelong friends. Fourteen years surely do make a difference. A short way down the corridor, by the door to the courtroom, Fitzpatrick stood looking puzzled, trying to figure out how and when Edgar Smith and Walter Spahr suddenly became buddies. Hell, I was just as puzzled myself. With a few more words, telling me he had to catch a 7:00 P.M. plane back to Florida, the former detective wished me luck and was gone. Ours not to reason why. . . .

Fitzpatrick's next witness was George O'Har, a detective at the time of my arrest and interrogation. O'Har contributed little except to outline further and detail the organizational aspect of the investigation—who did what, when, where and by whose orders—and he was quickly dismissed.

There was time left in the day for one more witness, if his testimony was kept short. Harold Springstead, Fitz's assistant, called Chief of Bergen County Detectives Richard Kikkert.

Outside of my own family, there are not many people in this world who have known me as long as Dick Kikkert. He is a few years older than I, went to grammar school with my brother, and often was somewhere around our house when I was a little kid trying to get my first pair of long pants. I can still remember him in the kitchen with my brother, each with a huge bowl of Campbell's vegetable soup filled with soggy, crushed crackers. They used to eat the stuff like Campbell's was going out of business.

Tall, husky, good-looking, not at all the detective "type," Kikkert came down the side aisle smiling in my direction, then waved to my mother, sitting in the first row. Fitz looked as if his mind could use a blowout patch. (In an age of tubeless tires, *that* dates me!)

After identifying himself as an investigator in the prosecutor's office in 1957, Kikkert described his first contact with me on the morning of March 6, when I was being interrogated by Spahr and DeLisle.

SPRINGSTEAD: "And do you recall who was in the room at that time?"

KIKKERT: "There were several people. The only one that stands out in my mind is Walter Spahr and, of course, Edgar Smith."

SPRINGSTEAD: "And where was Walter Spahr at that time?"

KIKKERT: "As I recall, he was half-seated on the edge of a desk facing Edgar Smith."

Kikkert went on to say that he had had a short conversation with me, asking me if I remembered who he was.

SPRINGSTEAD: "And what occurred subsequent to your conversation with Edgar Smith?"

KIKKERT: "After I finished the short conversation with Mr. Smith, Walter Spahr began talking to him again. He had been talking to him when I walked in. What the conversation was I can't recall. However, Edgar got up out of the chair and Spahr seemed to react and he put his hand out against Edgar's chest and said 'Sit down' or 'Stay there.' Edgar went backwards into the swivel chair, it spun out from under him, and he fell to the floor.

Umin, satisfied with Kikkert's testimony, asked only a couple of clarifying questions, one establishing that Kikkert had seen me twice that morning. When Umin was done, Judge Gibbons had a few questions.

JUDGE GIBBONS: "At the time you first saw Edgar Smith, was he dressed in street clothes?"

KIKKERT: "To the best of my recollection, he was in jail coveralls."

JUDGE GIBBONS: "Was he in jail coveralls both times you saw him?"

KIKKERT: "Yes, to the best of my recollection he was."

Court was adjourned for the day immediately after Kikkert left the witness stand, and if Fitzpatrick was surprised by the way the detective greeted me when he entered the courtroom, he was astounded by what happened after the adjournment. Judge Gibbons had hardly left the courtroom when there was a reunion going on behind the railing separating the spectator area from the counsel tables—myself, my mother, Dick Kikkert, my lawyers, and several friends, all laughing and smiling and seemingly having a happy time. Several newspaper reporters tried to edge near to find out what was going on, but at a wink and nod of my head, the federal marshals chased them away. Fitz just stood and glared.

Arthur Ehrenbeck, a certified court reporter and one of the wittiest, nicest, most delightful people it has been my pleasure to meet, was the first witness when court resumed Wednesday morning. Ehrenbeck had stenographically recorded the statement I had given the police the afternoon on March 6, 1957, the key piece of evidence at my trial and the focus of the habeas corpus hearing.

Ehrenbeck's testimony, including the playing of the tape recording of my statement, with numerous stops to check the accuracy of the tape against the stenographer's original notes, took all day. At one point, during a break in the proceedings, with Ehrenbeck on the witness stand and myself sitting at the counsel table a few feet away, he and I engaged in a short conversation regarding *Brief Against Death*. He had been pleased by my mention of him in the book and by the fact that I had spelled his name correctly. With both Fitzpatrick and Springstead able to hear clearly, Ehrenbeck told me that he had enjoyed the book, and that whatever else I did in life, I should not give up writing, that I had a talent he wished he had.

As I said, a very nice man.

Just before Ehrenbeck was excused and court adjourned for the day, Umin asked him to identify the photo taken of me while I was giving my statement to the police, the photo I had pointed out to my lawyers during the prehearing preparations, showing me being helped into a police car by two detectives, a cigarette dangling from my lips. The witness identified it immediately, and later it was put in evidence. It would be important.

The day did not end peacefully. One more incident would take place that would earn me a lecture from David Webster. There were twelve minutes left in the day's session when Ehrenbeck stepped down from the witness stand. Fitzpatrick, looking tired and unhappy, asked the judge to allow us to recess right away. He had an appointment, he said. Fair enough. But then he added that to stay twelve minutes longer "would be somewhat of a hardship."

That was the wrong thing to say, for sure. I was already in a bad mood, mainly because I felt that the playing of the tape recording in open court had not been for any evidential purpose, not because it had any bearing on the voluntariness of my statements to the police, but simply as Fitzpatrick's grab at the next day's headlines, an attempt to play to the press corps and, if the state lost the hearing, to get across to prospective jurors and the public, prior to a retrial, a statement that would not be admissible at that retrial. So when I heard Fitz weeping that twelve minutes longer would be a "hardship" for him, I leaned back in my seat and said loudly enough for everyone in the courtroom to hear: "It's been a hardship for me for fourteen years."

Fitz looked toward me but said nothing. That night, however, when I got together with my lawyers for our nightly conference, David Webster told me that after court Fitz had buttonholed him and complained that I had "embarrassed" him in front of the judge and press, that I had made a fool of him, and that he was not going to stand for that sort of treatment from me.

"I've apologized to him for you and assured him it won't happen again," David told me, "but don't you say anything to him because he doesn't want you to know that he complained to us."

In other words, he didn't want me to know that I had gotten

under his skin. That sounded to me like the sort of funky, behind-the-back thing Fitz would do. If he had a bitch, he should have been man enough to say so in court or tell me himself, not sneak over and cry on my lawyer's shoulder after I left the room.

"Promise me you won't do that again," Umin asked. "Fitz isn't doing well at this hearing, not giving us a very difficult time, and we're far out in front. Let's not get him angry. He may get better if he is angry."

Chapter
Eight

When I returned to court Thursday morning, I could see that something was wrong. Fitzpatrick was sitting at the prosecution table, his hands folded across his middle, looking utterly self-satisfied, while at our table Umin and Webster were thumbing furiously through our trial plan books—thick looseleaf binders containing all our research materials and also proposed cross-examinations for each of the witnesses expected to testify for the state, indexed in the order the witnesses were expected to testify. Umin had planned the hearing strategy with all the care and attention to detail that Eisenhower and his staff had planned D-Day.

"What's up?" I asked, leaning over Umin's shoulder to see what he was reading.

"Not now," he answered abruptly. "We've been surprised. Fitzpatrick is putting Galda on this morning."

Galda, Frederick C., Judge, Bergen County District Court, the man my lawyers had been waiting for, but who was not supposed to testify until Friday.

In 1957, as First Assistant Prosecutor for Bergen County, the number-two man in county law enforcement, Fred Galda had been the man effectively in charge of the investigation of the Victoria Zielinski murder case. He had questioned me through the night of March 5 and the following day had interrogated me during the statement Arthur Ehrenbeck had stenographically recorded.

A politician through and through, seven times the mayor of Paramus, unsuccessful candidate for the State Senate, Galda and the county prosecutor, Guy Calissi, had been "partners" for many many years—Calissi as the borough attorney of the town where Galda was mayor, Galda as first assistant in Calissi's office, each supporting and pushing and defending the other. It was, for the most part, Calissi's use of his office and title to support Galda's candidacy for the State Senate that had been a major factor leading the New Jersey legislature to bar prosecutors from political activity.

When Galda—since becoming a judge he has been known to courthouse hangers-on as Friendly Freddie—entered the courtroom and settled himself in the witness chair directly in front of me, he did not look in my direction, nor would he through the many hours he was to sit there, only four or five feet away. But I looked at him, and I was amazed by the physical change in the man since last I had seen him fourteen years before. Once he had been a husky, vigorous, domineering redhead with a wisecracking, wise-guy attitude matched only by my own. Now, squirming in the chair as he waited for the questioning to begin, he looked as if the good life had been tough on him, aging him two or three years for every one since I had seen him last. His once red hair was now a sandy-rusty gray, thinning noticeably, his face lined and old and tired, and when in response to the first few questions he identified himself, his voice came out a hollow croak. I had heard stories over the years that he liked to live fast and well, enjoying whatever pleasures were available. Rumor or not, he looked it.

Under Fitzpatrick's questioning the witness described his first meeting with me, at the Mahwah police headquarters on the night of March 5, 1957—"He came in, and kind of pretty cocky, I recall that"—and how the questioning had been done through the early morning hours of March 6. Much of his testimony repeated earlier testimony. He did his best to show that I was a willing, cooperative witness, that the interrogations were nothing but friendly, routine conversations, and that the police were so solicitous that at one point he permitted me to wear his topcoat when I was taken to the scene of the crime at 2:30 A.M.—but only because it was below freezing, I was wearing only a thin shirt, and I had complained of the cold, he admitted.

At approximately 5:00 A.M., Galda testified, it was decided to take me to the prosecutor's office, in the county courthouse in Hackensack, but first I was taken to the county medical examiner's office in Hackensack for a physical examination. "For Smith's protection as well as ours," he added.

Sure.

At approximately 9:00 A.M., he related, he had asked me to identify the pair of pants the police had found not far from the scene of the crime.

FITZPATRICK: "What did Edgar Smith say when he saw them?"

GALDA: "He initially denied they were his."

FITZPATRICK: "Did there come a time when Edgar Smith's wife came to the prosecutor's office?"

GALDA: "Yes."

FITZPATRICK: "Did Mrs. Smith identify those pants?"

GALDA: "Yes."

FITZPATRICK: "Identified as whose pants?"

GALDA: "Her husband's."

JUDGE GIBBONS: "Did [Smith's] denial take place before Mrs. Smith was brought to the prosecutor's office?"

GALDA: "That's my recollection, Your Honor. I think that was one of the reasons I brought her down."

There was much questioning regarding the time when Galda first believed that he had sufficient evidence to charge me with the crime, but his answers being altogether equivocal, Fitzpatrick turned to the matter of the stenographically recorded statement taken by Ehrenbeck and asked what arrangements had been made for that.

Arrangements were made with Judge Wallace Leyden, the county assignment judge, for an extra member of the monthly prospective jurors' panel to sit in and witness the taking of the statement, as a disinterested observer, Galda explained. Arrangements were also made, before the statement commenced, for a detective to obtain a motion picture camera and film the events when later in the day I was taken to the scene of the crime and then again when I was taken to Mahwah police headquarters to be arraigned.

The witness was turned over to Umin for cross-examination shortly before the luncheon recess. Umin began right off by asking what standards the prosecution had used to determine whether to charge me with the crime, a crucial point, for when the police have sufficient evidence to make an arrest and bring formal charges, that is when they *must* bring those charges, notwithstanding the fact that they might not feel they have sufficient evidence to get a conviction. To continue interrogating a suspect to obtain more evidence, to build a stronger case, is not permissible except under rigid controls, the most important of which is that the suspect must be advised of his rights and given access to his attorney. He has, the law says, ceased to be a mere suspect; the evidence has made him the person *in fact* charged with the crime even though formal charges have not yet been brought, and at that point he is entitled to all the protections afforded to those who have been formally charged.

Galda explained that when he spoke of "evidence" he felt was needed to bring formal charges, he meant "evidence with which you could go to trial." Then realizing his mistake, he tried weaseling out of the answer, shifting about like an all-pro running back, dodging and turning and refusing to take

Umin's questions head on. But if Galda was a nifty running back, Umin was a middle linebacker who knew damn well that if you hit the guy hard enough and often enough, you were going to slow him down, and that's when you could wipe him out.

Umin hit him often enough. Over and over and over, filling page after page after page of the official transcript, Umin went on hitting him with the single question: If you had sufficient evidence to convince yourself that Smith committed the crime but insufficient evidence to get a conviction, would you have charged Smith with the crime? And over and over and over Galda danced around a direct answer. Then he made a mistake.

"Many people entered into this phase of the discussions [whether or not to charge Smith]. I feel that once it was established that the pants were identified that *we could go no more, that this was now in the accusatory stage*, as far as I was concerned. *It was beyond suspicion. This was where we now had to accuse him.*"

But as the record of the hearing already showed, the prosecutor did "go" more, at least another seven and a half hours more, interrogating me in an attempt to get evidence to support a first-degree conviction, holding my wife in custody, denying me access to my lawyer. The prosecutor had not, as the Supreme Court rulings require, brought me to court for formal arraignment and warnings as to my rights once the investigation had reached the "accusatory stage"—a phrase Galda had lifted directly from the Supreme Court's famous *Escobedo* decision.*

---

* "We hold only that *when the process shifts from investigatory to accusatory*—when its focus is on the accused and its purpose is to elicit a confession—our adversary system begins to operate, and, under the circumstances here, *the accused must be permitted to consult with his lawyer.*" [Emphasis supplied] *Escobedo v. Illinois*, 378 *U.S.* 478; 84 *S. Ct.* 1758; 12 *L. Ed.* 977 (1964).

UMIN: "When in your mind the investigation reached what you called the accusatory stage, what did that mean?"

GALDA: "Can I hear that again?"

Umin repeated the question, adding: "What consequence does that decision that the investigation has reached that stage have—"

"If you ask me to my mind, when the pants were identified," Galda replied, not waiting to hear all the question.

JUDGE GIBBONS: "What do you mean by 'accusatory stage'?"

GALDA: "We were in a position at that time, as I see it, to formally charge Edgar Smith."

UMIN: "Did you at that time formally charge Edgar Smith?"

GALDA: "He was formally charged in Mahwah."

UMIN: "At what time of day?"

GALDA: "Pretty close to five o'clock."

UMIN: "At what time did the investigation reach the accusatory stage? Was it when Mrs. Smith identified the pants?" [9:30 A.M.].

GALDA: "That would be substantially correct. We were satisfied at that time that that was it, and there was nothing more that could be done. . . ."

UMIN: "Did you advise him of his rights at that time?"

GALDA: "I did not."

UMIN: "Do you know whether he was advised at that time of any rights of his?"

GALDA: "When you say any of his rights . . . we didn't do that. His rights, *he could go to the john*, he couldn't leave the building, to be sure, but we didn't go X,Y,Z, if that's what you're driving at."

That's exactly what we were driving at.

Umin next brought out the fact that since I was being interrogated in the county courthouse, it would have been possible at the accusatory stage to arraign and charge me right there, before a county judge, rather than delaying the arraignment and continuing the interrogation for another seven and a half hours before finally taking me to be arraigned in Mahwah before a part-time municipal magistrate, where they did not even bother to keep a record of the proceedings.

UMIN: ". . . Is there a husband and wife privilege, or was there a husband and wife privilege, in the law of New Jersey [at the time you asked Smith's wife to identify the pants]?"

GALDA: "Surely."

UMIN: "Did you advise Mrs. Smith of the privilege?"

GALDA: "I have no recollection of ever having suggested that to Mrs. Smith."*

For the rest of the afternoon Umin questioned Galda about the police methods when investigating a crime and established with greater emphasis that the police could have, and indeed should have, brought me before a magistrate for arraignment long before they actually did. It was during this questioning that Galda made an offhand remark even Umin failed to notice.

At my trial in 1957, I testified that I had been with Vicky Zielinski the night she was killed but that I had left her alive in the company of a man named Hommell. Hommell testified that he had not seen me that night, that he had at the time been in a Mahwah tavern with a man named Rockefeller. Rockefeller also testified and corroborated Hommell's story. No mention was made by the prosecutor of the fact that Rockefeller had once been confined to a mental institution. The prosecutor put him on the stand as a trustworthy, reliable witness, and the jury apparently believed him. But at my habeas corpus hearing in 1971, Galda, in the offhand comment,

* In New Jersey, as in most states, one many not be forced to testify against one's spouse in a criminal proceeding, and Steve Umin's question was intended to establish both that such a privilege existed and that the police did not warn my wife of her right to refuse to give evidence against me.

referred to Rockefeller as not being "the most stable man in the world and we couldn't rely much on what he said." Unfortunately, the prosecution never bothered to tell that to my trial jury.

For all intents and purposes, the hearing was over by the time Galda stepped down from the witness stand Friday afternoon. The state would make an effort on Monday to neutralize Galda's testimony with that of Guy Calissi, who was county prosecutor at the time of my arrest, even going so far as to provide Calissi with the transcript of Galda's testimony to study before taking the stand and having Calissi's law partner sit in the courtroom during Galda's testimony, both violations in spirit if not in fact of the witness exclusion rule set at the start of the hearing. But not even this little bit of cheating could help Fitzpatrick. Umin and Webster were simply too good, too capable, too well prepared, for the state to repair the damage. A demonstration of my lawyers' careful preparation, as contrasted to the state's sloppiness, came near the end of Prosecutor Calissi's testimony.

WEBSTER: "Mr. Calissi . . . didn't you ask Edgar Smith to go to the morgue?"

CALISSI: "No, I did not."

WEBSTER "Did you on the night of the 5th ask him to go to the morgue?"

CALISSI: "No, I didn't."

WEBSTER: "To view the body of Victoria Zielinski?"

CALISSI: "I did not. I wouldn't ask him either question for my own—"

WEBSTER: "Pardon?"

CALISSI: "I wouldn't ask him either question for my own personal reasons."

WEBSTER: "You would not have asked either question?"

CALISSI: "That's right."

WEBSTER: "By that you mean to go to the morgue and view the body?"

CALISSI: "That's right."

WEBSTER: "And your feelings now are the same as they were in 1957?"

CALISSI: "Absolutely."

That is what is known as a setup. Everyone but Calissi seemed to be aware that he was about to be clobbered. David waited, taking his time, milking suspense, waiting until the reporters in the courtroom were silent, ball-point pens ready, aware they were watching a pro at work. I sat grinning at Calissi. I knew what was coming because I had suggested it in a letter to Umin just a couple of days before the hearing began.

WEBSTER: "On page 778a of the transcript [of my 1957 trial] did you put these questions to Edgar Smith? Question by Mr. Calissi: 'As a matter of fact you refused to go on the mound in the sandpit.'

"Answer [by Smith]: 'I did not.'

"Question [by Calissi]: 'And you refused to go down to the morgue when you were asked, the night of the 5th.'

"Answer [by Smith]: 'I did not.'

"Question [by Calissi]: 'You refused when *I asked you to go down to the morgue.*'

"Answer [by Smith]: 'That's correct, but I did not refuse. . . .'

"Question [by Calissi]: 'When I asked you to go down to see the body of Victoria Zielinski. . . .'"

Calissi sat stunned. It was difficult to tell whether he had forgotten the incident or if he had forgotten it was in the record of my trial. Whatever his reason for denying the incident had taken place, he knew now that he was trapped, his credibility severely damaged. David just stood and waited, in no hurry, then Calissi blurted out: "If that's what the record shows, that's what it shows."

WEBSTER: "The question I am putting to you now, sir, having heard your statement—*'I asked you to go and you refused*'—don't you remember now that you did ask him to go?"

CALISSI: "No!"

Calissi's time on the witness stand was not the only time Fitzpatrick's lack of preparation of a witness would show. At another point, a former jail guard, now a prosecutor's detective, testified that when I was first confined in the county jail, one of the other guards had asked me why I had "done a thing like that." The witness stated that he heard the question asked and that at the time it was asked he was standing "four or five feet" away from me, and "Mr. Smith was taking off his undershirt." My lawyers did not even bother to cross-examine the witness. Everyone in the courtroom, including the judge, had heard the former chief of detectives testify that prior to confining me in the county jail, my undershirt had been taken from me and held as possible evidence because of a suspicious stain on the neckband.

Even before the first week of the hearing ended, my lawyers were telling me, "All we can do from here on in is lose it," and one newspaper quoted Umin as telling Fitzpatrick, "You've just nailed your own coffin shut." Fitz knew it. Desperate to halt the flow of damaging testimony from his own witnesses and do something that might sway the judge, he turned on Tuesday of the second week to so-called "professional witnesses"—three psychiatrists who had spent untold days testifying for prosecutors from one end of New Jersey to the other. Each was to swear that he thought my statements to the police were voluntary, though not one of them had any knowledge of the conditions under which the statements were made or pretended to have such knowledge. Once more David Webster demonstrated his skill and savvy at waylaying prosecutors.

When cross-examining one of the psychiatrists, David went into a long series of questions as to what could constitute coercive influences. Was frustration a coercive factor on "a person"? Was cold a coercive factor on "a person"? Can the physical discomfort of "a person" be a factor? Is constant police presence a coercive factor on "a person"? Can the physical condition of "a person" be a factor? On and on he went, asking if this or that or some other thing could be a coercive factor on "a person," always mentioning factors present in my case but never once mentioning me. Then he sat down.

"Thank you. That's all I have."

Gorgeous. He had left the biggest question of all unanswered. Harold Springstead, Fitz's assistant, couldn't wait to jump up and ask it.

"Doctor, I believe you testified that constant police presence could be a coercive factor on an individual—could be a coercive factor on *some* individual?"

"I said it could be both, coercive and a protection."

I turned in my seat and looked at Springstead, standing there rocking on the balls of his feet, looking entirely pleased with himself. *Ohmigawd! He's really going to ask THAT question.*

"Under the circumstances I outlined in my hypothetical question, what would be the effect on Edgar Smith?"

"The effect, in all probability, would be one of coercion . . . in all probability the presence of the police would most probably be interpreted by him as coercion, not protection."

Springstead looked bewildered. He had violated one of the cardinal rules—never ask a crucial question unless you are pretty damn sure in advance what the answer will be—and now he had been zapped by his own witness, his own *expert* witness.

There is another rule equally important. When you get in trouble with a question, stop, leave bad enough alone, don't keep digging in to try to repair the damage or you might dig yourself a deeper hole. Springstead never learned that rule either.

"If Mr. Smith were cooperative with the police, would your answer still be the same?"

"Yes."

I have to give Springstead credit for tenacity. He kept trying, kept asking questions, but the damage had been done
and he was never able to recover. He didn't even smile along
with the rest of us when later, during recess, a reporter leaned
over the railing and asked David why the prosecutor had
asked so many hypothetical questions, and David had replied
loudly enough for everyone within ten feet to hear: "Because
he can't think of real ones."

There are times when Little Fitz (one of my lawyers had
nicknamed him New Jersey Fats) isn't to be believed. Just as
he was about to rest the state's case on Thursday morning, he
decided it was time to put a small part of my book, *Brief
Against Death*, into evidence. Obviously my lawyers weren't
going to sit still for that, and it didn't seem the judge would
either. We argued that if the book went into evidence, all the
parts relevant to the period I was in police custody should be
put in, since after all, that's what the hearing was all about.
That stopped Fitz cold. If he offered the book as his exhibit
and offered all the portions in which I had described my custody and interrogation by the police, then in fact he would be
putting my story on the record, safe from cross-examination,
and there would be no need for me to testify at the hearing.
But on the other hand, if he did not offer the book, then perhaps the judge would strike from the record testimony of the
three psychiatrists, each of whom had based his testimony in
part on his reading of the book.

Fitz argued and argued and argued and got nowhere. The
judge offered to read the book and decide what was relevant,
thereafter admitting into evidence only those parts. Fitz
backed off from that, telling the judge that if he read the book,
he would never be able to forget it (I took that as an unin-
tended compliment!) and it would affect his ultimate decision.
Then Fitz came up with a bright idea. He would "tentatively

rest" his case, see if I took the witness stand to tell my story
and be available for cross-examination; then he would decide
whether he wanted to put the whole book in evidence. No way.
My lawyers were not about to buy a gig like that. "Either rest
or don't rest," David told him. "We aren't going ahead with
our case until you tell us we've seen all of yours."

It was a farce. The judge finally had to declare a long
weekend recess to give Fitz time to think it over and make up
his mind.

When we returned to court on Tuesday, February 9, the
first order of business was a motion by David Webster to quash
a subpoena served upon me the previous day—a nice birthday
present—requiring me to produce in court all the working
drafts of *Brief Against Death*. David moved to quash more in
fun than anything else, arguing that under the federal rules
the subpoena was void for failure of the prosecutor to pay me
a witness fee. Fitz took it all very seriously, as always, and
once more went into his "weeping" act, bemoaning the fact
that I wanted a subpoena fee when I had been "living off the
taxpayers for fourteen years." Judge Gibbons told him to pay
the fee. Fitz promised he would. He never did. So much for
his reliability.

The next bit of business should have been the state's decision on my book, but instead Fitz asked to be permitted to
put in additional testimony via depositions, telling the judge
his witnesses were still in Florida. Judge Gibbons denied the
request, telling Fitz it was his own fault for not having the witnesses under subpoena and present in court. With that, Fitz
called a couple of minor witnesses and then rested his case,
deciding not to put my book in evidence. It was time for Steve
Umin to call the star witness for my side—me!

A great deal of effort had gone into preparing for this
moment, and we had a nice surprise in store for Fitzpatrick.
For four weeks—surely not unknown to the prosecutor—my

lawyers had been going over my testimony with me, the weekends spent at the prison before the hearing began, then each night after court for four hours. But on the night of February 8, Umin decided on a last-minute, abrupt change of strategy. During all our pre-hearing preparations, it was assumed that I would spend a great deal of time on the witness stand, with Umin taking me through my story step by step, in chronological order, from the time I was first taken into custody until I was lodged in the county jail, charged with the crime, just exactly as I had recounted the story in *Brief Against Death*.

There were three thoughts underlying such a line of procedure: (1) We went into the hearing assuming that I would have to tell a detailed, complete story in order to convince the judge that coercion had indeed been a factor in my interrogation by the police. (2) We assumed Fitz would keep me on cross-examination for a considerable period of time, several days possibly, bringing out the details in an attempt to trip me up, and it would be better if the details came out under my lawyer's questioning than Fitz's. (3) Umin felt quite certain that Fitz would make an all-out attempt to discredit my book and in doing so discredit its author, so it would be better in the long run, we thought, if any inconsistencies were brought out by my own lawyer.

As the hearing had progressed, however, Umin's thinking changed. He came to realize that (1) we were so far ahead, winning so handily, that there was no need for me to make more than a token appearance on the witness stand; (2) the shorter the direct testimony, the less Fitz would have to cross-examine; and (3) so much of the state's own evidence and testimony verified *Brief Against Death* that Fitz could not do much damage by going into the book on cross-examination. All Umin asked of me, he said, was that I break even, simply hold my own with Fitz. I intended to do every bit of that.

On the night of the eighth, sitting in the jury room planning my testimony for the next day, Umin used a yellow legal pad to work out a short series of questions, none of them in chronological order, to make it more difficult for Fitz, who we were sure would be expecting chronological testimony, to follow and keep track of. Such a change would make it tough for him. He would be trying to cross-check my testimony against my book and the record of my trial, and we were going to force him to jump back and forth until he didn't know where he was.

While my lawyers were planning legal surprises for Fitzpatrick, I decided to do my own part.

The prison suit I had been wearing the first week of the hearing had been a disaster, the pants ending three inches above my ankles, the jacket too tight to button, a good thing, since all the buttons were cracked or missing. The last week I had a different suit, too large for me, originally an olive-green color but nearly black with dirt and use, so shiny from being pressed and repressed it looked as if I were wearing a mirror. That would never do for my big day on the witness stand. Never. Fitz would already be off balance because of the type of testimony my lawyer would draw from me, and it seemed appropriate that when I sat up there on the stand, looking down at my former friend, waiting for him to begin, I should be better dressed than he was, at least.

A friend had been shopping for me all weekend. When I walked into court Wednesday morning, ready to testify, I was properly magnificent in a slightly moddish black suit with pinstripes as thin as wires, a yellow-gold Cardin shirt, a matching yellow-gold and black silk tie, gold mesh cuff links, and black shoes with gold buckles that picked up and reflected the overhead fluorescent lights. It had cost me a large loaf of bread, but the look on Fitz's face made it all worth it. Even John Selser, my trial lawyer in 1957 and my lawyer for several years after, didn't recognize me when we met in the corridor before court opened.

My testimony began and was over before Fitz knew what

was happening. Umin, the master strategist, who had been so precise until then, finally made a slight error. He had estimated my testimony would run 18 minutes. Actually, it ran 23 minutes.

Yes, I had been taken into police custody late at night with no warnings as to my rights. Yes, I had several times requested a lawyer. Yes, after demanding repeatedly and finally getting permission to telephone my wife, I had asked her to contact a lawyer for me, a former county judge named Dwyer, with whose son I had gone to school. Yes, immediately after the phone call my wife was taken into custody by Detective Graber and prevented from contacting the lawyer. Yes, Spahr had pushed me over a chair. Yes, I had been asked to take a lie detector test and to go to the morgue. Yes, I had been ill with a virus for several days before being taken into custody. Yes, the police had suggested that I would be given a break if I cooperated. Then the big question.

Each time I had seen Umin during the preceding four or five weeks there was one question he had never failed to ask, usually more than once: "Why did you give the police a stenographically recorded statement?"

It is a near-impossible question to answer, one involving so many factors, from the conditions of my detention to the complexities of my own personality, dozens, perhaps hundreds or thousands of factors, literally a lifetime of experiences all contributing to the atmosphere and my state of mind at the moment I gave in to the police and agreed to give a statement. Each time Umin asked me that question he had got a different answer, the same answer basically, but each time in a different form, mentioning different factors, each stemming from my effort to recall that single moment in time fourteen years before, when everything had come together to create a state of mind, an atmosphere, an instant in time that could never be duplicated, never be fully recalled. I tried, tried like hell to recapture the emotions of that moment, the thoughts, the pressures, the whole tone of the experience, but in the casual, relaxed atmosphere of a conference room, rapping with my lawyers, it never quite came back to me. I knew exactly when Umin would ask the question while I was on the witness stand, at the very end of my testimony, to leave it clear in the judge's mind, but right up to that instant when the question was placed, I hadn't the slightest idea what I would say. I had made up my mind the night before, lying in my cell in the Federal Detention Center in New York City, that I would not worry about it. Forget it, I had told myself, don't sweat it. When Umin asks the question, just let the answer *happen*.

It happened.

UMIN: "There came a time later that morning, Edgar, when you participated in a question and answer session that was stenographically transcribed and conducted by Mr. Galda?"

SMITH: "Yes."

UMIN: *"Why did you do that?"*

I shifted sideways in the witness chair, arms folded across my chest, head down, eyes squeezed shut, fingernails digging into my palms, rooting in my mind for the memories, calling back all the sensations, tearing through the fourteen years of mental cobwebs, forcing myself back in time, my eyes now open but fixed on a point in space, my voice low and hoarse as the words started to come, and as I spoke, I was, for that minute or two, reliving what had happened to me.

"That is a very difficult question to answer. It involves everything that happened to me all night long. When I had first been taken into police custody, I felt compelled right off the bat to answer their questions. I felt that if I didn't answer the questions that that in itself was going to be suspicious and perhaps they would take it as incriminating against me. And during the night I had lied to the police. I had given them misleading information, and once having told them something, and once they had found out that not everything I had said was true, then I felt compelled to explain, to talk some more. And this went on through the night, and by morning I had gotten myself so tied up in contradictory stories and at that point I was beginning to feel a whole range of pressures on me that I didn't really feel I had any choice other than to attempt to give them one more explanation. I was there. I was not being allowed to contact anyone. All through the night there had been pressure, like a little pressure from being asked to take a lie detector test, or Mr. Calissi wanting me to go down to the morgue. I believe that came up again during the night. I don't know, it's sort of an overwhelming feeling of being in police custody, that was the thing that bothered me more than anything else. It was like being in a cocoon, you are cut off from everyone, you are cut off from everything, you do only what they want, you go where they say you go, you do what they say you do, you can't even go to the bathroom without asking them, and when they do allow you to go to the bathroom, they send somebody with you to stand in the open doorway as if they were afraid you were going to commit suicide or try to escape. It was the now and then glimpses of my wife I was given, the attempts to contact an attorney— they let me call my wife and then they would take it away from me. All these pressures in addition to the feeling that I was compelled to answer the questions. At some point I couldn't take it any longer. I knew that unless I went along with them I was going to sit there and they were going to keep hitting me with questions and hitting me with questions and my wife was going to sit in an office. And they told me she was being questioned, that she had identified my pants. They told me she was going to stay there until I did give them what they wanted, until I did cooperate with them. They told me that if I wanted a lawyer I would have to cooperate with them. If I wanted anything I had to cooperate with them. If I wanted a cigarette I had to cooperate with them. And at some point I just gave in and gave them what they wanted. I just didn't know what else I could do."

I looked up and saw Fitzpatrick standing behind the railing on our side of the courtroom, smiling as if it were all a joke. But it was no joke. He knew it. I knew it. The courtroom had been as silent as a tomb during my answer, not a person moving. It had been impressive. A friend later told me that Judge Gibbons had not even blinked all the while I was talking.

Umin had one more unrehearsed question.

"Did you think that would help you in some way?"

"I just don't think that at that point it mattered. What mattered was getting out of it, getting out of that office, getting away from the questions, getting to a lawyer, getting to see my wife. Just doing what they said. It is difficult to explain to anyone who hasn't gone through it. You are just in a box and there is no way out of it."

Umin paused, shuffled some papers, let my testimony sink in, let me relax. I was wound up like a 39-cent Swiss watch about to bust my mainspring, sweat covering my forehead and running down my back, the palms of my hands damp and cold. There wasn't a sound in the room yet, and when I glanced over to where Fitz now sat at the counsel table, a somewhat puzzled expression on his face, I realized that even *he* had been affected by my testimony, even he looked willing to concede at that moment that perhaps the police had coerced the statement from me.

My mind felt numb as I sat waiting, wondering what Umin was going to do next, and suddenly a wildly weird thought occurred to me: If he asked the same question again, I couldn't remember a goddamn word of what I had just said. (The next morning the first thing I would do when I entered the courtroom would be pick up the overnight transcript and read my answer, to see what I had said.)

Then I looked at a friend, and when she smiled, I relaxed, satisfied that everything was all right. Umin saw it, sat down, and said: "No further questions."

I have absolute confidence in *Brief Against Death*. When the book was published and Prosecutor Calissi, his assistant prosecutors, his detectives and investigators, and other police officials were asked to comment on it, all declined, citing court rules about discussing pending cases. I never accepted that excuse, and not merely because I knew the court rules as well as they did. To me, *Brief Against Death* was and still is, in all its essential facts, charges, and conclusions, an untouchable presentation of my side of the story. They could do a lot of nit-picking—perhaps the rug in the prosecutor's office was maroon instead of red, or it was this officer instead of that officer who denied me my request for a lawyer—but in its essentials, I am convinced the book can stand up under any attack by anyone.

Umin told me prior to the hearing that Fitzpatrick would attack the book, that he would go through it point by point, and that I should be prepared. He said Fitz would even want to compare the various rough drafts of the book with the published version, seeking contradictions, seeking to show I had changed my story here or there, or that facts had changed in the various tellings. My response was that Fitz didn't have the heart to try that, not with me, not with the guy who wrote the book. No way. Umin disagreed. I was right.

Fitz is a slow worker. God! Is he *slow*. He will ask a question, shuffle around in his notes, ask a question, check his notes, ask a question, go looking for something in his notes, ask a question, check an affidavit or transcript, ask a question, hand the clerk a document to be marked for identification, ask a question, fumble around with his papers, think, look confused, look puzzled (he always looks puzzled), and on and on and on. He kept me on the witness stand all afternoon Tuesday and most of Wednesday, but with all his stalling and fumbling, there were relatively few questions asked, and even fewer of real importance. I haven't counted how many times he referred to *Brief Against Death* and questioned me about it, but it was infrequent, perhaps a dozen or so times, and most of those questions were simply to show that my story differed from the stories told by his detectives. He seemed not to know where he was going, not to have a clearly defined line of questions prepared, and rarely did he follow up a question with the next obvious question. At one point he got so fouled up that he put his copy of my book into evidence and asked the clerk to hand it to me for reference, then stood there without a second copy to refer to. He borrowed another, but since I had his copy, with all the portions he wished to refer to marked off and checked, and the copy he had was "clean," I usually knew where he was going before he did.

By Thursday afternoon the hearing was over and I was ordered back to the State Prison at Trenton to await the decision. Judge Gibbons ruled that there would be no closing arguments, that instead each side should submit its closing arguments in brief form, both sides to file them March 17.

Before leaving the courtroom, David and Steve Umin stopped to talk with me for a few minutes. I had one question I wanted answered. And answered straight. "Who won?"

"We did," David replied.

"We did," Umin agreed.

Some friends and I were allowed a five-hour visit in the federal detention room on the third floor, and then around 6:00 P.M., Sam Maples, a U. S. marshal assigned to the Trenton office, arrived with his big new Oldsmobile to chauffeur me back to the state jailhouse.

Sam Maples is one of the world's great characters, louder than a tornado about to swallow Frisbee, Kansas, and usually funnier than John Lindsay when he's being serious seriously. And he is hell on hippies and radicals. ("Those dirty bastards want to run the whole damn country and they can't even get themselves straight.") The first time I met him was in April, 1970, in the U. S. marshal's office in the Trenton courthouse. At that time he walked into the office, took one look at me and said: "Jesus Christ! Another one of these guys claiming his constitutional rights were violated."

Now it was a year later and we were sitting in the car at a Burger King just outside Trenton, eating a "Whopper" that tasted like raw kangaroo meat on a bun. Sam turned in the front seat and said: "Hey, Smitty, from what I hear around the courthouse, you've got yourself a winner."

Play it again, Sam!

Chapter Nine

Our brief was filed the third week of March, as ordered by Judge Gibbons. Weeks went by without any sign of Fitzpatrick's brief, which was supposed to be filed the same day as ours. By Easter my lawyers were telling me that Judge Gibbons was already at work on his opinion, notwithstanding the prosecutor's failure to file the state's brief, and the guessing was that as soon as Fitzpatrick did get around to filing, the judge would immediately thereafter hand down his ruling.

On May 14 Steve Umin visited me at the prison, and in the course of our conversation, when I expressed concern as to how Judge Gibbons would rule on the habeas corpus petition, Umin told me: "There won't be any bad news in this case." The next day Fitzpatrick filed his long-delayed brief. Then on Friday, May 17, while I was having a visit with my mother, a sergeant interrupted the visit to tell me that Frances Bronson, Bill Buckley's secretary, had phoned with a message. "She told me to tell you 'We won,'" the sergeant advised me.

The ruling by Judge Gibbons was everything we could have hoped for, complete victory on every point raised during the January-February hearing, and the speed with which he handed down his ruling provided a stark contrast to the delaying tactics of the judges who had had the case before him.

For the first time a court had ruled on the merits of my claims after a full and fair hearing of the witnesses and evidence, and for the first time I had proof of the claim I had made in *Brief Against Death*, that if a court heard my appeal on the merits, "there was no way under the facts and law the court could avoid reversing the conviction."

Judge Gibbons voided my conviction and ordered that the writ of habeas corpus freeing me would issue "unless within sixty days the State of New Jersey shall grant to the petitioner Edgar H. Smith a new trial on the indictment charging him with the murder of Victoria Zielinski. . . ." Judge Gibbons had found that the period of my interrogation on the evening of March 5, 1957, and continuing through the morning and afternoon of March 6 was coercive in nature, and that the statements elicited from me during that period had been unconstitutionally obtained and could not be used at a retrial. Moreover, the judge ruled that the actions of the police in 1957 were illegal and unconstitutional under 1957 law, not under any new constitutional rules established after my conviction. In other words, what the police did was wrong when they did it, not something that was wrong retrospectively.

To say I was elated by Judge Gibbons' ruling would be like saying that it must have been nice to be the first man to set foot on the moon. When one struggles as long as I struggled, giving up so much over the course of fourteen years, living more than a third of one's life caged like an animal, persistently maintaining the position that a State Supreme Court had been repeatedly and clearly in error, vindication in the form of a ruling like Judge Gibbons' is indescribably sweet. I didn't laugh or cry or jump up and down shouting. I had *known* I would win sooner or later, and when victory came, I simply smiled and began looking ahead to the next round in the fight. I didn't have long to wait.

Less than a week after Judge Gibbons' ruling, my lawyers filed an application for bail under the federal rules allowing bail where a habeas corpus petitioner has been successful. A hearing on the bail application was scheduled for June 9, just 14 years and 5 days after I was sentenced to death by Judge Arthur O'Dea of the Bergen County Court. Steve Umin advised me that, while nothing could be guaranteed, there was a good chance that bail would be granted, if only because Judge Gibbons wanted my case closed permanently and realized that if I were given bail, that would probably be the end of the battle. That was something I could understand.

Having lost the battle to keep me under sentence of death and with a new trial ordered, the state of New Jersey had only one thing to offer me in return for a negotiated deal—my freedom. As long as the state had me in prison, there remained the possibility that I would forego a new trial, instead entering some sort of plea that, in return for my immediate freedom, would allow the state to close the books with a conviction. If, however, the federal court granted bail, then the state would have nothing to offer me, and through various legal motions I could delay the start of a new trial almost indefinitely, at least long enough that a new trial would be so difficult the state would be forced to give up and dismiss the indictment. I felt that, at a minimum, I could delay the start of a new trial for three years, simply by filing pretrial motions and appealing any denials.

In view of the widespread publicity given Judge Gibbons' ruling in May, when the story was front-page news in the New York *Times*, I expected more reporters and photographers than were waiting when I arrived at the federal court building in Newark on the morning of June 9—my handcuffed wrists attached to a leather belt around my waist and two prison guards escorting me, as always. But the absence or presence of media representatives was not my main concern. Steve Umin's optimism about the prospects for bail had so infected me that all my belongings at the prison were packed and stored in an empty cell, and I had made plans to fly to the Virgin Islands for a rest immediately after my release.

The large courtroom in which Judge Gibbons would hear

the bail arguments was crowded when I was brought in from the United States marshal's detention cell, where I had waited for nearly an hour. Bill Buckley, also apparently optimistic, was sitting in the front row with Warren Steibel, the producer of his TV show. When I leaned across the railing to shake hands with Bill, it marked the first time we had had any direct contact in the nine years he had been helping me fight for my freedom. Previously, each time I had seen him at the prison, we were separated by a glass window, and our conversations had been carried out over a telephone.

As newspaper reporters took notes and a couple of artists made charcoal sketches for the evening television news, Steve Umin presented a short but powerful argument in favor of the granting of bail. Umin argued that my fourteen-year record of accomplishment in prison had shown that I would not be a danger to society if released, that I had no intention of fleeing if set free on bail, and that if the state retried me, there was "no fair likelihood that Edgar Smith could be convicted of first degree murder" a second time, and that "one more unconstitutional day in prison would do irreparable harm to Edgar Smith." In addition, Umin pointed out that Bill Buckley had filed an affidavit with the court, in which he agreed to take custody of me and guarantee my availability any time the court called for me. Judge Gibbons was impressed.

Ed Fitzpatrick opposed the bail application in his usual style—a combination of restrained hysteria and professional arrogance. He argued that the federal court had no authority to grant bail to a state prisoner, that I was guilty of the crime, that the state would retry me, and that if I were set free, I would flee or go into hiding and be a "danger to the community." The hypocrisy of that argument was beyond belief. More than a year before Fitzpatrick had indicated his willingness to allow me to go free if I were to enter a guilty plea to second-degree murder, and I am certain he would not have been willing to do that if he *really* believed, as he told Judge Gibbons during the bail arguments, that I was a danger to society. But of course the press and public knew nothing of the plea bargaining a year earlier.

I don't think I'll ever forget the moment when Judge Gibbons rendered his decision. I sat with my hands flat on the table, looking straight ahead at the court clerk, and it was all I could do to keep from jumping up and shouting "WHOOOOPEE" when the judge said an order would issue granting me bail in the amount of $5,000.

Little Fitz looked as if the courthouse had fallen on him. He asked that Judge Gibbons limit me to the state of New Jersey. The judge said there would be no travel restrictions. Fitz then asked that I be denied the right to appear on television. Judge Gibbons said he couldn't repeal the First Amendment. Then Fitz asked that the order be held up to give him time to appeal. The judge agreed to hold the order for twenty-four hours.

Twenty-four hours. That's all. Just twenty-four hours and I would be a free man. I may have appeared calm when the state prison guards took me downstairs and turned me over to the federal marshals and while I was changing the prison suit for my own clothing, but inside I felt like a high school kid about to get laid for the first time. Not the purest, best Mexican grass could have floated me higher. Tripping? WOW!!! I was on a FREEDOM trip.

An hour after the judge ordered bail, the federal marshals took me out of the courthouse for the trip to New York City, where I would be held in the federal detention center until my release the next afternoon. I think it was then that I realized for the first time that I had become a sort of antihero, a "celebrity" of some kind. The street outside the courthouse was filled with photographers and TV cameramen, and everywhere I looked someone was sticking a microphone in my face and asking how it felt to be a free man. Workers from the courthouse hung out windows to watch the "celebrity" being hustled through the mob and into a car parked in front of the Newark Police Headquarters across the street, and all along the sidewalks people clustered with curious expressions on their faces. "What's going on?" "Who's that guy?" "Is he some kind of Mafia boss or something?"

We stopped once on the way to New York City, for a roast beef with horseradish sauce on sesame seed bun at a roadside restaurant just before the entrance to the Holland Tunnel. Ten minutes later I was checking into the Federal Detention Center on the Lower West Side. One more night in jail. Just one more long, hot night in a cell. After 5,180 nights as a numbered animal, 5,180 nights as the property of the state of New Jersey, I had just one more night to go. It would be the longest night.

Like most jails, the detention center was overcrowded, and as a result I would have to spend the night in the segregation section—the section of the jail in which they confined the men most difficult to handle, the ones who refused to conform to the rules. What did I care? By the time the cell door closed behind me I had less than eighteen hours to go before climbing into the back seat of Bill Buckley's limousine and riding off to greener pastures—for lack of a better way to describe where I was headed after my release.

Four other men were in the cell with me. We played blackjack for a while, then three of us played casino. One fellow— a hijacker—had a watch, and every couple of minutes I asked him what time it was. He got so tired of telling me after the 150th time that he took the watch off and hung it on the bedspring of the top bunk, where all I had to do was look up from my cards (we were using the bottom bunk for a card table) to see it. I discovered something that night about the relativity of time: The faster one wants time to pass, the slower the hands of a clock will move.

One more night in jail. The cards were put away, the last

cigarettes were smoked by my cell mates, and then it was quiet in the segregation wing. By 2:00 A.M. everyone was asleep but me, the guy who had less than twelve more hours to go before the handcuffs came off for the last time. Lying on my bunk, chain-smoking borrowed cigarettes, staring up at the hands of the wristwatch hanging above my head, I waited. And I waited. After fourteen years on Death Row I was still waiting. But this was the last wait. And the longest wait.

Wednesday, June 9, the day that was to be the first day of the rest of my life, came on hot and humid. By 6:00 A.M. I was taking a shower and getting dressed in a cell for the last time, assuming all went well, and by 8:00 I was downstairs in a small room waiting for the U.S. marshals to pick me up and take me to Newark. A young fellow, not more than nineteen or twenty, was waiting with me, also to go to Newark—but he was to be arraigned on charges of holding up a New Jersey bank. We talked as we waited, and I told him I was going to be released on bail.

"That's great," he remarked. "What were you in for?"

"Murder."

The eyes, especially the young kids' eyes, always get bigger when they hear that.

"Oh! Well, gee, uh—wow, you know."

I stood there, smoking my cigarette, not saying anything, waiting for the next question. Finally he asked how long I had "done."

"Fourteen and a half years."

Before he had a chance to recover from that, from the fact that I had been in prison since he was five or six years old, I told him that before the day was over, he was going to be a TV star, that when we went out of the detention center with the U.S. marshals, there would probably be a lot of photographers and TV cameramen waiting for us.

"By tonight all your friends and relatives will know you

got busted for hitting on a bank," I told him, "but don't worry about it."

The marshals were late, not arriving until after 9:30 because of the early morning traffic. The kid with me was scared stiff when we walked out the door, but when he saw there was only one photographer from the New York *Post* waiting to take our pictures, he got a bit cocky.

"Ahhhh, I knew you were bullshittin'. That wasn't anything."

Newark was a different story. We had to park half a block from the courthouse entrance, and by the time we had run the obstacle course of photographers, TV film cameras, audio cables snaking all over the sidewalk, and reporters with notebooks and tape recorders, the kid was white-faced. When finally we were in the detention room on the third floor and he was locked in a cell, he seemed to sigh with relief. It was the first time I ever saw anyone happy to be locked up.

I must confess that the attention being given me by the news media came as a surprise. During my previous trips to court I had grown accustomed to having cameras poked in my face and being asked dumb questions, but Newark was something else. All the New York TV stations had camera crews there, filming for themselves and the networks, and there seemed to be at least two reporters and photographers from every newspaper within a hundred miles. It bothered me at first. I would have preferred to have been released on bail with less fanfare, so that I could sneak away and relax for a few days before accepting some of the many requests for interviews, but before the day was over, I would be thankful that what was about to happen would happen in full view of the media and public. The image of "Jersey Justice" was about to be given another layer of tarnish.

For two hours that morning I nervously paced the floor at the detention cell, waiting for the twenty-four-hour period to expire and the bail to become effective. I was to be released at 1:00 P.M. I knew, of course, that Assistant Prosecutor Fitzpatrick was in Philadelphia, asking the United States Court of Appeals for the Third Circuit to revoke Judge Gibbons' grant of bail, and I knew also that he was being assisted by a Deputy Attorney General, the first time the state had intervened at that high a level, but the odds against Fitzpatrick's success were so outrageous that no one gave his appeal the slightest chance.

The intervention of the Attorney General's office came about as a result of the suspension of the Bergen County prosecutor on charges of accepting bribes and obstructing justice—charges he would later beat at trial. Under New Jersey law, the prosecutor of the county in which a crime takes place has total authority for apprehension, arrest, and prosecution, except in cases where the prosecutor is, for some reason, superseded by the Attorney General, as in this case where my prosecutor had been arrested and his office was being run by the Attorney General pending trial.

When the Attorney General took over the Bergen County Prosecutor's Office—coincidentally the day after Judge Gibbons reversed my conviction and ordered a new trial—he put one of his own men in charge but allowed the assistant prosecutors, such as Fitzpatrick, to continue to handle the cases then pending. Hence Fitzpatrick remained on my case, but he now had available assistance from the AG's office.

At the time I was waiting to be released on bail, I did not know that Fitzpatrick was being assisted by a Deputy Attorney General, nor do I think it would have made any difference to me had I known. I *knew* I was going to walk out of that courthouse at 1:00 P.M. Anthony Greski, the chief United States marshal for New Jersey, apparently shared my confidence, for an hour before the twenty-four hours was to expire, he took me to his office, told me I could leave as soon as the $5,000 bail was posted, and let me use his phone to call Bill

Buckley's office. I immediately phoned Frances Bronson, Buckley's secretary, and told her I was free to leave whenever the money was posted. She told me to sit tight, that Buckley's limousine was on the way back from taking him to the airport, and that as soon as it got back, she would send someone over to post the bail and get me out.

"How long will that be?" I asked.

"Perhaps an hour," she told me. "The money is here waiting to be picked up."

What an incredible hour that was to be.

I was returned to the detention cell as soon as the phone call was completed and resumed my pacing, every few seconds, it seemed, asking one of the marshals for the time. Chief Marshal Greski returned to the detention room at 12:15, and when I saw the look on his face, I knew something was wrong. I don't know what it is men in jail develop, some sort of sixth sense, I suppose, but when you've been behind walls as long as I had been, you can smell trouble about to happen.

As soon as the chief marshal approached the front of the cell, I asked him what the trouble was. "Don't bullshit me," I told him. "What happened?"

I'll say one thing for the man: He had a lousy job to do and he wasn't enjoying it.

"I have a telegram I've just received from the clerk of the United States court of appeals," he told me. "I have to read it to you. It reads as follows: 'No one is to disturb the custody of the prisoner until further order of this court.'"

"That's it?"

"That's all there is right now, but I understand from the clerk that another telegram will follow this one. I'm afraid you're going to have to wait some more."

I didn't have to wait long. Thirty minutes later Greski was back with another telegram, and the second one put the lock on the box:

It is further ordered that the relator [Smith] is remanded to the custody of the State of New Jersey pending disposition of the appeal on the merits or further order of this court without prejudice to relator's rights to apply to the courts of the State of New Jersey for release on bond.

What all that meant was that Judge Gibbons' bail order had been revoked and I would go back to the Death House to wait until the court of appeals decided Fitzpatrick's appeal from Gibbons' ruling reversing my conviction and ordering a new trial. Beautiful! For fourteen years I couldn't find a single judge in the state of New Jersey who had anything but praise for the way my arrest and trial had been handled, so now the court of appeals tells me it's okay with them if I can find a New Jersey judge who will set me free on bail. That's something like George Wallace telling Angela Davis that it's okay with him if she can find an Imperial Wizard of the KKK who will give her the American of the Year Award.

Getting me out of the Newark Courthouse for the trip back to New York City, where I would be held overnight before being returned to the prison in Trenton, turned out to be an exercise in muscle. The street outside was jammed from one side to the other, and from one end of the courthouse to the other, and people were hanging out the windows of all the surrounding buildings, including the Newark Police Headquarters across the street. There must have been a couple hundred reporters and photographers, and several times that many curious onlookers. I didn't realize it at the time—I was too depressed—but the events of that day, the way I was given bail and then it was taken away at the last possible moment, would result in a significant shift in public and media opinion.

Chief Marshal Greski used all the personnel available to him, including Post Office police and men from other federal agencies, to get me through the crowd and into the car parked on the sidewalk across the street. Thirty minutes later I was again in the Federal Detention Center in New York. The people there, inmates and guards alike, were sympathetic when they heard what had happened, and when I asked to use the telephone, the captain in charge of the center granted permission at once.

The first call was to Frances Bronson, Buckley's secretary, who told me that one of my lawyers, Steve Lichtenstein, was on another line talking to the producer of Buckley's TV show. My other lawyers, Steve Umin and David Webster, were still in Philadelphia, where they had argued before the U.S. court of appeals that bail should not be revoked. Frances had her switchboard connect me with Lichtenstein, and my first question was: "Okay, what do we do now?"

"Nothing," Lichtenstein told me. "We could petition the United States Supreme Court to reinstate bail, but we feel that that would not be a wise move at this time. Umin thinks we will have a much better chance of having the bail reinstated if we wait until the court of appeals upholds Judge Gibbons' grant of a new trial."

"You mean we have to wait for the prosecutor to appeal *that* before you people try to get me out?"

"We think that's the best way."

I didn't like it, and I told Lichtenstein I didn't. Normally, an appeal of that type takes months to be heard, and it is not at all unusual for the court of appeals to take as long as a year to hand down a decision.

"That isn't going to happen," Lichtenstein told me. "You don't know the full story."

"Yeah, okay, so tell me."

"The court of appeals obviously understood that in revoking your bail they were simply highlighting the unfair treatment you have received thus far in the state and the federal courts and doing nothing for the image of the judicial system, and because they understood that, they have ordered the appeal expedited. Typewritten briefs, rather than the usual printed briefs, must be filed by both sides within two weeks, and oral arguments will be heard within thirty days. We have a tacit understanding that the decision will be handed down within a month or two of the oral arguments, and at that time we will be free again to seek bail."

I still didn't like it. Perhaps it was true that we would have a better chance of having the bail reinstated if we waited until after the appeal, but that didn't mean there was *no* chance to have it reinstated immediately, and I was not one for giving up. The only people who never win are those who never try. I insisted that we apply to the Supreme Court for bail, but Lichtenstein insisted just as strongly that I be patient until I had a chance to talk with my other lawyers and knew the full story of what had happened that morning in Philadelphia. Reluctantly, I agreed. Umin and Webster had done a hell of a job for me up to that point, and I was willing to give them a chance to do things their way.

I remained at the Federal Detention Center overnight, and a long, tough night it was. I was not half as angry with the courts as I was with myself. For the first time in fourteen years I had counted something before I had it, and that made it all that much tougher for me. But by the next morning, when the U.S. marshals came to pick me up for the ride back to Trenton, I was beginning to put the whole thing in perspective and feel a little bit better. Sure, I would have to wait a couple of months longer, but all I had lost was the bail. Judge Gibbons' order reversing my conviction and ordering a new trial still stood, and none of us could see any way the prosecutor could have that upset on appeal.

Although I did feel somewhat better the next day by the time I got back to the prison, enough of my anger and disappointment remained that it showed clearly in a letter I wrote that evening to Bill Buckley:

> Well, we came pretty damn close. And some good things did come out of it, not the least of which is an interesting swing in public opinion as a result of the way things were

done. I am told even the Bergen County papers thought it was a lousy show. If Fitzpatrick never did anything else in his life, he guaranteed me national exposure from here on in.

As you know, I had a phone available to me in West Street and got through to Frances. She put me on with Steve Lichtenstein. Losing the bail was a disappointment, but that isn't what bothers me now. What I am hot about is that after fourteen years of not quitting, of never conceding anything, of making every effort even though it was obviously hopeless, I now find my lawyers quitting on the bail question. We could have made an application to Supreme Court Justice Brennan, but we didn't. We were told by the court of appeals that we could apply to the State Court for bail, but we didn't attempt that either. I can take losing the bail; I cannot tolerate giving up, not trying, quitting.

As anyone who has ever been involved in a criminal proceeding knows, more goes on out of court—in judges' chambers, lawyers' offices, on the telephone, or in a bar across the street from the courthouse—than goes on in a courtroom where the public and media can see it. And so it was in my case. For more than a year there had been discussions of means to end the case through some sort of deal between myself and the prosecutor, and although those discussions continued all through the bail proceedings, nothing concrete seemed to be happening. The prosecutor still had hopes of reversing Judge Gibbons' ruling on appeal, and until those hopes were crushed, the state was not willing to concede that a deal was the only way out.

For my own part, I realized that no matter what happened in the court of appeals, it was likely that my case would end through a negotiated settlement. No one, not myself, not the prosecutor, *really* wanted to go through the ordeal and expense of a new trial, the outcome of which would be uncertain for both sides. But again, serious discussions to close the case would have to await the outcome of the state's appeal.

The state's appeal was argued before the United States Court of Appeals in Philadelphia on July 14. When I learned that one of the judges on the three-judge panel was J. Cullen Ganey, I knew the vote was already 1–0 in my favor. Judge Ganey had sat once before on one of my appeals, in 1963, and was the first judge in any court to agree with my arguments that my conviction was unconstitutional because of improper police procedures during my arrest and interrogation.

On August 1 Steve Umin advised me that we could expect a ruling on the appeal within the next couple of days, and on August 3 we got it. In a brief two-and-a-half-page opinion, the court of appeals held that all Judge Gibbons' findings of fact and law were correct, and that the order reversing my conviction and requiring a new trial would stand as issued. The vote was 3–0. The letter I wrote Bill Buckley that night reveals my pleasure at the victory:

> Christian charity has never been one of my strongpoints, so I might as well go ahead and tell you that it is great fun to throw a shutout at Fat Fitz. I hope he now takes it to the Supreme Court. Another shutout will do him good.

Unfortunately, while it is fun to win big and make a prosecutor look bad, as we did in the court of appeals, that does not get one out of prison, and getting me out remained the number one problem. It was obvious that the prosecutor would now be even more anxious to close the case by negotiation, and it seemed to me, as I wrote to Buckley, that we were now in a position to take a hardheaded attitude on a settlement.

> Steve Lichtenstein was in today and said—confidentially— that he feels Umin made some mistakes in approaching the state on an "arrangement," and he asked if I thought he, Lichtenstein, ought to try approaching the top man. I told him it was okay with me if Umin approves. But I also told him our position ought to be that we are preparing for a new trial and not looking for a deal, but we'll listen if the state has something to say.

With Umin's approval, Lichtenstein contacted the Attorney General and made arrangements for a meeting after Labor

Day, at which time we would find out for sure how anxious the state was to close the case by negotiation. Meanwhile, Fitzpatrick was going ahead and appealing to the United States Supreme Court, arguing that the court of appeals had been wrong in upholding Judge Gibbons' order reversing my conviction. It would be a silly appeal, one with absolutely no chance of success, not after a unanimous ruling by the court of appeals, and so it seemed to me at the time that Fitzpatrick was merely trying to prolong my stay in the Death House, trying to drag the case out as long as possible and get as much time from me as he could.

The only way to counter Fitzpatrick's delaying tactics would be to move immediately for bail from the Supreme Court. I spoke with Lichtenstein about that, and he assured me that if nothing came of the meeting with the Attorney General, if there was no prospect for an immediate settlement of the case, a bail application would be filed within a day or two after that. Again, it seemed to me we were just wasting time, that the Attorney General was not going to offer any settlement that would be acceptable to me, but I agreed to give the lawyers the time they needed.

On August 21, while I was waiting for my lawyers to meet with the Attorney General, George Jackson was killed at San Quentin. Bill Buckley had written to me a few days before Jackson's death, suggesting an analogy between Jackson and Richard Mayberry, a white prisoner in a Pennsylvania institution, who had been written about in a nationally syndicated article. Buckley asked for my comments. I replied the day after George Jackson's death:

I have the clipping on Richard Mayberry, and your letter asking whether there is an analogy between the Mayberry experience and that of the Soledad Brothers, so as to suggest that the difficulties encountered by the latter might be based on other than "purely" racial animosities.

I have read the Mayberry article, having already been somewhat familiar with the case, and of course you know that I reviewed *The Prison Letters of George Jackson* for *Playboy* and a couple of newspapers. There is no doubt that a column by you would be timely, particularly since last evening George Jackson enjoyed a properly spectacular death certain to be recorded on page one of the *Times* and guaranteed to make him a revolutionary martyr. I say "enjoyed" because it was apparent to me after reading the last letter in Jackson's book, the letter written immediately after he learned that his kid brother, Jonathon, had been wasted (isn't that an appropriate slang word?) in the Marin County Courthouse shootout, that sooner or later George would go out the same way, with a gun in his hand, taking someone with him and doing it as a matter of choice. To have died any other way would have been the worst sort of self-betrayal for a man like that. Everything he believed in required him to go out that way, a truly fundamental difference between the George Jacksons of this world and, say, the Abbie Hoffmans. It is the difference between talking revolution and being a revolutionary. After a Chicago or Kent State, the talking revolutionaries cry and say: "That ain't fair." After a Marin County Courthouse, the George Jacksons say: "The job isn't done. Pick up the guns, brothers, and carry on."

But getting back to your analogy. I would agree with you only if you insist in keeping in that one word—"purely." It is clear that Jackson's difficulties were not "purely," or solely, the result of his being black. But whereas Mayberry's problems in prison seem to result from the single fact that he will not conform, George Jackson's are/were (I have to get used to the past tense) somewhat more complicated. His nonconformity was directly related to the fact of his color. Jackson refused to accept the system, refused to conform, because he was a revolutionary, and he was a revolutionary as a result of his black experience. You just can't say that (a) Mayberry is a nonconformist, and (b) Jackson was a nonconformist, and therefore (c) they are/were the same animal. No way.

I hope you don't plan to quote me because this is a mess. I am trying to give you a quick answer. Incidentally, I was intrigued by the comment of Mayberry's warden, who said the man would be less of a danger on the street than he was in prison. There you have another similarity with Jackson. Had Jackson been released years ago, before the Marin County shootout, he might never have become a revolutionary symbol, never would have become a martyr and rallying point, as he will now. In this respect, at least, the system is self-defeating as a result of its refusal to bend. I've always said the quickest way to destroy a budding revolutionary is not to hound him with the FBI and try to get him on a silly conspiracy rap, but rather it is to invite him to dinner at the White House, appoint him to a committee to effect whatever change he is pushing for, and then let him die of respectability, the fatal disease of radicals.

A messy letter to be sure, and not an altogether coherent one, but I think it answers your question: Yes, I don't agree with you, except in part!

Buckley replied a few days later and suggested that it was highly unlikely that anyone short of a moron would believe that the prison authorities in California arranged Jackson's death, that the man had been "set up." As usual, I did not agree with Buckley, and I wrote and told him so:

You are correct, of course. It is obvious that Jackson panicked when the gun was spotted. But you are wrong when you say it is unlikely people will jump to the conclusion that Jackson was set up. Most blacks are already convinced he was, and the charge will be repeated often enough that an awful lot of people will believe it. And to some degree perhaps he was set up—by the system. When you look at the sentence he got for a run-of-the-mill robbery in which no one was injured and the amount of time they were forcing him to do, with parole still nowhere in sight, plus the conditions under which he was confined, it is not too farfetched to say the system did set him up by forcing him into a state of hopelessness from which, sooner or later, he was bound to attempt something fatal. He was a young kid caught up in a system he didn't really understand, and the more he struggled against it, the more oppressive it became.

Then, almost as an afterthought, I added a paragraph that would prove unfortunately accurate:

I have a feeling, by the way, that the Jackson incident will be looked back on as one of the more significant events in the history of the American prison system. Just as it is true that California led the rest of the country in progressive penal reform, I think we will find over the next couple of years that what is happening in California prisons now is a forerunner of a period of violence and disintegration that will spread to prisons all over the country. I can see within a very short time the sort of situation in which the National Guard and the Army will be needed to quell prison riots, just as they were needed during the city disturbances during the sixties.

Less than three weeks after I wrote that letter, America's attention was fixed on a small town in New York State—ATTICA!

Chapter Ten

Through all of August and well into September I waited for my attorneys to make a move to obtain bail for me, but the more I pressed them for action, the more they insisted that such a move would prejudice our chances of making a deal with the Attorney General. They argued that the Attorney General would have to oppose a bail application, if only for appearances' sake, and to do so successfully he would have to argue to the courts that he could still get a first-degree murder conviction in the event of a new trial. (Bail is permitted but not a matter of right in first-degree cases, and the courts rarely grant bail in such cases.) This, my lawyers felt, would make it difficult, perhaps impossible, for the AG to make a deal later that would permit me to go free at once. The Attorney General could not, in effect, say to the public: (a) We know that Smith is guilty of first-degree murder, and (b) we don't feel he can safely be released on bail, therefore (c) we are reducing the charge to second degree and letting him walk out of the Death House.

I did not agree fully with my lawyers, and my doubts about their strategy were repeatedly expressed in my correspondence with Bill Buckley. On August 24 I expressed doubt that we should be holding any discussions at all with the state:

I generally object to any discussions with the state, and my objections have been expressed to Steve Umin. I do not think we should have initiated the discussions, nor do I think we should be talking while I remain in prison. At least we should have required some "good faith" showing by the state, either a holding back of its appeal to the Supreme Court or an end to its opposition to bail.

I think we must make it clear to the state that the longer it keeps me in prison, the harder my position will become, and the more determined I will be to demand a retrial. It should also be made clear to the other side that I consider the granting of bail the best way to reach a satisfactory resolution of the case. And from the standpoint of public relations it would be easier, and more practical, if I were first released on bail and the public became used to the idea of my being on the street.

On the question of whether we should apply to the New Jersey courts for bail, I wrote:

I simply have the feeling, as do others, that this has become the lawyers' case, and at this point the lawyers are thinking only in terms of dealing. For instance, no one has yet argued to me that we should not make a State Court bail application for the reason that I probably would not get bail. The whole argument against it seems to be that it will make negotiations more difficult.

My lawyers met with the New Jersey Attorney General shortly after the Labor Day holiday. The result of the meeting was an agreement to meet again after the United States Supreme Court had ruled on the state's appeal. The Attorney General seemed willing at that point to settle the case by negotiation, my lawyers told me, but he did not want to do so until the state had exhausted every avenue of appeal from Judge Gibbons' new trial order. Once again there was some hesitation about asking the Supreme Court for bail, and once again I expressed to Bill Buckley my doubts about the way my lawyers were handling the case:

It may be incipient paranoia, but I remain convinced that Steve Umin has so committed himself to making a deal with the state that he will not consider anything else, and that his reluctance on the bail question is the result of his belief that he can best sell a deal to me if I remain in jail, that the longer I wait, the more anxious I will be to get out of here by accepting anything the state offers—if it offers anything. At this stage, if I were the Attorney General, I would tell me to go to hell. We have made it plain that (a) we are not going to put political or media pressure on the state, (b) we are not going to fight to have me released on bail, and (c) my attorneys are reluctant to retry the case.

In retrospect I can see now that I was being terribly unfair to my attorneys, but at the time, sitting in a Death Row cell, I had very little patience for, or understanding of, anything that did not promise to result in my freedom as soon as possible. What I did not realize, of course, was that that was precisely what my lawyers were trying to do—get me out as soon as possible.

Toward the end of September the state's appeal was filed in the Supreme Court—the state's last chance to prevent Judge Gibbons' habeas corpus order from going into effect and therefore requiring the state to grant me a new trial—and within two days Steve Umin filed a petition with Associate Justice Brennan, asking that I be released on bail pending the outcome of the state's appeal. We argued that as long as the matter was in the federal courts, the federal courts had jurisdiction to grant bail and the state had no cause to complain that I should seek bail in the State Court, since it was the state, not me, who was keeping the matter in the federal court via appeals. To my surprise, and perhaps to Umin's, Justice Brennan decided not to exercise his authority on the bail issue, ruling instead that the question was one of such importance, since it involved an interpretation of the Supreme Court's procedural rules, that it should be decided by the full Court rather than by an individual Justice.

Although I was pleased that Justice Brennan agreed with our position that the bail question in my case was one of major importance, it seemed likely that the Supreme Court would never get to rule on the question because of the timing. When we filed our application in late September, the Court was still out for its summer recess and would not return until the second week of October. What would most likely happen, my lawyers told me, was that the Court, which always seeks to avoid difficult questions when that is possible, would move the state's appeal to the top of the Court's calendar and dismiss it at once, thereby ending the federal role in my case and giving jurisdiction back to the state courts. At that point, the Supreme Court could ignore the bail question on the grounds that the case was no longer in the federal courts and therefore they did not have jurisdiction. All we could do was wait and see.

Yeah, wait. Wait. Wait. Wait. Patience. Patience. Patience. That's all I seemed to be getting from the courts and my lawyers. Efforts at negotiations to settle the case out of court and obtain my immediate freedom continued, and the state was running out of courts to appeal to, but still, all I knew for sure was that I was still sitting on Death Row, and the end seemed nowhere in sight. I was getting so damned tired of the games lawyers play that each day brought me closer to accepting almost any deal the Attorney General wanted to throw on the table. All I wanted was OUT. As I told Steve Umin at one point: "If it means I'll get out right away, and it's what the Attorney General wants, I'm just about ready to confess that I loaded the rifle for Oswald."

The Attica revolt took place late in September, while I was awaiting the outcome of our bail application and the state's appeal. Bill Buckley wrote a column about the revolt shortly after Rockefeller's Storm Troopers went in and tried to shoot everyone but the bird in the warden's cuckoo clock, and once again Buckley and I disagreed. My letter to him in answer to his column was a long one, and I won't quote all of it here, but there are some parts I think are worth the reader's time and patience:

> Fewer pork dishes on the prison menu may seem "playful" to you as a demand, as you wrote in your column, but try eating pork three meals a day, day after day for several years at a time, and pork will cease to be funny. If I had a dollar for every time they have served pork in this prison [Trenton] for breakfast, lunch, and supper, I could retire. It ain't funny after a few days, especially if you are Jewish or Muslim, follow the dietary laws, and have to skip all meals containing pork. Hell, they even chop up the leftover pork and mix it in with the vegetables. Ever have pork stew? Try that sometime. Or pork chow mein!!
>
> Your comment about "religious freedom" and the Black Muslims shows a disturbing lack of knowledge about the Muslims. They are, for instance, just about the cleanest, neatest, quietest, most courteous inmates in the prison, and they are instructed by their leaders that as long as they are living under the white man's rules, they should follow those rules. If you have been paying attention to what the Attica guards have been saying, you would know that it was the Muslims who guarded the hostages in the early stages of the revolt and protected them from the other inmates, as well as giving them blankets and clothing. One guard said that as soon as he knew that a Muslim had been assigned to kill him, he knew he had a chance of coming out alive, and another said he was more afraid of the state troopers than of the Muslims.
>
> As for censorship of reading material and the right of free communication, they had had it in federal prisons for years, and they have nowhere near the problems the state prisons have with revolutionary elements. Rhode Island has been censorship-free for more than a year, and also free of trouble. You may not believe it, my friend, but black men don't have to read *Right On!* or *The Militant* to know they are low men on the totem pole. And finally, if you go back and read the communication demand the inmates at Attica made, you will see that they demanded freedom of *outgoing* communication "at their own expense."
>
> Gee whiz! Have you just discovered that prison inmates

are politicized? Is that really a surprise? You didn't believe me when I told you that in the *Esquire* article? Try to understand, Bill, most men in prison are not long-term prisoners who have been in prison all their life. Most are doing short sentences, and the majority have been outside in recent years. They don't need to become politicized *in* prison. Most bring their politics and ideology in with them. It's funny in a curious way that people jump to the conclusion that the men who rioted at Attica were longtime, "hardened" criminals convicted of horrible crimes of violence. No way. The key spokesman for the inmates was doing four years for third-degree robbery and petit larceny. Ask yourself what the system must have done to that man, a man who *knew* he was not far from walking out of that place, to make him put his life on the line and threaten to kill the hostages. That man could have done his time standing on his head, yet he risked everything, including his life. Why? To make "playful" demands?

As for Rockefeller believing the inmates would kill the guards if he waited any longer, look at the facts. Put aside the stories about the inmates standing with knives at the hostages' throats. Those stories come from the same people who told us the dead had had their throats cut, one man had been castrated, and that the inmates had zip guns—none of which was true. The *fact* is that after the original takeover, *no* guard was injured, and that the one guard injured in the initial disturbance was permitted to be taken out to a hospital. Perhaps the situation could not have been resolved peacefully, but it is a fact that as long as they were talking, however fruitlessly, no one was dying. Why do you suppose that if the state troopers had gone in the first day, or the second, they would have been any more careful about whom they were killing?

As I said, I am tempted to say a great deal about your column, but I think you already have your mind made up on this subject. I will drop the subject with just this one thought for you to contemplate: I absolutely believe that when Attica is put in perspective, when it is looked back on two or three or five years from now, it will be seen as a *minor* opening skirmish, and that we will be wishing we could have a prison riot in which *only* forty or forty-one would be killed. Why?

Because the result of Attica will be merely more talk about prison reform. Until the inmates *force* reform, there will be no reform. Believe it.

I was not totally idle while my attorneys were negotiating with the Attorney General. I had learned in 1957 the power of the news media to prejudice jurors and move public opinion in criminal cases, and I was determined that if I were to be tried again the local press would at least publish a fair and complete account of what was going on. But to do that I had to have access to the media, and particularly to the major newspaper in the Bergen County area—the *Record*.

Prison rules made it impossible for me to have visits with newspaper reporters or to have correspondence with them, but a liberalization of the correspondence rules in 1971 resulted in our being allowed to write to "friends." As a result, in August, while the state was filing its appeals, I was making arrangements with a *Record* reporter to correspond on a "friend" basis. It took time to set it up, to have someone outside the prison contact the reporter and brief him on what I wanted to do. Finally, later that month, we began corresponding, my letters going directly to his home rather than to the newspaper offices, to keep the prison authorities from realizing what was going on.

At first our correspondence dealt with the fact of the state's appeal and my reactions to that, but as time went by and we built up a mutual trust, I began letting the man in on the behind-the-scenes negotiations—who was saying what and offering what to whom. Much of it he was aware of from his contacts in the courthouse, but I was able to tell him some things he hadn't known and that no other reporter knew. My attorneys did not like the idea of my being in contact with a reporter; they were exceedingly publicity-shy and did not feel there was any constructive role the media could play in effecting my release, something I did not agree with at all. Even when I advised them on September 24 that the *Record* was planning an editorial page feature column calling for a negotiated settlement of my case, their attitude was cool. I doubt they really believed that the *Record*, a newspaper which, around the prison, had a reputation of being the prosecutor's mouthpiece, would actually come out in favor of my release.

The column was published on October 1, and for the first time I had a newspaper in my corner. A few of the paragraphs must have sent the Attorney General and prosecutor up the wall together:

> FACE IT: keeping Smith in prison will not undo the past, nor is it likely to protect anyone else from being murdered. If anything, keeping Smith locked up will make a sham of our penal system's professed goals of just and fair punishment, rehabilitation, and a new chance at life.
>
> There's a simple way out for both Smith and the State—a sort of strategic lie of the kind that freed the *Pueblo*. Smith can plead non vult or no defense, which is equivalent to a guilty plea without actually being one. The State, if it accepts such a plea, can impose a maximum sentence of life imprisonment.

My attorneys were unhappy about the column. They liked the idea of having a newspaper on my side, but they feared that suggesting such a deal and putting the deal down as a "strategic lie" might make it even more difficult to negotiate the case to a close. They reasoned that the Attorney General might hesitate to try to sell the deal to the public as a fair and honest one when the newspapers were saying it was all a gimmick, a "strategic lie."

I disagreed with my lawyers. My feeling was that if we were ever going to make a deal and have the public accept it, we first had to prepare the public for the eventuality and show the public that such a deal was favored even by a newspaper that everyone in the Bergen County area knew had always been opposed to me. And so, against my attorneys' advice, I continued to brief the reporter-friend on the status of the negotiations. It finally paid off.

On October 12 the United States Supreme Court unanimously rejected the state's appeal and remanded the case to the state courts for a new trial, and as expected, the Court ignored the bail request for the reason that the matter was again a case under state jurisdiction. Three days later the editors of the *Record* dropped the other shoe in a lead editorial calling for the state to dismiss the case against me and allow me to go free:

> Retrial would be costly in a time when there is much talk of holding down public costs, and it would amount to purposeless harassment. The State has nothing whatever to gain by putting Mr. Smith to a new trial. The ends of justice have been served by his years of confinement and his thorough rehabilitation of himself.
>
> Let's call the whole thing off. Nothing will restore the life of the murdered girl, and nothing can restore the 14 years of life Edgar Smith has spent in prison.

It was a good editorial and a sensible one, but unfortunately it did not take into consideration the reality of the situation, and that reality was that the state of New Jersey had to salvage a conviction from the Edgar Smith case. Victoria Zielinski had ceased to be important. I was not important. What mattered, what counted above all else, was salvaging some sort of conviction and saving what was left of the image of Jersey Justice. Look at what happened. . . .

For fourteen years the courts of New Jersey could find nothing in my case to criticize. Never mind that they couldn't find sufficient reason to void the conviction and order a new trial. They couldn't even find a single thing—nothing, nowhere in the case—to criticize. Appeal after appeal after appeal resulted in compliment after compliment after compliment for the way the police handled my case. Each and every time my case went before the New Jersey Supreme Court the vote against me was 7–0. And then in 1965, after the State Supreme Court refused even to *hear* an appeal from me, I took the *same* petition, the one it refused to hear, and I filed it in the federal courts.

The United States district court refused to rule on the petition for procedural reasons. The United States court of appeals upheld that refusal by a 2–1 vote. The Supreme Court ruled unanimously that the petition should be heard. Judge Gibbons heard the petition and ordered a new trial. The United States court of appeals upheld Judge Gibbons by a 3–0 vote, and the Supreme Court upheld that by a 7–0 vote. In effect, the federal courts held, with only three dissenting votes out of 24 votes cast, that from the time I was tried in 1957 until my conviction was overturned in 1971 the New Jersey courts had been repeatedly and unanimously wrong.

What could New Jersey do? Could it release me, as the local newspaper urged, and admit that all those years the courts of New Jersey had failed to do their job? Could it let me go and admit that the system had broken down, failed to do its job, failed to achieve substantial justice in my case? Could it just admit that for nearly fifteen years the New Jersey courts had been blind to illegal police conduct? Not likely. What New Jersey had to do was get another conviction, any kind of conviction, anything that would let the New Jersey courts off the hook. Convicting me again would do that, even if the conviction were the result of a backroom deal. Get me to plead guilty, somehow, to anything, and then New Jersey could say, "Look, folks, our police made a mistake, did some things wrong, and maybe our courts didn't quite do a good job, but look, Smith pleaded guilty, that means Smith did it, and therefore even though the system messed up a bit, you all can relax because we got the right guy, and that's what counts, not *how* we did it, and so therefore the system *does* work."

Immediately after the Supreme Court's dismissal of the state's appeal, the serious business of negotiating, or plea bargaining, began anew, and this time, with all the appellate avenues closed to them, the people in the Attorney General's office knew that they had either to make a deal with me or to obey Judge Gibbons' order and grant me a new trial. As before, my lawyers held back on a bail petition to the state courts for fear that such a move could upset negotiations for my freedom.

Plea bargaining. The little-understood process that keeps the American judicial system functioning. Generally speaking, plea bargaining begins when both sides in a criminal matter come to the conclusion that it would be to their mutual advantage to avoid a jury trial. For the prosecution, the factors that lead to negotiation can be the possibility of an acquittal at trial; the lack of sufficient personnel in the prosecutor's office to handle a trial; the cost to the taxpayers of going to trial; the shortage of judges; and the overcrowded court schedule. For the defense, the most common reason for entering into bargaining is that a defense lawyer decides that the odds against acquittal are too high to risk and the fact that defendants convicted at trial normally receive much harsher sentences than those who enter some sort of guilty plea.

Most often the way plea bargaining works is something as follows: A person is charged with a crime, say, first-degree murder, and is indicted and scheduled for trial. The prosecutor, looking at his case, decides that he doesn't have the evidence to get a first-degree conviction from a jury and that there is some chance the jury will vote for acquittal. The defense lawyer, looking at his case, reaches the same conclusion as the prosecutor, but he also sees the outside possibility that a stubborn jury—perhaps one that has been prejudiced by the news media coverage of the crime or by a similar crime taking place while the defendant is awaiting trial— might not merely convict his client but also bring in a first-degree verdict and a death sentence. The defense lawyer talks it over with his client, warns him of the possibilities, and suggests that it might be wise to bargain with the prosecutor,

perhaps for a reduced charge and light sentence. If the defendant agrees with that, and many a criminal defendant has done
so even though he was innocent of the crime, out of fear of
the outcome of a trial, the defense lawyer will then approach
the prosecutor on a deal.

Neither side is ever willing to admit its case is weak or that
it has doubts that it can win at trial. Both will bluff, neither
will come right out and say what it is looking for, and even
after the bargaining is under way, those concerned will insist
that there is no bargaining going on. Thus, months after my
lawyers began bargaining with the Attorney General and even
after we had got down to specifics, with the fact of that bargaining being reported by the newspapers, I would still tell a
reporter in an interview: "No deal could ever be good enough
to make me plead guilty to this crime. I expect to be retried,
and I expect to be found not guilty."

And that is how the game is played. You say one thing in
public, another in the back room.

In my case, the state's reasons for wanting to avoid a new
trial were many. Witnesses had scattered all over the country
in the fifteen years since my original trial, many had died,
others, like Victoria Zielinski's mother, had established new
lives elsewhere and the prosecutor did not want to put them
through the ordeal of a trial again, forcing them to relive the
terrible memories. Also, the tremendous publicity my case
had got since *Brief Against Death* was published, added to
the fact that no one had ever spent more time on Death Row
than I, virtually guaranteed that a new trial in Bergen County
would be something of a circus, covered by the news media
as no other trial in New Jersey since the trial of Bruno Haupt-
mann for the Lindberg kidnapping. The image of Jersey Justice, already tarnished by the federal court decisions granting
me a new trial, could not survive such an event, especially if
I were to be acquitted. New Jersey *had* to have a conviction,
and there was just too much risk of losing if it retried me.

For my own part, the reasons for avoiding a new trial were

as many and valid as the state's. First, there was money, roughly $50,000 in legal fees and expenses for a new trial, money I simply did not have. There was the fact that my former wife would have to be a witness in the event of a new trial, and if that happened, the new life she had established in Colorado, where her friends and neighbors knew nothing of her past, would be destroyed. Moreover, my daughter, now fifteen years old, knows nothing about *her* past, does not know about me, and thinks that her stepfather, whom I allowed to adopt her when she was ten years old, is her real father. Having destroyed their lives once, I did not feel I had the right to do it again.

And there were pragmatic reasons, self-serving reasons, such as the fact that I could not be *guaranteed* by my attorneys that I would win an acquittal if I went to trial again. All they could guarantee me was that I would spend more time in prison, months, perhaps even another year, while waiting for the trial preparations to be completed, for all the witnesses to be located, interviewed, brought back to New Jersey, and for all the technical, procedural pretrial motions to be heard and disposed of by the courts, including appeals, if necessary. For a guy who wanted OUT as badly as I did, the prospect of more time in prison made me want to throw up.

Finally, there was the realization on my part that whatever the result of a new trial, whether acquittal or conviction, not too many opinions as to my guilt or innocence would be changed. Those who always believed I was guilty would write off an acquittal as being the result of the passage of time since the crime, my access to high-quality, "slick" lawyers, the fact that some witnesses had died, and the fact that changing standards had made it impossible for the prosecution to use all the evidence used at the original trial—notwithstanding the fact that nothing of importance would have been lost in the way of tangible, or physical, evidence.

Those who always believed in my innocence or those who

came to that conclusion as a result of reading *Brief Against Death* would continue to believe in me even if I were reconvicted at a new trial. They would believe, as happens to be true, that the case was so fouled up at the start, back in 1957, that it was just too late fifteen years later to straighten it out and show the trial jury what the truth was.

Bill Buckley and I discussed these factors at great length over a period of months, and I found that he fully shared my confidence that if I were to make a deal with the state, a deal the result of which I would be required to plead guilty in order to obtain my immediate freedom, those who believed in me, who believed me innocent, would understand that what I had done had been a strategic necessity, a charade performed to get me OUT, and not something related to any reality. When a man has been in solitary confinement for nearly fifteen years, more than a third of his life, intelligent people discount anything he says as part of a bargain to regain his freedom.

On and on and on and on the discussions went between my attorneys and the Attorney General's staff. While the discussions were going on, Bill Buckley and I kept up our correspondence about this, that, and almost anything. Attica came up again in October. At one point I wrote and gave him a concrete example of why inmate complaints about the prevalence of pork in their menus were not as frivolous as he thought:

> Do you recall what I wrote after you characterized as "playful" the Attica demand for less pork? Well, my friend, yesterday's menu in this place [Trenton] was bacon for breakfast, pork chops and pork gravy for lunch, and ham for supper. Now, I ask you, just exactly what was a Jew or Muslim supposed to eat yesterday? Bread and water? It's no joke. I just can't imagine what these people are thinking of. They *know* that at Attica and the Tombs [a New York City prison] and at other prisons the abundance of pork is a complaint that has caused trouble and that a simple thing like

yesterday's menu is the sort that could spark a serious incident, yet they go right ahead and do it. It is as if the prison
authorities have some sort of death wish. I have no doubt
that many inmates feel that yesterday's menu was a matter of
spite. Ah, well, when this prison burns, I will be outside and
can cover the story as a reporter.

Just as I was about to mail the letter to Buckley, I added a
postscript:

> Speaking of such things, would you believe that tomorrow
> we have pork roll (that's right) and collard greens with bacon
> rind for lunch?

The first break came on Monday, October 20. I was sleeping when the guard on duty in the Death House woke me at
9:00 A.M. and told me that my lawyers were waiting to see me
in the conference room set aside for that purpose. When I
walked into the room a few minutes later, I found Steve Umin,
Steve Lichtenstein, and, much to my surprise, Bill Buckley,
who had got out of bed at 5:00 A.M. to drive to Trenton for
the visit. I knew as soon as I saw Bill that something important had happened. It turned out to be the first offer from the
Attorney General.

Steve Umin explained to me that he had met with the
Attorney General's staff on Friday, that a settlement of the
case had been worked out and put into writing, and that all
that was needed for the deal to go through was my acceptance
and the agreement of the Bergen County assignment judge—
the chief judge in the county. It would be the Attorney General's job to sell the deal to the judge, but no difficulty was
anticipated. Then Umin handed me a copy of the settlement
they had worked out. For those who wonder just how carefully such things are arranged, how much stage managing
goes into what appears to the public to be a spontaneous plea
made in open court, how much of it is justice and how much
off-Broadway theater, the following is the settlement as presented to me that morning:

PROPOSED PLEA PROCEDURE

I. Presentation of the defendant and the reading of the indictment. Placing the defendant under oath. Questions as to representation:

    1. Are you represented by counsel?

    2. If so, who are they?

II. Query by the Court as to how the defendant will plead to the indictment and the defendant will respond that he wishes to plead non vult.

III. The Court will then proceed to question the defendant as to the voluntariness of the plea and his understanding of the plea:

    1. You are charged with the crime of murder. Do you understand the nature of this offense?

    2. Have you discussed with your counsel the charge of murder and the nature and consequences of the plea of non vult to this charge?

    3. Do you understand that a plea of non vult is tantamount to a plea of guilty?

    4. Do you understand that the Court may impose such sentence as in his discretion he considers appropriate subject to the limits prescribed by law, but in the event the sentence exceeds the recommendation of the prosecutor, you will have the right to retract your plea?

    5. Are you entering the plea of non vult voluntarily?

IV. The Court then asks the prosecutor the nature of the facts the prosecutor intends to prove at trial:

    1. That the defendant was driving the car of Joseph Gilroy on the night of the murder—March 4, 1957—and that this car was at the scene of the crime.

    2. That front portions of the interior of the Gilroy automobile were spotted with blood.

    3. That the State will offer several items of clothing stained with blood connecting them with decedent and identified as belonging to defendant.

    4. That there was adhering to an item of defendant's clothing a thread similar in color to the sweater decedent was wearing the night she was killed.

    5. That moulage footprint impressions were taken at the scene of the crime which correspond to the size of the defendant's shoes.

6. That in subsequent writings the defendant has admitted the following:
> (a) His presence at the scene of the crime with decedent in Gilroy's automobile; and
> (b) That defendant discarded items of clothing he had worn that evening.

V. Following the presentation by the prosecutor, the Court addresses the following questions to the defendant:

1. Do you understand that a plea of non vult is tantamount to an admission of the facts the State has just outlined?

2. Do you admit that you killed Victoria Zielinski?

VI. The Court accepts the plea of non vult to the indictment.

VII. The Court asks the defendant and his counsel if they have anything to say as to the Judgment of Conviction to be entered or the sentence to be imposed. Mr. Umin will respond briefly.

VIII. The Court will then ask the prosecutor if he has a recommendation. The prosecutor will respond that he does have a recommendation, and his recommendation is that judgment of Conviction be entered of murder in the second degree and that the sentence imposed be of the time already served by the defendant. The prosecutor will comment briefly on the reasons for his recommendations.

IX. Entry of conviction of murder in the second degree and imposition of sentence of time served.

The entry of the plea of non vult in accordance with the above procedure is conditioned upon the entry of judgment of Conviction of murder in the second degree and an imposition of sentence of time served without any form of continued supervision.

And that is how justice works. Umin told me I could have a few days to talk it over with my family, and Bill Buckley told me he thought it a reasonable offer from the state, the key component of which was that as soon as I said what the Attorney General and judge wanted to hear, I could pick up my marbles and go home. I went back to my cell to think about it. Two days later I wrote to Buckley:

> My problem is with the guarantee. I have to be certain, and I am not yet, that the judge will do in court exactly what

he says in private he will do. Once a plea is entered, if the judge crosses me up, it is virtually impossible to retract the plea, so I am being asked to take a great deal on faith, and New Jersey judges rate somewhere near Charlie Manson on my Faith Meter.

And then, a few days later, on October 24:

As you know by now, I saw Steve Lichtenstein again on Friday and told him to go ahead on the understanding that I must have an ironclad guarantee against a double cross, and that everything must take place exactly as agreed upon.

I have to tell you, Bill, that you are in very exclusive company, since the only people who favor this thing are Umin, Lichtenstein, and yourself. I think it is the wrong thing to do —I am doing it for entirely selfish reasons, not because I think it is right. . . .

Selfish reasons? That's for damn sure. I wanted OUT!!!!

Chapter

Eleven

A few days after I agreed to go along with the deal offered by the Attorney General, Bill Buckley wrote me that he was pleased by my decision, that he thought it the correct decision under the circumstances. But I still had my doubts. On October 31 I wrote to Buckley:

> I wish I were as pleased as you are that I have agreed to go along with the deal. I agreed for one reason: because it became obvious to me that no attempt would be made to have me released on bail. . . . Had I been released on bail, no deal would have been necessary. I do not like this deal. I think it is as bad a deal as we could have made, but I do not see that I have any choice unless I want to sit in this place for the many months it would take to prepare for a retrial.

Things would get worse before they got better. No sooner had I agreed to accept the settlement as outlined in the written agreement with the Attorney General than Steve Umin advised me that a new condition had been added. The Attorney General apparently was having second thoughts about his ability to "sell" the settlement to the chief judge in Bergen County, who would have to approve it.

Further conversations had been held between Umin and the

Attorney General, the result of which was a request that I agree to submit to a psychiatric examination, the purpose of which would be to certify to the judge that I could be released safely back into society. Such a certification would have two effects: (1) It would make it easier for the Attorney General to convince the judge that the deal was an acceptable one, acceptable from the standpoint of public safety; and (2) it would allay the public's fears about having a man released directly from Death Row onto the street.

At first I balked at the new condition, thinking it unnecessary and perhaps even prejudicial in the event the deal fell through and I had to stand trial again, but finally, after long discussions with my attorneys, I agreed to go along with whatever was required to effectuate my release from prison—and that's when we all got shocked.

One day after I had agreed to go along with all the conditions set by the Attorney General, my attorneys informed me that the chief judge in Bergen County, a man named Morris Pashman, had refused to permit the settlement to go through. The Attorney General had tried, I was told, but the judge flatly refused to give his approval. More talks, more negotiations would be required to satisfy the judge.

Every effort to determine what the judge wanted, what would satisfy him, was unavailing until, finally in the second week of November, the word came down to me through my lawyers: As part of the proceedings in court, when I entered the *non vult*, or "no defense" plea, the judge wanted me to confess the crime. My immediate response was that I would not do so, that the most I would do would be to state in court that I understood the plea to be an admission of the material facts of the state's charges, and therefore, in fact, it was a guilty plea.

A few more days went by, then the judge's answer came back through Steve Lichtenstein: The judge would accept no less than a direct admission of guilt. He wanted to ask me:

"Edgar Smith, did you kill Victoria Zielinski?" And he wanted me to answer: "I did."

The judge's demand was half-expected—at least *I* expected it. For several weeks a newspaper reporter friend from Bergen County had been warning me that no matter what my lawyers were telling me, the judge was not going to accept any sort of settlement of my case that did not include a direct admission of guilt in open court, for only such an admission on my part could "vindicate" the New Jersey judicial system. The federal courts had thrown out the so-called confession extracted from me by the police in 1957, and so now the judge wanted to obtain a new confession to verify the first, to enable the state courts to say: "Look, Smith has again admitted the crime, made a second confession, which proves that the first confession was true. Therefore, the federal courts threw out a perfectly reliable confession. It may have been coerced, as the federal courts have ruled, and it may have been tainted by that illegality, as the federal courts have also ruled, but this second confession by Smith, made in open court, proves the first confession was true, and proves that the state got the right guy for the crime."

My lawyers realized what a difficult decision I had to make because of the judge's demand, and for that reason both Umin and Lichtenstein refrained from advising me. They simply explained the options and let it go at that: I could give the judge what he wanted and walk out the door five minutes later; I could refuse to go along with the judge and as a result sit in jail months longer while preparations were made for the new trial. It took me one day to make the decision. Bill Buckley was in Vancouver, British Columbia, visiting relatives when I phoned and informed him that I was willing to give the judge the answers he wanted if it meant my walking out the courthouse door immediately thereafter. I wanted OUT, and Bill understood. He told me he was pleased by the decision, that I had decided that my freedom came first, but he added, unnecessarily, I thought, that he had been prepared to back me whatever my decision.

Except that it wasn't that easy.

The judge was apparently caught unprepared by my decision, or perhaps he thought he could get more from me by stalling. Whatever the reason, both my lawyers and the Attorney General suddenly found themselves unable to obtain any sort of commitment from Judge Pashman. The more they talked to him, it seemed, the more he equivocated, the more uncertain he seemed to be as to what he should do, or what he was willing to do.

The fact that negotiations for my freedom were taking place became so obvious and so generally known that along about mid-November, in anticipation of my release, Harrison Salisbury, of the New York *Times*, asked me to write an article for the *Times* op-ed page for publication immediately after my release. I decided to write the article in the form of an open letter to New Jersey's Governor Cahill. Two events prompted that decision: (1) In the wake of the Attica revolt, New Jersey prison officials and spokesmen for the Department of Institutions and Agencies hastened to reassure the public, through the media, that a prison revolt in New Jersey was highly unlikely, that prison administrators in New Jersey had so liberalized the institution rules that the inmates were calm and content. (2) Shortly after the Attica revolt, David Rothenberg, executive director of the Fortune Society—an organization of ex-convicts dedicated to reforming the penal system and assisting men being released from prison—resigned from one of Governor Cahill's commissions studying the prison problem. In an eloquent letter of resignation, which he released to the press, Rothenberg chided the governor for failing to recognize that the time for studying had passed with Attica, that it was time to begin *acting* to alleviate the miserable conditions in New Jersey's prisons before an Attica-type revolt broke out.

As anyone familiar with the ways of politicians and bureaucrats might have guessed, Rothenberg's letter resulted in a statement from the governor expressing his sorrow that Rothenberg did not stay on the commission to work for reform within the system, and the bureaucrats in charge of the prisons denied that there was any serious possibility of trouble in the New Jersey institutions.

Those really aware of the mood in the New Jersey prisons at that time, and particularly those who bothered to listen to the complaints of the prisoners, knew that serious trouble was as certain as, say, the fact that George Wallace would win the Democratic Presidential primary in Alabama. My article for the *Times* was intended to alert the public to the danger and to put Governor Cahill on notice that, after he found himself with a prison rebellion on his hands, he could not excuse himself, or his administration, by claiming that he had not been warned. Unfortunately, on Thanksgiving Day, while the *Times* was preparing my article for publication, a revolt broke out at the Rahway Prison, one of New Jersey's two maximum-security institutions. A large portion of the prison facilities was wrecked, several guards and prisoners were injured, and the warden was taken hostage and stabbed.

Much has been said and written about Governor Cahill's handling of the Rahway revolt, contrasting his relatively bloodless resolution of that crisis with Governor Rockefeller's resort to uncontrolled force and violence. Cahill's response was to communicate directly with the prisoners, giving them his personal guarantee that there would be "no reprisals" if they would end the rebellion and release the hostages unharmed. The prisoners accepted, released the hostages, surrenderd to the state police, and within weeks, forty-one of the prisoners were indicted by a grand jury on charges stemming from the rebellion, an action generally considered by unbiased observers to be a direct and unconscionable violation of the governor's promise, a violation he shrugs off with the explanation that he meant by "no reprisals" only that the prisoners would not be beaten in retaliation for the revolt, something that should be understood, a matter of policy, not something a governor should need to promise.

The evil, for that's surely what it is, of Governor Cahill's betrayal of the Rahway prisoners is not so much that he broke a promise—he is, after all, a politician, and for a politician to fail to keep a promise is as normal as it is for the New York City Sanitation Department to fail to pick up the garbage— but rather it is that the next time the governor faces a crisis in one of the state's prisons, his promises will be valueless. That is something the governor seems not to understand. Efforts to convince him that he *must* keep his promise of no reprisals, even if that means he must interfere with a judicial process begun with the indictments of the prisoners, have been unavailing. And the prisoners, who were told by the outside advisers at the height of the rebellion that they could take the governor's word, now have a new rallying cry: "No more promises."

Even Governor Rockefeller, for all his faults and for all the mistakes he made in handling the Attica revolt, was not so stupid as to make amnesty promises he did not intend to keep. Cahill did, and when the next rebellion strikes New Jersey's prisons, as surely it will, it will be Governor Cahill who will have to bear the responsibility for the lives that are lost, for the next time he will not buy back the hostages alive with meaningless promises. The next time he will get them back dead.

Judge Morris Pashman proved to be nothing less than impossible. Every effort to deal with him, to determine what he wanted from me in return for my freedom, to get any kind of straight answer from him, ended with my lawyers' throwing up their hands in disgust. One minute the judge said this, the next minute that, the next something else, and when he couldn't think of something to say, he retreated to his chambers to think of some new way to do nothing. By the end of November Steve Umin was walking around with an expression on his face like that of a man who had just memorized Chairman Mao's Little Red Book, except that what he had been memorizing was Chairman Pashman's Little Meaningless Pronouncements.

Every effort to resolve the case through negotiation during the month of November had run into a brick wall named Morris Pashman, and by the first of December it was obvious to both Steve Umin and the Attorney General that there was no way a bail application to the state courts could be avoided. My lawyers did not want to file the application, knowing full well that it could bring an instant end to any possibility of a negotiated settlement and force a new trial, but neither could they in good conscience allow me to sit on Death Row indefinitely while Judge Pashman equivocated.

My lawyers' and the Attorney General's concern about a bail hearing in the state court was genuine. The only ground for refusing bail in a murder case in New Jersey is when, after a full hearing of the facts which the prosecutor believes he can prove at trial, the judge finds that there is a reasonable probability that the prosecutor will be able to establish a first-degree case and obtain from the jury a death sentence. Should the judge find that the probability is of less than a first-degree conviction, then bail must be granted. What makes it difficult for a defendant is that the rules of evidence governing a bail hearing are less stringent than those in force during a trial; that is, a prosecutor may introduce evidence at a bail hearing that he might not be able to introduce at a trial. An example of what that means:

At a new trial, the prosecutor would have had a very difficult time proving beyond a reasonable doubt that I had ever been with Victoria Zielinski on the night she was killed, or that I had been anywhere near the murder scene. The physical proof was minimal and could possibly have been overcome; there were no witnesses to place me in the girl's company or at the scene. However, at a bail hearing, the prosecutor could have introduced into evidence my first book, *Brief Against Death*, in which I had explained why I was with the girl the night she was killed, and how and why I was at the scene of the crime.

It might not make sense to one unfamiliar with the workings of the law that a prosecutor could use evidence to deny me bail but could not use that same evidence to convict me of the crime, but that is how the law works. The chances are that no judge would have allowed my book to be used as evidence against me at a new trial, or if he did, it was likely any resulting conviction would have been reversed on appeal; however we were concerned with the evidential rules at a bail hearing, and we knew damn well there was no way to be certain what a judge like Morris Pashman might do. The only thing we were reasonably certain about was that, however weak the prosecutor's proofs turned out to be at the bail hearing, Judge Pashman would find that bail should be denied.

Something about Morris Pashman. Reportedly a star schoolboy basketball player in the twenties, who played on the Passaic, New Jersey, high school "Wonder Team"—winners of 159 straight games, an all-time national record—he drifted into local politics after law school, eventually earning New Jersey's traditional political payoff—a judgeship. Now in his sixties, gray-haired, tanned from frequent trips to Florida, slightly moddish with long hair and bright shirts and ties, he has a reputation of being the canniest, most hard-nosed, fearless judge in the state, one who has the absolute support of Joseph Weintraub, New Jersey Chief Justice, whose job, it is said, Morris Pashman dearly covets.

Unfortunately for me, Judge Pashman's reputation as a

fearless, hard-nosed judge seemed more myth than fact. My own impression, shared by others, was that he was terrified of my case; afraid of how the press would react if he thwarted the negotiations and forced a retrial no one really wanted and which the press had editorialized against; afraid of how the public would react if he permitted the settlement and allowed me to walk out of the Death House; afraid of what the federal courts would do if he made any unfavorable decisions my lawyers appealed; afraid, in short, of what my case could do to the image and ambitions of Morris Pashman. Like it or not, I had become the Big Story of 1971, and whatever Judge Pashman did with my case would be reported, questioned, picked over, and discussed by both the press and the public. And so he tried to do nothing. He was damn good at that. Until we filed the bail application.

Forced into action by the long-delayed filing of the petition for bail, Judge Pashman scheduled a hearing at the Bergen County Courthouse for Monday, November 29, thus triggering a week-long series of events that would culminate in a dramatic, emotion-charged legal proceeding unlike anything that had ever before taken place in an American courtroom. Broadway was coming to Bergen County.

Forewarned by the near-carnival atmosphere that prevailed at the federal courthouse in Newark the previous June, when my attempt to obtain bail from the federal court had come so close (Close? Close counts only in horseshoes and hand grenades), the prison authorities decided that special and extreme security precautions would need to be taken when I was returned to the courthouse in Hackensack, where fourteen and a half years earlier I had been interrogated, arraigned, tried, convicted, and sentenced to death.

So concerned were the authorities for my safety—I can't imagine that they *really* thought there was any longer a chance I would try to escape—that they refused to tell anyone, including the prison guards who would escort me, when or how we would make the trip. All the escort guards were told was that they should report to work on Monday at 4:00 A.M., at which time they would be told why.

Monday, November 29, 1971

They woke me a few minutes after 4 in the morning. Two guards came to my cell, told me to take a quick shower, and while I was doing that, explained that for "security reasons" we would be leaving for Hackensack in thirty minutes. And to make doubly certain nothing would go wrong, we would not follow the usual routine of leaving the prison by the front door and getting into the car in the street outside; the car had been brought into the prison compound through a gate normally used by delivery trucks. In addition, the guards escorting me would not, as they usually do when they take someone to court, wear civilian clothes. For this trip they would be in uniform. And as always is the case when a man under sentence of death is being transported outside the prison, the state police were notified of our departure time, the route we would travel, and our estimated arrival time.

The drive to Hackensack was uneventful and unexciting. I slept most of the way. At my insistence, I was permitted to wear my own clothing rather than prison clothing, so at least I felt a bit better about that. One more trip in a baggy, or too-tight, filthy, shiny, buttons-missing prison suit, and I think I would have told them to go without me.

We arrived at the Bergen County Jail at 6:30, only to find the security precautions had been so successful that no one was expecting us; the courthouse was dark, all the doors locked, and the guard on duty at the county jail had no idea of where we were supposed to go or what we should do until the hearing began at 10.

I had an idea.

"Look in the phone book for the number of the assistant

prosecutor assigned to my case," I told one of the guards who had come from Trenton with me. "He lives in Allendale. He ought to know what we should do."

"He's probably still in bed," the guard replied, a bit dubious that my idea was a good one. "He might get pissed off."

"No way. He's a real nice guy, I've known him since he was a kid, and he's really super-gung-ho about this stuff," I assured the guard. "He won't mind at all."

The guard still wasn't convinced, but after thinking about it for a while and seeing nothing else he could do—prison guards aren't hired to set thinking records—he decided that my suggestion sounded reasonable.

"What's his name?"

"Edward N. Fitzpatrick," I answered, barely suppressing an insane grin.

No doubt about it, Little Fitz did not appreciate being awakened at 6:30 in the morning, especially not by a state prison guard who wanted to know what he should do with Edgar Smith. After an unhappy "Why ask me?" and a few "How should I knows?" Fitz's legal training came to his rescue and enabled him to produce a brilliant suggestion; he suggested that we just sit where we were until the courthouse was opened at 9, at which time we could go to the sheriff's office and ask them what to do.

And that's what we did.

Shortly after 9 I was taken into the courthouse adjoining the county jail, to a theaterlike room—a small stage and a dozen or so rows of plush seats—used by the Bergen County Sheriff's Department as a lineup room. There, with my two prison guard/escorts and several deputy sheriffs, I waited for the 10:00 A.M. bail hearing to begin. I would have been better off standing on the riverbank at Memphis, waiting for the *Robert E. Lee.* The hours went by. Ten o'clock. Eleven. One. In between a few messages from my lawyers. "We're talking to the judge." Or: "We're talking to the Attorney General."

And all the while I sat in the hot, stuffy, windowless lineup room, smoking, drinking coffee, yawning, playing knock rummy with the guards and deputy sheriffs.

At one point during the afternoon Steve Umin came to the room to tell me he had decided it would be better for me to have the bail hearing held *in camera,* meaning in the judge's chambers, with press and public excluded. He explained: The state would be permitted to do things at the bail hearing, such as introducing evidence or calling witnesses, that it might not be permitted to do at a trial because of the differing evidential rules at the two types of proceedings. If we allowed it to do as it pleased in a bail hearing open to the press and public, then if bail were denied and a new trial became necessary, things the state might do or say at the bail hearing could prejudice the prospective trial jurors, since the press would surely report everything that took place.

"As soon as Judge Pashman is ready to begin the hearing, I will make the motion for an *in camera* hearing," Umin told me. "Of course, I'll need your permission for that."

"The answer is no."

"No?"

"That's what I said. No secret hearings."

Umin was stunned. No doubt he had already made arrangements with the judge and prosecutor for the type of hearing he wanted, and they had agreed—that's the way those things are done, prearranged in private, then the motions are gone through in open court for the benefit of the press and public.

"Why?" Umin demanded. "Don't you understand that this way will be better for us? We might even have a chance to reopen the negotiations."

"No secret hearings," I told him. "I don't trust Judge Pashman, and I don't trust the New Jersey courts."

"I don't either, but what's that got to do with it?"

"Everything. I believe the only chance I have of a fair shake in this state is for us to demand that everything take place in open court, where the public and press can see and hear it all, and see and hear if I am getting a screwing. I know you wouldn't trust a jury picked in this county, but I would, and I am convinced that the only chance I stand is for me to get the public and press between me and Judge Pashman and keep them there. Anyway, a closed-door hearing would make it look as if we have something to hide, especially if we make the request for it."

"Edgar, you've got to trust me and do it my way. This is the kind of decision I have to make for you as your lawyer. I'll just have to make the request for an *in camera* hearing."

"You can do that if you want, if you think that's what you have to do, but after you've done it, I'll object."

"That would be suicide."

"I'm sorry, Steve, but that's how it is. You do what you think you have to do, and I'll do what I feel I have to do."

Umin begged, cajoled, threatened, reasoned, and threw up his hands in disgust, but in the end I remained adamant. The hearing must be held in open court. We could not ask for a secret hearing.

"What about a compromise?" Umin suggested. "Suppose we can talk Judge Pashman or the prosecutor into making the motion for an *in camera* hearing. At least that way it would not look as if *you* were trying to hide something."

"I don't like secret proceedings."

"I know that, but go along with me this time. I give you my word this will be to your benefit. We have to get the hearing started and put Judge Pashman on the spot. If we can do that, we can bring about the opportunity to renew the negotiations."

I hesitated, still not liking it, but finally I agreed on the condition that either the judge or the prosecutor must request the closed-door hearing. Umin took off out of the room as soon as I had made my decision. Thirty minutes later he was back to tell me the guards would be taking me upstairs to the judge's chambers. Judge Pashman had agreed to hold the hearing *in camera* on his own motion and would cite an obscure New Jersey Supreme Court ruling as justification for excluding the press and public. It would appear, Umin told me, as if the closed hearing were a requirement. That was good enough for me.

The hearing turned out to be a nonhearing. I was taken upstairs by the guards and sheriff's deputies, through a corridor filled with newspaper photographers and TV cameramen, past open office doors from which curious secretaries and court functionaries stared, along another corridor filled with persons waiting to attend what they thought would be a hearing in open court, and finally into Judge Pashman's chambers. Only the guards, the judge's secretary, the sheriff's deputies, a couple of court attendants, and the lawyers for both sides were allowed inside. Fifteen minutes later it was over.

Judge Pashman opened the proceedings by stating that my lawyers would be given a full opportunity to present whatever they felt would have a bearing on the bail question, and that included, he repeated several times, the calling of any and all witnesses. The issue was whether or not the state of New Jersey could show there existed a reasonable assumption that if I were retried on the murder charge, the state could obtain a first-degree conviction. Barring that, bail would have to be granted.

Naturally, as soon as Judge Pashman offered to allow us to call any witnesses we wanted, Steve Umin made it plain that we wanted to call *every* witness the state intended to call in the event of a retrial. Umin could do no less. Assuming Judge Pashman were to deny bail, the opportunity to question the state's trial witnesses in advance would be invaluable when we finally went to trial. In effect, we would be using the bail hearing as a means of preparing for trial, as a means of obtaining all of the state's trial testimony in advance. It also meant that the bail hearing could run on for two weeks or more.

Judge Pashman's next move was a surprise to everyone.

First, he stated that he had never read the transcript of my 1957 trial, and therefore he was unfamiliar with the strengths and weaknesses of the state's evidence. As a result, he was going to recess the hearing until the following day in order to give my lawyers and the lawyers for the state time to sit down, go over the trial transcripts, and Xerox those portions they felt the judge should read prior to taking any testimony at the hearing or that could be put in evidence by mutual agreement. The lawyers were to take care of that immediately so that the judge could read the material overnight.

Before recessing for the day, the judge turned to me and asked where I wished to be held overnight. Did I want to stay in the Bergen County Jail, or did I want to be returned to the prison in Trenton?

"I'll go back to Trenton, if that's all right. All my legal materials are there, and there are things I want to go over for this hearing."

The judge ordered that, for as long as the hearing ran, I would be transported each day back and forth from Trenton to Hackensack, and within an hour the guards and I were back in the car on the Jersey Turnpike, having eluded a swarm of photographers by sneaking out a back door of the courthouse.

Chapter Twelve

Tuesday, November 30

More of the same. Again the guards awakened me at 4:00 A.M. for a quick lukewarm shower before the ride to Hackensack, where arrangements had been made for someone from the sheriff's department to meet us and let us into the lineup room in the courthouse. And then we did what we had done most of the previous day—played cards, drank a lot of bad coffee brought over from the county jail, talked, paced the floor, and took turns catching short naps. Several times during the day Steve Umin came in to tell me that negotiations seemed to have reopened, that Judge Pashman was beginning to understand that it was in the state's interest, as well as mine, to close the case without going through the expensive, difficult process of a retrial.

Working with Umin was Mark Segal, a partner in Steve Lichtenstein's law firm and the youngest member of that office. It was the first time Segal had ever worked so closely with Umin, and by the end of the week Umin would tell me that he might not have got through the week without Segal's assistance. Judge Pashman was slowly driving Umin up the wall.

Tuesday passed with nothing seemingly accomplished. The bail hearing was not resumed, my lawyers were apparently hopping back and forth from the prosecutor's office to the judge's chambers, trying to find some area of agreement, and both the prison guards and I were getting bored and tired of the whole routine. It was not until after 6 that night that we were told we could return to Trenton, but were to be back in the courthouse by 8 the next morning.

Wednesday, December 1

We left the prison a bit later Wednesday morning, about 5:30 A.M., and arrived in Hackensack shortly before 8. The first thing I heard when I walked into the lineup room was that Bill Buckley was in the courthouse. Obviously something had happened the previous day, or in the evening after the guards had taken me back to Trenton, that I did not know about. It wouldn't take long to find out what that something was.

Buckley, Steve Umin, and Mark Segal came to the lineup room at 8:30, and we immediately moved to a corner of the room for a private talk, out of hearing of the guards and deputy sheriffs. Umin laid it out: No concrete agreement had been reached with the judge, but an outline of a settlement had been drawn up and agreed to by the Attorney General and representatives of the Bergen County Prosecutor's Office. If I would enter a plea of *non vult*, in effect a guilty plea to an unspecified degree of murder, and would admit that I had committed the crime, Judge Pashman would find that the crime had been no more than second-degree murder, would sentence me to a period of 25–30 years in prison, would give me credit for the time I had already served, and would suspend the remainder of the sentence subject to my being placed on probation for that suspended period of time.

"How long would that be?" I asked.

"With credit for time served and time off for good behavior while you were in the Death House, you would be on probation for about four years," Umin told me. "There would be no special restrictions. For a period of six months or so you'd have to report to a probation officer about once a week, but then they would taper that off. Also, Judge Pashman has agreed to waive the travel restriction, which means you'd be free to travel anywhere, anytime you wished."

I turned to Bill Buckley and asked what he thought of the offer, but Mark Segal interrupted to say there was more. I had been hearing that for months. Each time an arrangement had been agreed upon and each time I had accepted the terms, one or another of my lawyers came back to tell me that the judge or prosecutor or Attorney General wanted "one more thing." I sighed, leaned back in my chair, and asked Segal what it was this time.

"Judge Pashman wants to make a speech after accepting the plea, some kind of thing for the public, probably an act of absolution for the New Jersey judicial system. He will probably tear you apart, declare that you are guilty as sin, but in the end he will find that the prison experience has rehabilitated you and you are fit to be released back into society. It will be a show for his benefit. There is nothing Morris Pashman wants more than for Morris Pashman to come off looking good in this thing, to come off looking like the one man who, after fifteen years or whatever it's been, was able to step in and solve the terrible problem your case has been for the state."

"I'm getting a bit weary of this bullshit. Every time you come in here there's something else they want. If I didn't want out so badly, they could all go to hell."

"We understand how you feel, Edgar," Bill told me, "but it won't hurt to let Judge Pashman have his little say before he sets you free."

"That's fine," I replied. "He can vote himself an Academy Award for all I give a damn. I just want out."

"Right, but in order to shift the burden of your release onto someone else, he wants you to submit to a psychiatric examination," Umin told me. "He wants his own doctor to certify that you are rehabilitated. It's the same sort of thing the Attorney General suggested a couple of months ago, at which time you agreed, so there shouldn't be any question of your agreeing now."

"I told you before I'd go along if it were necessary to get the deal through. That's no problem."

"Good. It is simply a device so that Judge Pashman will feel he is covered if anything went wrong later," Mark Segal explained.

"In other words, if I went out and fouled up some way, Pashman could say it was the doctor who said I was okay to be released, and that way get himself off the hook."

"That seems to be it."

"How do I know the doctor is going to go along with the thing?" I asked. "What if there is some sort of double cross?"

"There won't be," Umin assured me. "The doctor is going to know, just by the fact that you are being sent to him, what it is Judge Pashman wants to hear. The question for the doctor will be something like: 'Can Edgar Smith be released back to society with safety for the public?' And just to play it safe, we'll have our own doctor present, a man I know from New York City."

"You don't have to worry about a double cross," Mark Segal promised me. "There is nothing Judge Pashman wants more than for this thing to come off well and make him look good, as I said before. He is probably more worried about you double-crossing him in open court than you are about him doing it to you. He has told us that he must be assured that you will play the part exactly as it is written and that you must trust him to act like a judge at all times."

"All right, Bill, what do you think?" I asked Buckley.

"The offer sounds fair to me, and Steve has assured me that you will be fully protected at all times. I think we can take his word for that. The important thing is for you to get out of here."

I thought about the offer and felt that it was something less than I would have liked, but in the end, after more discussions about the details and the procedures to be followed in court, told Umin I would go along.

"There's just one thing I must warn you about," Umin said. "This is not a normal judge we are dealing with here, so don't get your hopes too high that everything is settled. He could change his mind in a minute."

Umin's warning was to prove well founded. Late Wednesday afternoon, following additional discussions between my lawyers and the people from the Attorney General's office, I was returned to Trenton with the expectation that we would return to Hackensack on Friday to iron out the final details and go through the courtroom proceedings. Within an hour of the time I returned to my cell in the Death House, one of the other men on the Row called me to say he had just heard on the radio that Judge Pashman had ordered my retrial to begin the following Monday and that he was going to hold the bail hearing the next morning, Thursday, convening day and night sessions if necessary to complete the hearing before the start of my trial.

An unbelievable judge, for sure. An hour after the guards and I had left to return to Trenton, Judge Pashman had summoned my lawyers and Assistant Prosecutor Fitzpatrick into court, and with the press and public present he had accused Umin of deliberate delay for the purpose of extending the negotiations beyond the time set by the federal courts for the start of a new trial. Incredible. After stalling for months, vetoing every agreement my lawyers had reached with the prosecutor and Attorney General, and constantly adding new conditions to the agreements that were reached, suddenly Judge Pashman was telling the world that my lawyers were at fault, that they were negotiating in bad faith. And with that accusation in open court, he all but guaranteed that if I did go to trial a second time, it would be held somewhere other than in Bergen County.

From what I was told later by other lawyers and members of the local press corps, Judge Pashman's accusations caused Steve Umin to blow his cool for the first time since Federal Judge Barlow had made the same sort of accusations after we had tried to have him removed from my case because of his delaying tactics. I am told that Umin and Pashman got together in the judge's chambers after the courtroom scene, and that the shouting could be heard all over the courthouse.

Thursday, December 2

At noon on Thursday I was told by the prison authorities I was to shower and dress at once, that I was being taken to Bergen County for the continuation of my bail hearing. An hour later, for the seventh time that week, the same guards and I were in the car on the New Jersey Turnpike. None of us realized how long a day it would be.

By three in the afternoon we were again in the courthouse lineup room, waiting, waiting, and waiting some more. At six o'clock I was taken upstairs to Judge Pashman's chambers, expecting that finally, at last, the bail hearing would resume, but just as we reached the judge's chambers, my lawyers came out and told me I was going back to the lineup room while they went to Newark to see Federal Judge Gibbons. I would have to wait until they returned from Newark to find out what it was all about. It was all a big secret of some sort.

At seven o'clock, in the middle of a knock rummy game, Judge Pashman walked into the lineup room, told the guards he had to leave to attend a "half-ass judges' conference," and said that when my attorneys returned, they were to do as my attorneys said with regard to returning me to Trenton and bringing me back to Hackensack the next day.

"How long will the lawyers be gone?" one guard asked.

"I don't know," the judge told him. "You just wait here for as long as it takes."

It took another two hours. Mark Segal arrived without Umin, who was near exhaustion and had gone home to bed. The deadlock had been broken, Segal told me.

"We went to Judge Gibbons and asked him to specify exactly when the sixty-day deadline for the state to retry you would run out. He refused to set a date. It was his feeling that the federal court should not decide abstract questions of that sort, that he would only make the decision if we made a formal motion for your release and charged that the state had gone beyond the time limit. But that isn't important; the important thing is that Steve and I both came away from the meeting with the feeling that Judge Gibbons was ready to give the state whatever time it needed to retry you if it would simply assure him that a trial was a certainty."

"In other words, they have all the time they want."

"That's about it," Segal conceded. "But never mind that. Pashman has accepted the deal."

I had been told by newspaper reporters with access to confidential information that there had been a telephone call between Judge Pashman and Chief Justice Weintraub, of the New Jersey Supreme Court, whom we had known all along would make the final decision as to whether there would be a negotiated settlement. Judge Pashman could do nothing without the Chief Justice's approval, and the Chief Justice did not feel that a deal would look too good for the much-heralded "Jersey Justice." Now, apparently, Weintraub did not like the manner in which the press was speculating openly about the behind-the-scenes wheeling and dealing in my case, and he wanted it ended as quickly as possible.

"You'll be brought back here tomorrow morning. We'll work out the details of the psychiatric examination," Segal explained. "Then we'll all go to Menlo Park, where the judge's doctor will make the examination."

"Who is 'we'?"

"You'll go down with the prison guards. Steve Umin and I will go in my car and bring our doctor with us."

"What is his name?"

"His name is Ryan. He will be with you when the examination takes place, and Steve and I will be right outside the door if any questions come up."

"And everything will be settled Monday morning?" I asked.

"Monday afternoon, but we don't know yet what time. Judge Pashman has scheduled the proceeding for two o'clock Monday afternoon, but Bill Buckley has a lunch date on Monday with the Vice President. We have asked Pashman to hold off the proceeding for however long it takes Bill to fly up from Washington."

Friday, December 3

Friday morning the guards and I were back in Hackensack, again in the sheriff's lineup room, by nine o'clock. Two hours later we were on our way to the New Jersey Diagnostic Center at Menlo Park.

Dr. Ralph Brancale, the doctor chosen by Judge Pashman to examine me, was a short, pudgy, elderly Dutch-uncle type, who sat in a large leather armchair with a clipboard on his lap. After introducing himself, he proceeded to ask me questions about my background—my schooling, family life, military service. That completed, he asked me what I intended to do after I was released, how I planned to make a living, where I intended to live, whether I thought I had been rehabilitated, and how good a prospect I thought I was for release. At no time did the doctor ask me directly if I had committed the crime. Nor did he ask me any questions as to the details of the crime. Two hours after it began, the examination was over. The instant diagnosis was that I had "passed."

As one of the persons who had been present that day put it immediately afterward: "I have just witnessed a man pretending to be a patient being examined by a man pretending to be a psychiatrist."

By five thirty Friday afternoon I was back in the Death House, gathering my belongings and settling down for what would be the longest weekend of my life. After fourteen years and nine months as a caged number, as property of the state of New Jersey, I had three full days to go.

I spent most of that last weekend on the telephone, calling friends and family to tell them what arrangements had been made with the Attorney General for my release. During the last two or three months of my confinement, when the negotiations with the state were taking place, I had virtually unlimited use of the prison telephone. I was permitted to phone my attorneys almost every evening, and several times a week I called my family or Bill Buckley's office to keep them posted on the progress of the negotiations. And even though the prison rules forbade it, I was often permitted to receive calls.

It was exceedingly important that I be permitted to use the phone. Not only was it impossible for Steve Umin to run up from Washington each time something developed and he needed to speak with me, but also in the background was the fact that as the negotiations were taking place, the New Jersey Supreme Court had before it a series of cases dealing with the death penalty in New Jersey, and there existed the probability that within a short time the court would abolish all plea bargaining in murder cases. It was imperative that the plea bargaining in my case be completed before the process was abolished by the court. Any delay, such as might have been occasioned if my lawyers had to come up from Washington each time they needed to speak with me, could have been disastrous.

Much of the credit—if that is the correct word—for my

being permitted free use of the telephone must go to Sergeant Donald Bourne, one of the officers supervising the second shift—2:30 P.M. to 10:30 P.M.—at the prison. There was never a time when he refused to allow me to use the phone, and rarely did he place a time limit on the calls. The importance of what he did for me, simply because he was a nice guy, became apparent only one month after I regained my freedom, when, as expected, the New Jersey Supreme Court did abolish all plea bargaining in murder cases. Had I not been able to reach my attorneys whenever there was something to discuss or a decision to be made, the negotiations could have been dragged out for another month or two, beyond the court's ruling, at which point a settlement of my case would have been impossible, and I might still be in prison awaiting a retrial.

How I felt about Sergeant Bourne and what he did for me became apparent just two months after my release, when I learned that he had been killed during a fight in the prison mess hall. The next day I phoned the New York *Times*, and with the approval of Harrison Salisbury I wrote the following piece for the *Times* op-ed page. It speaks for itself:

> In a magazine article last year I wrote that among America's state prison guards there is a small but growing cadre of highly motivated, well-educated, bright young men who are the hope for the future as far as meaningful prison reform is concerned, men who are dissatisfied with the record of the past and who have earned for themselves what the old-timers, the hardhead guards could never earn—the support and respect of the inmates.
>
> Donald Bourne was one of the good ones. I remember vividly his first day on the job at the New Jersey State Prison at Trenton in 1958 when, as is done with all new guards, he was taken on a tour of Death Row. I watched as he worked himself up to sergeant and became a supervisor on the second shift. Tough when he had to be tough, he still managed to treat the prisoners as men rather than as numbered animals, always going out of his way to help a prisoner if he

could, even if that meant working overtime or bending a rule or two. He was a man we knew we could go to when we needed help.

Now Donald Bourne is dead. A few nights ago, while riding a taxi across Central Park to my office, I heard on the radio that there had been another in a long series of fights and stabbings in the Trenton prison's mess hall, and when it was over, Donald Bourne, forty-four years old, married and the father of two young children, lay dead on the cold tile floor, stabbed to death with the sharpened handle of a bucket. A prisoner who only that morning had appeared in court to plead guilty to stabbing another guard several months before was accused of the crime.

The tragedy of Donald Bourne is more than the tragedy of a nice guy dying too soon, more than the tragedy of a grieving widow and two children suddenly left fatherless. The real tragedy is that those persons who have the authority to change our prison system, those politicians who learned nothing from Attica and San Quentin and Rahway, will learn nothing from the death of Donald Bourne. They will bury him, give him a nice funeral with lots of his brother officers forming an honor guard, say some great things over his grave about how they will work to prevent such a tragedy from ever happening again, will pat his widow on the back when they hand her the folded American flag that had draped his casket, and then, as they always do when they bury a nice guy, as they did after burying a lot of nice guys at Attica and San Quentin, they will go home and forget it.

After Attica they promised new facilities to isolate the troublemakers, more funds for better libraries and rehabilitation facilities, and greater efforts to eliminate tension and frustration—all good things—but on the day Donald Bourne died, it was announced that the New York prison budget for the coming year would be cut by $22,000,000.

After Rahway they promised more good things, including elected prisoner representatives who would sit down with the administration and talk out the problems, but we soon found out that what they really wanted was prisoner representatives who would say "Yassuh, Boss Man" each time the warden sneezed, and who could be counted on to go back and try to talk the other prisoners into saying "Yassuh, Boss Man."

It's a shame, a deadly shame, that more good men like Donald Bourne are going to die because our politicians and administrators will not learn, will not move NOW to change the old, obsolete penitentiary system that grinds a man down, dehumanizes him, driving him into the sort of mindless frustration that will cause him to stab a guard to death with a hundred or more witnesses looking on.

I liked Donald Bourne, and I try to tell myself that when a man dies doing his duty, doing the work he has chosen to do, his life has not been wasted. I hope that's true. And I hope Donald Bourne rests in peace. A nice guy deserves at least that much.

Monday, December 6, 1971

I left Death Row for the last time at 7:00 A.M. There were no handshakes, no good-byes. I had not told any of the men, all of whom knew that negotiations were taking place, that the fight was over, that this time I was going out and not coming back. It would have been tougher for me had I walked around saying good-bye to men who I knew would sleep that night in their cramped, stuffy cells, eating prison slop for dinner while I ate steak, drank champagne, and slept in the luxury of a New York hotel suite. Anyway, I was leaving behind guys I knew, not friends.

It is difficult to explain the relationship between men in prison and more so between men on Death Row, who live every day in the shadow of the electric chair, never knowing whose turn it would be next to die, eating, sleeping, laughing, crying, suffering year after year within a few feet of each other. One unfamiliar with the situation would assume, probably with good reason, that such men would form close and lasting bonds of friendship, but that is not so, particularly on Death Row. Their relationship is based almost completely on the fact that they face the same situation, that each has a common enemy—the state which is trying to kill them. Beyond that, I have found, there is no relationship. The analogy that fits most closely, I suppose, is that of military service friendships. One serves at a particular duty station for a year or two, gets to know a certain group of men, hangs out with them evenings and weekends, goes drinking with them, maybe chasing girls, plays poker with them, but when it comes time that one man is transferred to another duty station, he leaves and that is that. He knows he will never see the others again, except by accident, and within a few days he is somewhere else, with new friends and a new life, the previous life, the previous friends no more than a memory that has already begun to fade.

One must remember, also, that men on Death Row, unlike the situation in a prison's general population, where daily survival, actually keeping alive, is not such an immediate concern, do not have time, not really, to spend on forming deep and lasting friendships. Death Row is a unique, intensely personal experience. One lives almost exclusively within oneself, always struggling to remain sane, to keep active, to fight boredom, and to stay alive. If another man doesn't make it, if another loses the fight and is executed, as three men were during my stay on the Row, the others feel badly about it for a while, and it makes them wonder if they will be next, but there are no tears. The others say, "That's too bad about Charley," and then they go back to their own struggle. On Death Row, every man *is* an island, and if the bell doesn't toll for you, that is all that counts. A tough philosophy, for sure, but it is the only one that enables you to survive.

The escort guards and I arrived at the Hackensack courthouse at 9:30 A.M., this time preceded by a state police escort car. It was no secret that this was to be the day I won my freedom, and already the state was putting on a show for the press and public. Broadway was no longer coming to Bergen County; Bergen County *was* Broadway. And Judge Pashman was to be its David Merrick.

Shortly after our arrival at the courthouse, again in that
same lineup room, Steve Lichtenstein, who had canceled all
his other appointments and appearances to be present at the
end of the case he had worked on for ten years, came in and
told us that the matinee performance had been scrubbed in
order to give Bill Buckley time to have lunch with the Vice
President and fly up from Washington. Instead, Judge Pashman had decided on an early evening performance. The
guards sighed, I sighed, everyone sighed, a pot of coffee was
gotten, the deck of cards was broken out, and the knock
rummy game was resumed. It was cold and windy and rain-
ing outside. Who was in a hurry to go out into that? *I* was.

Late in the afternoon one of my attorneys came into the
room and took me aside for a conference. He had just come
from Judge Pashman's chambers. For a week the judge had
insisted that he was not going to tell anyone what questions he
would ask me during the courtroom proceedings, that we all
had to trust him to act properly, "to act as a judge." But then,
at the last minute, he had disclosed precisely the questions he
would ask me, and I was told what the judge wanted to hear
from me in response. God forbid that any of the actors should
miss a line. Also explained to me at that time was the plea
bargaining setup in New Jersey.

I must give New Jersey credit for one thing: The courts
have taken the hypocrisy out of plea bargaining in New Jersey.
Unlike the situation in many other states, where everyone
pretends that there has been no dealing, where the judge asks
the defendant in court, "Have any promises been made to you
in return for this plea?" and the defendant answers, with
everyone present knowing he is lying, "No, sir," at least in
New Jersey they face the truth, that there has been dealing,
that promises have been made, and the judge asks, "Have
any promises been made to you *other than those made in the
course of plea bargaining?*" Moreover, the defendant is protected against a double cross in New Jersey [something I had

not known at the time of my original concern about a double cross], for if the prosecutor does not recommend what he has promised in the way of a sentence and the judge does not pass that sentence, or less, then the defendant may automatically retract the plea and nothing that has taken place in the courtroom can be used against him at trial. All in all, a much more honest system than prevails in most other states.

Bill Buckley flew from Washington to Newark Airport in a private jet, helicoptered in the rain from Newark to Teterboro Airport, just outside Hackensack, was picked up there by his limousine, and just after 5:00 P.M. arrived at the courthouse. The cast was complete, the stage set, the audience in place. Sheriff Joe Job entered the lineup room at 5:30 and announced it was curtain time. Then, taking me aside, he said: "Don't worry, Edgar. There will be plenty of security. There won't be any Dallas in Bergen County."

Ohmigawd! Not even Judge Pashman would have come out with a line like that.

I was taken upstairs to the courtroom by the two prison guards and what seemed like seven hundred armed deputy sheriffs and court attendants. At the door to the courtroom, one of the prison guards stopped me and took off the handcuffs· I had worn on the way up from the lineup room. I don't know if the guard realized it at the time, but the handcuffs had come off for the last time.

Every seat in the courtroom was filled by news reporters and courthouse employees, and the walls of the room were lined with armed guards. It was so crowded that Bill Buckley and eleven other reporters had to sit in the jury box off to Judge Pashman's left. I sat at a long table with Steve Umin, Mark Segal, and Steve Lichtenstein. Little Fitz and a couple of people from the Attorney General's office sat at a table to our right. Judge Pashman began the make-believe by asking Fitzpatrick if he had a matter to present to the court. Fitzpatrick, with a straight face, informed the judge that the state was bringing me before the court on my indictment for murder. Then Pashman asked Umin if my side was ready to proceed.

MR. UMIN: May it please the court, Your Honor, the defendant at this time wishes to withdraw his plea of not guilty to the indictment and enter a plea of non vult *subject to the agreement negotiated and jointly agreed upon with the State of New Jersey, which will be articulated by Mr. Fitzpatrick in his recommendation to the court.*

After some "household chores," Judge Pashman asked Fitzpatrick for his recommendation.

MR. FITZPATRICK: If Your Honor please, *the State has an agreement with counsel and the agreement arrived at is that upon the acceptance of a plea of non vult to this indictment, the State will recommend a sentence for Mr. Smith as would provide for his immediate release from incarceration under the terms of whatever probation the court might wish to impose.*

Judge Pashman then asked the representative of the Attorney General if that office was in accordance with Fitzpatrick's recommendation, and the reply was that they "concur with it wholeheartedly."

There it was, the settlement was on the record for all to see: I would plead *non vult* and give the judge the answers he wanted, and in return the state was willing to let me walk out the door, climb into Bill Buckley's limousine, and ride off into the sunset—or in this instance, into the rain. I don't know what anyone else would have done or what people expected of me, but at that point in my life, after fourteen years and nine months behind bars, that was a good enough deal for me.

Judge Pashman called me to the witness stand, had me sworn in by the clerk, and proceeded to tell me that my attorneys and the Attorney General had been negotiating for an end to my case.

THE COURT: *For the past five weeks your attorneys and the representatives of the Attorney General's office have been conferring. That is known as plea bargaining. It is known as sentence bargaining.*

More technicalities, such as reading the New Jersey Supreme Court directive authorizing plea and sentence bargaining, the rights of both sides under that directive, the right of the judge to accept or deny the prosecutor's recommendations, and then the judge asked me if I fully understood everything he had said, everything that was going on in court. Then Judge Pashman asked the big questions:

THE COURT: *Mr. Smith, did you and you alone kill Victoria Zielinski?*

A. *I did.*

THE COURT: *Was anyone else there, Mr. Smith, when you killed her?*

A. *No.*

THE COURT: *Did you see anyone else in the area during the time you were with Victoria Zielinski?*

A. *No.*

THE COURT: *How did you get to the sand pit, Mr. Smith?*

A. *By automobile.*

THE COURT: *And whose car was it?*

A. *Joe Gilroy.*

THE COURT: *Joseph Gilroy, G-I-L-R-O-Y. And approximately what time did you get to the sand pit?*

A. *Nine* P.M.

THE COURT: *Would you tell us briefly how did it happen that Victoria Zielinski got into your car?*

A. *She asked me for a ride.*

THE COURT: *Was there any kind of prearranged meeting?*

A. *No.*

THE COURT: *After arriving at the sand pit, Mr. Smith, and a space of time thereafter, did you strike Victoria Zielinski?*

A. *I did.*

THE COURT: *At that time were you wearing tan khaki pants when you killed her?*

A. *I was.*

THE COURT: *Where and when, where and when, Mr. Smith, did you discard those tan khaki pants?*

A. *Same night, Oak Street, Ramsey.*

THE COURT: *Did you leave the sand pit after this and go home?*

A. *I did.*

There were more questions, and each time, as before, I answered as briefly as possible. The judge had what he wanted, the state had what it wanted, and in a few minutes I would have what I wanted. There was nothing left to do except for Judge Pashman to make his speech.

Judge Pashman summed up the fact that he had read the transcript of my 1957 trial, had read the medical and laboratory reports about the evidence, had examined the evidence, had evaluated it all, and had done so in light of the answers I had just given a few second before. Then he stated that in his opinion "the physical and scientific evidence was devastating in light of Mr. Smith's answers today."

At that point Judge Pashman said something that even today, looking back over the transcript of the proceeding, I find difficult to believe. First, he stated that he did not necessarily agree that the crime had been more than a second-degree murder, that there had been any intent or premeditation involved. He felt, he told everyone present that day, that I had been charged with first-degree murder simply because I had stated that I had left the girl alive and with another man. I was not, in Judge Pashman's opinion, charged with first-degree murder because it had been a first-degree murder or because the prosecutor felt it had been, but rather, and solely, because I had not confessed guilt, because I had said I had left the girl alive and with someone else.

"I truly believe," Judge Pashman stated, "I believe that

you and you alone, Mr. Smith, brought on the first-degree murder charge and that you alone, as it were, are responsible for the ultimate jury verdict of death."

WOW! If that is true, if a murder is second degree if one confesses but first degree if one denies guilt and blames another, then it says something about the American legal system, or at least New Jersey's legal system, that none of us should want to hear.

Judge Pashman was not done, not by a long sight:

> Perhaps the wheels of justice grind too slowly and we do despair at times. But grind they must, and they must grind with determination regardless of the continuing costs. This is the price, we hope, for a reasonably safe Bergen County. I do not advocate the expenditure of any public funds for the harassment of a defendant, whether it is Mr. Smith or anyone else. That is not the goal of the State of New Jersey. It is not the goal of the County of Bergen and certainly it is not the goal of this court.*
>
> I have read the original probation report of Edgar Smith. I have re-read it. I have read and re-read the classification material forwarded to me by the Principal Keeper of the State Prison at Trenton, Mr. Yeager, and I have read and re-read the report of Dr. Ralph Brancale, who is the Director of the Diagnostic Center at Menlo Park. The classification material indicates no serious deviations of any kind by the defendant in his years in the Death House at Trenton. There are some minor infractions through the years, but nothing of any consequence. The original probation report is not too helpful, of course, at this time, but that too has been included in the classification material.
>
> But among many requirements, I insisted that Edgar Smith be examined by a doctor of my choice, one whose expertise in psychiatry is undisputed in my opinion. Mr. Smith agreed to this. His attorneys agreed to this. This was done in the presence of Dr. James Ryan of Columbia University, who was designated by the defendant, but he merely stood by. The examination and report belonged to Dr. Brancale. I should

---

* See footnote on page 233.

say that Edgar Smith's willingness to undergo this examination, with frank admissions to Dr. Brancale, that willingness was to his credit. I arranged for his examination and for the report over the weekend and of course copies of the report were arranged for and were delivered by the State Police to all counsel likewise over the weekend.

During that same period of time, from Friday, Saturday, and yesterday, I have discussed this matter with Dr. Brancale more than several times. There have been other meetings and discussions with counsel during this time.

Dr. Brancale states, amongst other observations, and I quote him:

"There is nothing in the personality pattern that would suggest the probability of a recurring similar offense, or that manifests any antisocial behavior."

Despite the problems of readjustment, and obviously there will be problems like that, the doctor says, and I again quote him:

"The overall picture looks quite promising and the prospects for the future are good."

He tells me the interview went real well. The report indicates, and I quote Dr. Brancale again:

"No manifest disturbances in either his emotional make-up or his mental processes. It is quite evident that the defendant examined today is a different man than the one who entered the Death House fifteen years ago.

"There is no evidence of serious psychiatric pathology and he does not appear to have any malignant psychosexual process. The examiner feels that this defendant may be returned to the community without posing a danger to the public."

Well, I have great faith in Dr. Brancale. I have great faith in his experience. I have great faith in his evaluation and generally speaking I have great faith in his release prognosis if you will.

I think that Edgar Smith's years have been of a stabilizing type. From everything that I have read, and it is rather extensive, he generally may be evaluated as being in good shape for a man who has been bottled up for fifteen years.

I think it is fair to say that it is normal for any man to attempt to gain his freedom, and it is ludicrous to believe that one will not contend that he is innocent. But, in an effort to

gain one's freedom, it is no answer to say that the life of
Victoria Zielinski cannot be restored and that Edgar Smith
cannot be tried for his life under existing law. And we are
not seeking to restore the fourteen years and nine months
that Edgar Smith has spent in prison. From my vantage point
he brought that on himself. Vicky Zielinski did not. That
cannot be the test to determine whether Edgar Smith can be
released at this time. The test is whether the interest and
ends of justice have been served by his fourteen years and
nine months of confinement in the Death House and by his
thorough and productive rehabilitation of himself.*

This is a man who developed from a high school dropout
to a self-educated writer, a writer in prison without even the
assistance normally provided sentenced inmates. It may be
said that Edgar Smith is an outstanding example of the meaningful changes that a prisoner may undergo as to render
him a useful, productive citizen upon his return to society.
We hope for this. We definitely hope for this.

So far so good, as far as I was concerned. I was content to
let the judge be the star of the show, to have all the lines he
wanted, to spotlight himself. But then he said something that
came close to blowing the whole show:

I think Edgar Smith's example can give us reason to be
optimistic about the very beneficial function of our correc-
tional system, and I say that even during these days when
that system is unjustifiably in many respects under criticism.

That was too much. To say that my getting my head straight
proves that the prison system works, that the *system* rehabili-
tates prisoners, not only is untrue but is dangerously misleading to the public. What I did for myself in prison I did *despite*
the system, not as a result of being subjected to the system,
or as a result of anything the system did for me. Pashman had

* This paragraph is perfectly illustrative of Judge Pashman's concern for
the news media's reaction to the proceedings under way, for in fact, rather
than being a relevant comment on the matter before him, the judge is using
the proceeding to answer, from the judicial bench, the newspaper editorial
quoted on page 188 of this book.

me angry, and had not Steve Lichtenstein put his hand on my arm to calm me, I would have gotten up and said some things to Judge Pashman that would have blown the whole proceeding. The American penal system's insane refusal to do anything constructive for the men it confines and indeed its seemingly suicidal effort to stifle any attempt by prisoners to do something for themselves are an issue about which I feel so strongly that it was all I could do to sit silently, eyes closed, fists clenched, as Judge Pashman went on with his production:

> But in the final analysis rehabilitation is the objective. We hope this is an example of the objective being achieved. This must be the reason and this must be the only reason for accepting this plea—not any of the easy reasons.
>
> It is important to point out some of the economics, all of which is part of a defendant's problem when we talk about rehabilitation and release. Mr. William F. Buckley, Jr. has filed an affidavit in this matter with the court. He is an internationally known editor of National Review and a commentator. He has detailed his interest in Edgar Smith. He states in his papers that he is prepared to assist him with his literary career. He makes other statements for and in behalf of Mr. Smith in support of an application that is being made today.
>
> A Mr. Arthur Kretchmer, who is an editor likewise states that Mr. Smith will be offered some paid writing assignments. That being so, I believe the economic picture in that sense, the requirements, has been satisfied.
>
> I think it should be noted that the Court is not myopic. The Court is aware of the highly-charged nature of these proceedings. I am fully sensitive to the very justifiable concern of our citizens in permitting this plea and approving of the Prosecutor's recommendation. As I view this case, the popular decision might be to continue the confinement of Edgar Smith only because of doubts perhaps in the minds of those citizens. But I do not believe that law should be administered that way and I do not think that law should be administered for the moment. It is intended, in my opinion, that is, the law is intended and this disposition, as another

solid section in a foundation of freedom, compassion, fairness, propriety in human emotions and opportunity.

So there we are.

Mr. Smith, it has been said that a man is the sum total of
his actions. If a person's actions have changed, then we now
have a new person. Well, Jean Paul Sartre had this to say and
it will only take thirty seconds and I pass it along to you. I
am paraphrasing his observations (and some of mine):

Man is the only being in the universe who is totally free.
His freedom is a promise as well as a frightening burden. On
the one hand, man's total freedom implies that he can be
anything, he can do anything, he can change himself into any
form. This same freedom is also a terrible weight. It is the
weight of responsibility. To be totally free in each act is to be
totally responsible also. There are no more excuses for man.
He must bear the total consequences of his free act, for he
and no one else performs them.

But along with the tremendous burden of responsibility,
let us not forget the promise of that freedom. I can do better
—I can change—I define myself anew.

Would you please stand, Mr. Smith.

Before imposing sentence, Edgar Smith, the Court is
required to comply with Rule 3:21-r (b). In accordance with
that rule, do you wish to make any statement in your own
behalf and to present any further information at all of any
kind concerning this matter?

THE DEFENDANT: No, sir.

THE COURT: And you do understand the nature and the
meaning of this offense and the plea, the plea that has been
taken, a plea which is tantamount to a plea of guilty?

THE DEFENDANT: Yes, sir.

THE COURT: And I ask you finally, Mr. Smith, whether
that plea was voluntarily entered, that it was not the result of
any promises, threats or other inducements made by the
prosecuting attorney or anyone else other than the promise of
the State's recommendation as to sentence, which, of course,
was previously outlined? Is that a correct statement?

THE DEFENDANT: Yes, sir.

THE COURT: Then, Mr. Smith, on Indictment S-276-56,
charging you with murder, it is the sentence of this Court
that you serve not less than 25 years nor more than 30 years

at the New Jersey State Prison in Trenton. You have spent 90 days in the Bergen County Jail in the year 1957. You have spent 5,296 days in the death house at the New Jersey State Prison. You will receive credit for all this time spent in those institutions. In addition, in accordance with law, you are to be credited with 3,966 days for what is called good time. This gives you a credit of 9,352 days. The expiration date for your sentence under this formula is April 26, 1976. The remaining balance of that sentence is 4 years, 4 months, and 20 days. That balance on the 30-year sentence is hereby suspended. You are placed on probation for that period of time, 4 years, 4 months, and 20 days. During that time you will be subject to the rules and conditions of probation, all of which have been fixed by the court pursuant to N.J.S.A. 2A:162-2, except that I have agreed that there will be no travel restrictions on travel outside the State of New Jersey so long as there is full compliance with the rules and conditions of probation.

You will return to the State Prison forthwith for processing out forthwith.

And so it was over, fourteen years and nine months after it began. I had given the judge what he wanted, he gave me what I wanted, and twenty minutes later I was in the car with Bill Buckley and my lawyers, speeding down the New Jersey Turnpike to Trenton, to go through the formality of signing out of the prison. They were waiting for me when I came out. TV film cameras whirring, flashbulbs lighting the entrance-way and reflecting off the bulletproof glass of the front door, a few dozen rain-drenched reporters, notebooks in hand trying to muscle their way past the photographers to ask their mindless questions.

"Mr. Smith, how does it feel to walk out of Death Row after fifteen years?"

"Could you tell us if you are happy to be free?"

"What do you think of Attica? Was Rockefeller right?"

I tried to ignore their queries, gave up, answered a few as briefly as possible, then escaped into the rear seat of the limousine waiting at the curb. As the car pulled away and rounded the corner of the ugly, red sandstone, walled prison, Bill Buckley handed me a paper cup filled with a cool rosé wine and pointed to a few grease-stained brown paper bags on the floor.

"There's roast beef in those," he told me. Then deftly extracting the cork from a fresh bottle of wine, he held it aloft with a triumphant grin and added, "And plenty more wine. Welcome back to the free world."

It had taken me fourteen years and nine months, but finally, on December 6, 1971, I was again a free man. Physically free.

Few people have ever undergone, in the space of twenty-four hours, the sort of transition I went through the day of my release. To begin a day on New Jersey's Death Row and end it in a suite in New York's St. Regis Hotel is mind-boggling, but that was only the half of it.

For months prior to my release and in anticipation of that event, tentative arrangements had been made for me to appear on Buckley's television show, *Firing Line*. Now, as the car sped northward on the New Jersey Turnpike, it was time to do the last-minute planning. We would begin within an hour to tape two shows, the first show with just myself and Buckley, the second with a panel of newsmen; the two shows were to be aired on consecutive Sundays.

What a scene it was! The car's interior lights were switched on, a typewriter was set up on a jump seat, the mobile phone was activated and a call put through to the television studio, the sandwiches and wine bottle shoved into a corner. It was time to work. With his jacket off, his sleeves rolled up, the phone between his head and shoulder, Bill began to type the introduction to the first show while at the same time speaking on the phone with his producer, deciding which newsmen would appear on the second show. Then, as we approached the entrance to the Lincoln Tunnel, the fuse blew and the interior lights went out. The last few lines of the introduction were completed with me holding a match over the typewriter.

The photographers were waiting for us when we arrived at the television studio, but none of them recognized me as I got out of the car. Instead, ignoring me, they began to photograph John Carley, a young lawyer friend who had accompanied us from Trenton and whom the photographers mistook for me. As they shot dozens of still photos and hundreds of feet of newsreel film of Carley, Buckley's chauffeur and I walked casually into the studio and up the stairs to the makeup room. Ten minutes later the taping of the first show began.

I had been awake for nineteen hours, with only two hours' sleep the previous night, when the taping of the first show began. The bright lights, the heat, the studio audience, the hordes of newsmen waiting to hear how I would explain a guilty plea made after fifteen years of protesting my innocence, the simple fact of being free after so many years, all contributed to my tenseness and the drama of the situation. And to make it worse, ten minutes into the hour-long show I found I didn't have a cigarette.

Both shows completed, it was back into the limousine for the short ride to the Buckley home on Park Avenue and a reception Bill had arranged for me. As the handshaking subsided and the champagne bottles emptied, the Death House seemed farther and farther away. A curious thing. While I was on Death Row the outside world seemed somehow unreal. I knew it was there, but it seemed just a vague memory. Then, suddenly, I was out, and reality seemed reversed; it was the outside world that seemed real and familiar, while the years on Death Row were rapidly becoming the diminishing memory.

At 2:30 A.M. I borrowed the limousine and driver to take my mother home to Ramsey, the small New Jersey town in which I had lived prior to my arrest. I wondered how the place had changed in the fifteen years I had been away, and I was surprised, as we rolled down the deserted main street at 3:00 A.M., to find that few changes had occurred since I last saw Ramsey. Stores had different names, and there were a few new buildings, but on the whole the town had changed very little.

By 4:00 A.M. I was back in New York City. Exactly twenty-four hours after I had walked out of Death Row to go to court, I walked into the lobby of the St. Regis and asked for the key to my suite. I was exhausted, physically and emotionally, and all I wanted was to slip into a comfortable bed and sleep until I couldn't sleep another second.

I got to bed all right, a huge, soft, marvelous bed, but tired as I was, I couldn't fall asleep. I was still tossing and turning, strangely nervous and uncomfortable, at 6:00 A.M. Then I realized what was wrong. The lights were out!

After fifteen years of sleeping on Death Row, where the lights never go out, I was utterly unable to sleep in the dark.

I could have turned on a light, that would have been easy enough, but to have done so would have been to surrender, to return myself to prison, to put myself back in the Death House. No way. I was a free man, and I was going to sleep like a free man or I would not sleep. And I didn't. Not until the sun came up. Then 27 hours, 70 miles, and another world away from Death Row, sleep came to me. I think I fell asleep with a smile on my face.

Many people were shocked by the full realization of the sort of deal that had been made, by the fakery of the whole thing, and of course the state authorities were angry that I did not continue the charade once I had regained my freedom. There were reports out of the Attorney General's office that the state would prosecute me for perjury, but those reports were squelched by the Attorney General himself, in a hastily called press conference. Obviously, to prosecute me for perjury the state would have had to prove I lied when I confessed the crime, and it was not about to do that. The Attorney General acknowledged the reality of the situation the next day when he told the press:

"It would be grossly unjust for any sovereign state to prosecute a defendant for perjury for statements he made under oath to keep from going to the electric chair.

"There will be no further comment from the Prosecutor's Office or the Attorney General's Office in connection with the Edgar Smith matter. Let's hope it is put to rest."

No such luck. Editorials in two of New Jersey's major newspapers, published within days of my release, made it plain that few people were fooled by the Bergen County version of a Broadway production and that the state had failed in its effort to restore the image of the New Jersey system of justice.

A December 8 editorial in the *Trentonian*, published in the state capital, said:

A CONVINCING PERFORMANCE

Monday night, author Edgar H. Smith, and author-editor William F. Buckley, sat in a television studio and casually discussed why, after 15 years of incandescent truth-telling, Edgar was forced to lie, lie, lie to a court of law.

You may recall that in addition to being an author, Edgar H. Smith is probably the most celebrated convicted murderer in the history of New Jersey. He and Mr. Buckley, his patron saint, benefactor and now devoted friend, maintained his innocence at the top of their lungs. Their dauntless crusade persuaded hundreds of thousands that Edgar was the victim of a barbaric justice.

Only God (and Buckley) know the cost of that crusade in money and time. But if the truth shall make men free, and if promoting the truth is costly, so be it.

Well, Edgar H. Smith is free. But it wasn't the truth that got the job done, according to Edgar Smith. It was a lie. To be accurate, it was several lies, according to Edgar Smith.

The way he tells it, the price of Edgar's freedom was the admission that he bludgeoned a 15-year old girl to death in a Bergen County sandpit on March 4, 1957. "It was a difficult choice," says Edgar, "but I wanted to be free."

So, his face reddened, his voice low, he told Judge Pashman he killed the girl, and he told how he killed her. It was a hell of a convincing performance.

But after all, he couldn't afford a new trial, so better to be a free liar than a jailed martyr. The judge gave him his freedom because the judge was convinced that Edgar will not kill again, that he is thoroughly rehabilitated. The judge is also convinced the evidence against Mr. Smith was "devastating."

Devastating enough to make a liar out of an honest man, a confessed murderer out of a professed innocent?

If Edgar's next book doesn't answer that one to your complete satisfaction, Buckley's next book will.

Four days later, on December 12, the Asbury Park *Evening Press* added its voice:

COURT THEATER

There is something about the release of Edgar H. Smith, Jr., on probation which offends one's sense of truthfulness and honesty. The man who had spent more time on Death Row than any other man convicted of murder was released by Judge Morris Pashman of the Superior Court after he pleaded guilty to a first degree murder charge. But the judge gave him a second degree sentence of 25-30 years, then calculated that he had enough credit for good behavior and other provisions to release Smith on probation.

So far, so good. There is precedent for bargaining with a convicted person to save the State the expense of a second trial, which had been ordered in Smith's case because a federal court had ruled that the confession upon which he had originally been convicted had been coerced. Smith was still maintaining his innocence of the crime.

But in open court, under the questioning of Judge Pashman, Smith said that he and he alone had killed the victim, Victoria Zielinski, in a Bergen County gravel pit. Judge Pashman then said: "The defendant admits this to be a fact. The facts in the case firmly and convincingly establish that the defendant caused the death of Victoria Zielinski. An impartial mind must conclude this."

Now William F. Buckley, Jr., the columnist and editor, who has befriended Smith for the past six years and has assumed responsibility for him, says that the confession Smith made before Judge Pashman was "simply court theater" and was made only to achieve Smith's immediate release from the Death House. Yet, if Smith were really innocent of the charge, but confessed it under oath, he was guilty of perjury.

Will he stand trial for that? Not likely, says a state prosecutor, who predicted that state officials and the courts probably would be content to let events "cool off" in the likelihood that public furor over the case would eventually subside, as no doubt it will.

But the record of bargaining and cynical disregard of the truth remains to cause distress to all those to whom the legal process should be conducted on a far different, and more admirable, plane.

Since my release from Death Row I have been living quietly, traveling to fulfill speaking engagements and reacquaint myself with the country that for so long was little more than photographs in newspapers and magazines or images on a television tube, making new friends, and working at my writing career. Perhaps no question arises more frequently when I speak about my case than: "Do you regret what you had to do to regain your freedom?"

In all honesty, the answer must be that I have not regretted it for a second. I have found, without exception, that those who have taken the time to familiarize themselves with the case are both understanding and sympathetic of what I had to do to be free, and invariably I have been accepted by my new friends on my own terms, for what I am, and for what I can bring to our relationships, rather than for anything the state of New Jersey says I am as a result of the negotiations that brought about my release.

It was a long fight and a costly one, costly in more ways than anyone other than myself could understand, but I am proud of it, I have learned from it, grown through it, and now, without regrets, I close the door on the past and look forward to the Great Perhaps.

Appendix I

UNITED STATES DISTRICT COURT
DISTRICT OF NEW JERSEY

UNITED STATES OF AMERICA: Civil No. 766-65
ex. rel. EDGAR H. SMITH   :
       vs.
HOWARD YEAGER, Warden,   :   *OPINION and*
New Jersey State Prison, Trenton   :   *ORDER*

By GIBBONS, Circuit Judge*

Petitioner Edgar Smith is before the court seeking a writ of habeas corpus. His petition was filed in 1965. He is confined in the New Jersey State Prison at Trenton awaiting the execution of a death sentence imposed by the Bergen County Court on June 4, 1957, after a jury trial for murder. Since that time petitioner has sought unsuccessfully to have the conviction set aside.[1] Heretofore this court, without an evidentiary hearing on the allegations of the petition, relying on the contents of the state court trial record, declined to issue the writ. The Third Circuit Court of Appeals affirmed, holding that petitioner's attorney had waived a federal evidentiary hearing. *United States ex rel. Smith v. Yeager*, 395 F.

---

* Sitting in the United States District Court by designation.

[1] Petitioner's conviction was affirmed by the Supreme Court of New Jersey. *State v. Smith*, 27 N.J. 433, 142 A.2d 890 (1958). A petition for habeas corpus was subsequently dismissed by the United States District Court for failure to exhaust state remedies. A motion for a new trial chiefly on the ground of newly discovered evidence was denied, and the denial affirmed by the Supreme Court of New Jersey. *State v. Smith*, 29 N.J. 561, 150 A.2d 769 (1959), *cert. denied*, 361 U.S. 861 (1959). Habeas corpus was again sought and denied in the district court. *United States ex rel. Smith v. New Jersey*, 201 F. Supp. 272 (D. N.J. 1962), *aff'd*, 322 F.2d 810 (3d. Cir. 1962), *cert. denied*, 376 U.S. 928 (1964). A Petition for Post-Conviction Relief was denied by the Bergen County Court on April 17, 1964 and that denial was affirmed by the New Jersey Supreme Court, *State v. Smith*, 43 N.J. 67, 202 A.2d 669 (1964), *cert. denied*, 379 U.S. 1005, *reh. denied*, 380 U.S. 938 (1965). A subsequent application for post-conviction relief was denied by the Bergen County Court on March 29, 1965, and leave to appeal was denied by the New Jersey Supreme Court on April 13, 1965. A Petition for Reconsideration was denied on June 22, 1965.

2d 245 (3 Cir. 1968). The Supreme Court reversed. *Smith v. Yeager*, 393 U.S. 122 (1968). The case was then remanded to this court for reconsideration of petitioner's request for such a hearing. Following the remand petitioner's attorney, relying on *Greenwald v. Wisconsin* 390 U.S. 519 (1968), urged that even on the state court record the totality of circumstances surrounding the taking of a statement by petitioner used in evidence against him at the trial compelled the issuance of the writ. On August 3, 1970, this court ruled that it was bound by a prior ruling of the Third Circuit[2] upholding the conclusions of voluntariness based on the state court record.

That state court trial was the only previous opportunity petitioner had to present evidence on his Fifth Amendment claim. On November 30, 1970, this court ruled that evidence crucial to the adequate consideration of that claim was not fully developed in that record, and that an evidentiary hearing must be held. 28 U.S.C. §2254(d) (3); *Townsend v. Sain*, 372 U.S. 294, 312 (1963). The November 30, 1970, opinion also delimited the scope of the factual issues to be determined. At issue is the voluntariness under federal constitutional standards of all admissions by petitioner which were used against him in the course of his state court murder trial. These admissions may be divided for purposes of discussion into the following categories:

1. Verbal admissions made by petitioner while in the company of various police officials operating at and out of the police headquarters, Mahwah, New Jersey, between the time he was taken into custody at Ridgewood, New Jersey at about 11:30 p.m. on March 5, 1957, and the time he was taken to the office of the Bergen County Prosecutor in Hackensack, New Jersey, at about 8:30 a.m. on March 6, 1957. Various police officers testified at the trial to such admissions.

2. Verbal admissions made during petitioner's interrogation at the Prosecutor's office on the morning of March 6, 1957. Detectives Charles DeLisle and Walter Spahr testified at the trial to such admissions.

3. Verbal admissions made first at the Prosecutor's office and thereafter at and around the scene of the homicide on the afternoon of March 6, 1957, which admissions were in the form of answers in an interrogation conducted by the First

[2] 322 F.2d 810 (3d Cir. 1963). See note 1 supra.

Assistant Prosecutor of Bergen County, Fred Galda. These admissions were recorded by a court reporter, were transcribed, and the transcript was read into evidence at the trial.

4. A verbal admission made by petitioner to Detective DeLisle in the Bergen County jail on March 11, 1957, with respect to the accuracy of the transcript of the interrogation on the afternoon of March 6, 1957. Detective DeLisle testified at the trial to such an admission.

5. Verbal admissions made to three psychiatrists, Drs. Zigarelli, Spradley, and Collins, during the course of their separate examinations of the petitioner. These examinations were made for the purpose of determining petitioner's sanity. The admissions were referred to during the cross-examination of petitioner at the trial and in the State's closing argument to the jury as tending to verify the admissions of March 6, 1957.

Petitioner contends that each of the separate categories of admissions was obtained in violation of his privilege against self-incrimination guaranteed by the Fifth Amendment, and hence was improperly admitted in evidence. Respondent contends that every incriminating statement was voluntary.

At the hearing on the petition twenty-eight witnesses testified, one by deposition, and fifty-six exhibits were received in evidence. From the testimony and exhibits, giving due regard to questions of credibility and the strength of recollections, I find the facts relevant to the disposition of this petition for habeas corpus to be as set forth hereinafter.

On the morning of March 5, 1957, the body of Victoria Zielinski was discovered in a sand pit in Mahwah, Bergen County, New Jersey, near her home. She had been killed by a severe blow to the head which crushed her skull. Guy W. Calissi, the Prosecutor of the Pleas of Bergen County, took charge of the investigation, centering investigative activities at the headquarters of the Mahwah Police Department in the municipal building of that borough. Assisting Mr. Calissi in the investigation were First Assistant Prosecutor Fred Galda, a number of detectives and investigators of the Bergen County Prosecutor's office, and police officers of Mahwah and of the adjoining Borough of Ramsey. Investigation of various persons who might have been acquainted with the deceased continued through the day and into the evening. The case received widespread attention from the press, representatives of which were present at the Mahwah municipal building on the evening of March 5, 1957.

At about 10:00 p.m. John Gilroy came to the Mahwah police headquarters in the company of an officer of the Ramsey police department. He informed Mr. Galda, who was then in charge, that on the evening of the previous day, March 4, he had loaned his Mercury car to Edgar Smith after Smith, Gilroy and one Rockefeller had spent the afternoon bowling; that Smith returned the car late that evening and that on March 5 he had noticed some stains on the floor mat and seat cover; that on March 5 at Smith's request Gilroy, accompanied by Don Hommel [sic], had picked up Smith, his wife and baby at the home of Smith's mother-in-law in Ridgewood and had driven Smith to his trailer home in Mahwah; that Smith had left his wife and baby at the trailer and accompanied Gilroy and Hommel to Ramsey; that Hommel had commented, with respect to the investigation of Victoria Zielinski's death that the police were looking for a Mercury car; that Hommel's comment about the Mercury car had produced a startled look on Smith's face; that Smith had told Gilroy that on March 4 he had vomited on his pants and had thrown the pants away; that on the trip to Ramsey from the trailer Smith had carried a pair of shoes which he said he was taking to a shoe repair man; that Smith separated from Gilroy and Hommel for a time in Ramsey, taking the shoes with him; and that Smith was then at his mother-in-law's house in Ridgewood.

Detectives Graber and Garabedian were dispatched with Gilroy to where his car was parked. At about 10:45 p.m. they examined it, concluded that some of the stains which Gilroy pointed out could have been blood, took the floor mat, and secured the vehicle. They asked Gilroy if his tires had been changed within the last two years and he told them they had not. By this time the Prosecutor's office had had plaster impressions made of certain tire tracks near the place where the body had been found. The detectives reported back to Galda, with Gilroy, and advised him of their suspicion that the stains were blood.

Galda directed Graber and Garabedian to go to the house in Ridgewood where Smith was staying and bring him to Mahwah headquarters. Gilroy accompanied them to give directions, but remained in the car when Graber and Garabedian entered the house at about 11:30 p.m. They identified themselves as Prosecutor's detectives, told Smith that the Prosecutor would like to speak to him at the Mahwah Police Department and asked him to return with them. They had no arrest warrant. They gave no warnings of any kind, but they did inform Smith that they were bringing him in for questioning with respect to the murder of Victoria Zielinski. Smith said he was not surprised since he expected the police to question everyone with whom Victoria had been acquainted. Smith was not informed that he was free to refuse to accompany the detectives. In Garabedian's investigation report on March 12, 1957, he states that he and Graber "picked up Edgar Smith . . . and brought him to Mahwah Police Headquarters." (Ex. R-1). Graber's report of March 15, 1957 (Ex. R-3) states: "Edgar Smith was brought back to the Mahwah police station for questioning." Beginning at 11:30 p.m. March 5, 1957, Smith was under the impression that he was in police custody, and he was in fact in such custody.

Upon arriving at the Mahwah municipal building Smith and Gilroy were asked to wait in the municipal council chamber adjoining the room used as police headquarters. In that room were policemen and several newspaper reporters. When one of the reporters attempted to interview Smith a police official chased her away. Gilroy described Smith's demeanor at about this time as cocky or self-assured.

After a short wait Smith was taken into the room used as police headquarters. At the outset of the interrogation Smith was observed by Officer Brennan of the Mahwah Police Department to be calm. He sat in a chair and placed his feet upon a desk. Mr. Galda ordered him to remove his feet. Smith asked a policeman whom he knew for a cigarette and was given one. He was questioned by Mr. Galda and other police officers including Graber and Captain DeMarco of the Bergen County Prosecutor's office. He was given no warnings. He was questioned about the information obtained from Gilroy and he admitted that he had spent the afternoon bowling with Gilroy and Rockefeller, had borrowed the Mercury car, had used it to drive to a service station for kerosene to fill the heater in his trailer, had become ill and vomited, had discarded a pair of pants on which he had vomited, and had disposed of a pair of shoes in Ramsey. During this interrogation Captain DeMarco observed an injury to Smith's fingers, which he said he incurred fixing a tail pipe. DeMarco told Smith to lift his trousers to see if he had any lacerations on the shinbones, and discovered contusions and lacerations on his knees. Smith explained that he had fallen while getting out of the car to vomit. Shortly after midnight on March 6, 1957, during the interrogation at Mahwah police headquarters, Officer Russo of the Mahwah police department was dispatched for a dozen coffees and sandwiches for the party at headquarters. Smith denies that he consumed either coffee or food at that time and there is no credible evidence to rebut this denial, although there is testimony from which it may be concluded that he was offered coffee and a sandwich. During the course of the interrogation on several occasions Smith was returned to the council room while Gilroy was questioned in the headquarters room. At about 2:00 a.m. on March 6, 1957, Captain DeMarco pulled from Smith's head a sample of hair. At about 2:30 a.m. Graber observed Smith's demeanor. In his words, "He was quite subdued, he was hanging his head, where he hadn't done that previously. He was very quiet." (tr. at 209). The level of interrogation by this time was far from casual or routine. Galda had asked Smith to take a lie detector test. Calissi had asked Smith to go to the morgue. It is not clear how Smith could have aided the investigation by complying, and it must be assumed that Calissi was then seeking to wear down his resistance to meaningful interrogation. As a result of the first interrogation at Mahwah Smith was directed to accompany Galda, Captain DeMarco and Detective Graber to show them where he had vomited and where he had discarded his shoes. In Ramsey Smith disclosed the location of the shoes in a garbage can in back of some stores on Main Street. The shoes were placed in a box and impounded. A red fiber which appeared similar to the red sweater worn by the victim was found stuck to the instep of one of the shoes. Smith was then taken to the vicinity of Chapel Road and Ferndale Avenue, near the entrance to the sand pit, an area where he claimed to have vomited on the evening of March 4. No evidence of vomit was found. Smith was asked if he had ever been further back on the road into the sand pit and denied that he had ever been back there. He observed in the road the discarded plaster bags, the contents of which had been used to make plaster impressions at the scene of the homicide.

While Smith, Galda, DeMarco and Graber were traveling about seeking confirmation of Smith's story about vomiting, Detective Russell Ridgeway and Lieutenant Charles Haight of the Mahwah Police went to Smith's trailer in an attempt to find the vomit stained pants, where Smith said he had discarded them. They had no search warrant or consent. In the garbage pail alongside the trailer they found a pair of gray cotton pants saturated with kerosene and in the trailer a pair of brown cotton gloves. These were not the pants Smith had described. (Ex. R-34).

At that point Smith was questioned by Mr. Galda and Captain DeMarco and told a different version of how and where he had discarded the pants. He explained that he had changed pants and had gone back to Pulis Avenue where he discarded the vomit covered pants. He was taken to the Pulis Avenue location, where a search for the pants was made. Smith, who was attired in light clothing, complained of being cold. The search for the pants was fruitless. Questioning with respect to the clothing Smith had worn on March 4 continued in the car, and Smith disclosed that he had worn a blue jacket which he had since washed and which was at his mother-in-law's house. Detective Graber was dispatched to that home at about 3:30 a.m. and obtained the jacket from Mrs. Smith. Galda, Captain DeMarco and Smith returned to the Mahwah police headquarters where Smith's interrogation continued. At this time Smith proffered an explanation with respect to the shoes:

"If it's those shoes that you are worried about, I think I can explain that. * * * * If those shoes have any blood on them, I can explain how it got on there * * * ." He said that when he got home and his knees were bloody, he wanted to change his shoes and his good shoes were under the bed and rather than soil the rug with his bloody knees, because his pants were off, he pulled the old shoes over by his knees and he leaned on them with his knees and pulled his new shoes out from under the bed." (Ex. R-59, p. 481-482)

It was now between 3:30 and 4:00 a.m. Lieutenant Haight and Detective Sinatra were detailed to return to Smith's trailer and measure the kerosene in the fifty-five gallon tank beside Smith's trailer. They found it to be three-fourths full. They had no search warrant and no consent. The measurement of the tank tended to cast further doubt on Smith's version of his whereabouts on the evening of March 4. At about 4:00 a.m. Mr. Galda gave instructions to obtain powerful searchlights. Smith was taken out for a further search for the trousers on which he claimed to have vomited and for evidence of vomit. Smith was first taken by Captain Wickham, Detective Sinatra, Detective Garabedian and Detective O'Har to another location on Wyckoff Avenue near a church where he claimed to have vomited. Next he was taken to Pulis Avenue, where he was asked to assist Mr. Galda and Captain DeMarco in a search for the pants. Finally he was taken back to the area near the sand pit and asked to assist in locating vomit there. All of these searches proved fruitless. Smith was then taken back to Mahwah police headquarters.

It was now after 5:00 a.m. At 5:20 a.m. Captain DeMarco made arrangements to have Smith examined at 7:30 a.m. by the county medical examiner, Dr. Gilady. He called Investigators Nunno and Perrapato and instructed them to be at Dr. Gilady's office at 7:30 a.m. He detailed Detective Sinatra to guard the suspect. The physical evidence which had been gathered from the murder scene and elsewhere was transferred from Mahwah to the Bergen County Prosecutor's office. Gilroy was driven home. The Mahwah phase of the investigation ended at about 5:40 a.m.

With Smith in the car, Sinatra, whom Smith knew to be armed, drove DeMarco to his home in Wyckoff so that DeMarco could refresh himself and change his clothes. Sinatra then took Smith to a diner in Midland Park where both ordered breakfast. Sinatra's best recollection is that Smith ate breakfast. Smith testified that he was too tense and ill to eat. Probably Smith did eat something, although by this time he was undoubtedly tense and ill. Smith contends that while he was with Sinatra in the diner he asked Sinatra if he could telephone his wife, or perhaps drive to his mother-in-law's home which was a few blocks away, and that Sinatra told him his instructions would not permit this. Sinatra denies that either request was made. From all the surrounding circumstances including the fact that Smith had been away from his wife all night, the geography and the fact that when he arrived at the Prosecutor's office later in the morning he made a similar request (to call his wife), which was granted, Smith's contention is more credible than Sinatra's denial. After breakfast Smith was taken back to Wyckoff where Captain DeMarco rejoined them. They then drove to Dr. Gilady's office in Hackensack where they were met by Investigators Nunno and Perrapato. Smith was given no warnings. Dr. Gilady's report (Ex. R-32) discloses and I find that Smith was stripped of all his clothing and examined for marks of injury. This examination took place in the presence of Captain DeMarco. The other four detectives were present, although not in the examining room. The doctor discovered indications of traumatic injury of recent origin on the left knee, the right knee and the left index finger. With respect to Smith's mental state he found "He was very restless and apprehensive and markedly agitated." Dr. Gilady's written report discloses that the examination took place at about 7:55 a.m. The report was received at the Prosecutor's office on March 6, 1957, exact time unknown. However, almost immediately after completing the examination and certainly no later than 9:00 a.m. Dr. Gilady telephoned the same information to Mr. Calissi or Mr. Galda.

Meanwhile at about 6:30 a.m. the Ramsey Police Department had found, in quite a different location than any to which Smith had made reference, a pair of blood stained pants. Arrangements were made to photograph the pants at that location and then to bring them to the Prosecutor's office at the courthouse in Hackensack.

At about 8:30 a.m. Detective Sinatra and others brought Smith from Dr. Gilady's office to the Prosecutor's office. About this time Mr. Galda, who was already at the office, had learned from a police source that Smith had a juvenile court record, and made efforts to obtain from the Juvenile and Domestic Court of Bergen County a copy of that record. He ultimately did obtain it (Ex. R-33) through the Midland Park Police Department.

Shortly after his arrival at the Prosecutor's office Smith's knee injuries were photographed for Captain DeMarco by a newspaper photographer. Thereafter Detectives Kikert [sic] and Garabedian took fingerprints, fingernail clippings and scrapings from Smith. Also, shortly after Smith's arrival, the bloody pants were delivered from the Ramsey Police Department. They were shown to Smith by Galda and Calissi and he denied they were his.

Shortly thereafter Smith asked for and received permission to call his wife. In the presence of one or more of the Prosecutor's staff this call was made. Smith told his wife he was in the Prosecutor's office, and that she should go to the office of Judge Dwyer, an attorney in Ridgewood, tell Dwyer who she was, tell Dwyer where he was, and ask Dwyer to get him out.

After this call was made the Prosecutor instructed Detective Graber to pick up Mrs. Smith and bring her to the Prosecutor's office. She was picked up promptly, before she had an opportunity to speak to Judge Dwyer, and taken by a back entrance to the Prosecutor's office. She was shown the bloody pants and identified them as Smith's. Smith was made aware of her presence in the Prosecutor's office. Thereafter she was taken back to her mother's house for the purpose of finding the flannel shirt which Smith had worn on March 4 and washed on March 5. She was brought back to the Prosecutor's office with the shirt. Mrs. Smith was given no warnings of any kind. In particular she was not advised that she could not be compelled to be a witness against her husband.[3]

Some time after 9:30 a.m. Smith was placed in a smaller office. At about the same time two detectives who had not previously figured in his interrogation arrived on duty. One of them, Detective DeLisle, inquired if there was a suspect in the Zielinski homicide. Captain DeMarco informed him Smith was the suspect. DeLisle suggested that too many people were participating in Smith's interrogation, and that he should be placed in less congenial surroundings. He was thereupon placed in a small office normally occupied by Captain DeMarco. DeMarco instructed DeLisle and Detective Spahr to continue Smith's interrogation. This interrogation commenced about 10:00 a.m.

At that time the Prosecutor had evidence (1) that Smith was acquainted with the victim, (2) that he was in the vicinity of the crime on the evening of March 4, (3) that he had used a car that evening which now contained suspicious stains, (4) that he had lied about his movements that evening and in particular about vomiting on his pants, (5) that he discarded a pair of shoes to which was adhered a fiber similar to that of a sweater worn by the victim, (6) that he had discarded a pair of pants, (7) that a pair of bloody pants, identified by Smith's wife as his, were found in a location other than the place where he said he discarded his pants, (8) that he had injuries consistent with having engaged in a struggle in a sand pit, (9) that he had washed a jacket and a shirt on the morning of March 5. Smith had been the prime suspect and focus of the investigation since 4:00 a.m. at the latest. Clearly the Prosecutor at 10:00 a.m. had sufficient information to charge Smith with murder, and to have him taken before a committing magistrate. The Prosecutor admitted that he was well aware of the New Jersey requirement that persons taken into custody be brought promptly before the nearest available magistrate.[4] The Prosecutor's office was in a courthouse where there were numer-

---

[3] See L. 1900, c. 150, p. 363, §5, as amended, L. 1940, c. 22, p. 96, §1, as amended, L. 1953, c. 231, p. 1695, §1, repealed, L. 1960, c. 52, p. 465, §49. The marital privilege is now governed by Rule 23(2) of the New Jersey Rules of Evidence.

[4] N.J.R.R. 3:2-3(a) (1953), as amended, R.R. 3:4-1 (1969), required that a person arrested without a warrant be brought "without unnecessary delay, before the nearest available magistrate." As contrasted with the federal courts, noncompliance with this rule does not vitiate a confession subsequently obtained. Compare *Mallory v. United States*, 354 U.S. 449 (1957), with *State v. Taylor*, 46 N.J. 316, 328, *cert. denied*, 385 U.S. 855 (1966).

ous judges, any one of which could properly have acted as a magistrate. At such an appearance it would have been the duty of the court to advise Smith of his right to counsel, his right to appointed counsel in a homicide case, his right to remain silent, the use to which any statement he made could be put and his right to make a statement not under oath.[5]

There were, however, certain evidentiary holes in the State's case. First, Mrs. Smith could not be compelled at a trial to testify against her husband.[6] Thus the identification of the bloody pants might be difficult. Second, no one placed Smith in the sand pit with the victim. Third, even if the pants were identified as Smith's and blood typing associated the blood stains with the victim, placing Smith with her, there was not sufficient evidence of the surrounding circumstances to show premeditation. Thus despite the mandatory language of N.J.R.R. 3:2-3(a) Smith was not taken before a magistrate and the interrogation continued. The purpose of the interrogation after 10:00 a.m. on March 6, 1957, was not to determine who committed the offense, but to obtain evidence of first degree murder.

Shortly before this new interrogation began, but after he had been confronted with the bloody trousers, and had been photographed, fingerprinted and had had his fingernails scraped and clipped, and after he spoke to his wife on the telephone about an attorney, and after she had arrived at the Prosecutor's office too soon to have called an attorney, Smith, by this time transferred to the smaller DeMarco office, said, "I am getting out." He started to get up but was pushed by Detective Spahr into a chair and fell backwards onto the floor. Thereafter Spahr noticed a small bloodstain on the collar of his T-shirt. Spahr ordered that his clothing be removed and prison coveralls were substituted.

Spahr and DeLisle conferred outside Smith's presence on an agreed line of questioning of the suspect. They were both experienced interrogators. It was agreed that at an appropriate point in the interrogation DeLisle would afford the suspect, unexpectedly, an opportunity to state any justification for what had happened by asking "What did she do to you?" or something to that effect.

Spahr explained the technique which was pursued, both in his 1957 report (Ex. R-47) and in his testimony in this proceeding. First it was necessary to establish a common ground with the suspect. In Smith's case, after obtaining some personal history, this

[5] N.J.R.R. 3:2-3(b) (1953), as amended, R.R. 3:4-2 (1969).
[6] See note 3 supra.

proved to be religion. Their common faith, and the fact that DeLisle also was of the same faith, though not practicing, served this purpose. At the same time it was necessary to maintain an authoritarian position between interrogator and suspect. This was accomplished by discussing in detail all the scientific aids which would enable them sooner or later to solve this crime. The suspect was led into a discussion of degrees of murder and the ensuing penalties. Reference was made to a file on another homicide, the Ledwin or Ludwin case, in which a man had killed his brother. Spahr explained that all murders are presumed to be second degree, and "there is a case where this man killed his brother and look what he got" (seven years) (Tr. 360). Then Spahr mentioned that whoever committed the act must have done so with great provocation. At this point, as planned, DeLisle asked, "What did she do to you?" Smith answered, "She hit me." The cat was out of the bag. Smith broke down and cried.

The interrogators then spoke with Smith about whether he wanted to see a priest for confession. Smith asked for a specific priest from Don Bosco High School in Ramsey. The Prosecutor was informed of Smith's breakdown. He agreed that the priest should be summoned, and sent a staff member to pick him up. Smith was given a cigarette and a glass of water. The interrogation continued, and Smith gave an incomplete but incriminating verbal statement which is recorded in Spahr's report (Ex. R-17) and to which Spahr testified at the trial. This statement admitted Smith's presence in the sand pit and an altercation with the victim, but did not admit killing in as many words and claimed a blackout or loss of memory for the crucial period following the altercation.

A priest, not the one for whom Smith had asked, but one of similar name, arrived at the Prosecutor's office some time after 11:00 a.m. He was admitted through the same rear entrance through which Mrs. Smith had been admitted. Smith was permitted to confer with the priest in a private room.

There is a dispute in the testimony as to whether Smith was on March 6, 1957, permitted to speak with his wife. If such a conversation took place on March 6, it took place either immediately before he was closeted with the priest, or immediately thereafter. Galda's recollection, which I find the most credible is that he authorized a meeting between husband and wife in his presence, which took place immediately before the priest's visit, on March 6. At this meeting, confronted with his wife's prior identification of the bloody pants, Smith admitted they were his. (Tr. at 577-78).

Clearly now the time had come to charge Smith and take him before a magistrate. Instead, at about this time Detective Ridgeway was detailed to procure motion picture equipment to be used when Smith re-enacted the crime. He rented such equipment at 11:30 a.m. (Ex. R-34).[7] Smith had not been asked if he would be willing to undertake any such re-enactment.

The judiciary was not left out of the picture, however, for while Smith was closeted with the priest, Calissi and Galda conferred with the Honorable Wallace Leyden, a judge of the Superior Court of New Jersey, and the Assignment Judge of Bergen County. They advised him of their desire to continue interrogation of the suspect. Instead of directing the Prosecutor to take the suspect before a magistrate, Judge Leyden arranged for a member of the petit jury panel currently sitting to be dispatched to the Prosecutor's office to serve as a "disinterested witness" to Smith's further interrogation. He also arranged that one of the regular court reporters serving the courts in the building be relieved from his regular assignment in order to record the interrogation.

The desk in the Prosecutor's office was at that time equipped with two telephones. One of these was a dummy telephone, containing a concealed microphone. The microphone was connected by concealed wire to a tape recorder in an adjoining room. Spahr was instructed to set up the recording equipment with magnetic tape and he did so. It was arranged that Smith's further interrogation would continue in the Prosecutor's office, with Galda asking the questions and Calissi monitoring the recording equipment. The existence of the concealed microphone was not revealed to Smith.

Smith was told the Prosecutor was going to take a statement. He was given no warnings. He was brought into the Prosecutor's office at 12:50 p.m. Present besides Galda were Louis M. Kalstad, the "disinterested witness" procured from Judge Leyden, Arthur J. Ehrenbeck, the court reporter, Charles E. Smith, Chief of the Mahwah Police Department, Harry Voss, Chief of the Ramsey Police Department, and Spahr, the recently successful interrogator. These people were introduced. Kalstad was introduced as "from the jury panel of the Second State Session." Smith was asked, and answered:

> "Are you willing to give a voluntary statement concerning this incident? A. Yes.
> Q. Are you willing to give the statement under oath, Ed? A. Yes.

[7] Due to technical difficulties with the camera the film footage was never successfully developed.

He was sworn. Mr. Galda then undertook an interrogation about Smith's movements on March 4. Smith's answers embroidered upon the admissions he had previously made. At first he admitted only to the same altercation which he had admitted to Spahr, and continued to claim loss of memory. He was encouraged to detail his movements on the morning of March 5, and he spoke about a conversation with Gilroy from a phone booth, and said:

> "I went back in. That's when it dawned on me that I had been with her the night before and something snapped in the back of my head that I did it and I knew it in the back of my mind." (Ex. R-26 p. 19).

He was asked to continue the recital of the occurrences of March 5, and with respect to the conversation between Smith, Gilroy, and Hommel [sic] said:

> "First thing I said when I came out of the house I said to this fellow Don, I said, 'Was that Vickie that got killed?' I guess I was asking as if I didn't know myself, and he said, 'Yeah.'
> He said 'The place up there is swarming with cops and checking the registration of every Mercury registered in Bergen County.'
> That's when it hit me really hard I must have been the one who really did it." (Ex. R-26 p. 19).

The quoted admissions took place at about 1:20 p.m. They were the first, and the only time that Smith actually admitted doing anything more than striking the victim once with his hand. The interrogation in the Prosecutor's office was transcribed by Ehrenbeck, and was also recorded on magnetic tape by Calissi. It continued until 2:15. Smith identified various incriminating exhibits and made further admissions as to his activities in and around the sand pit.

The transcript of Ehrenbeck's stenographic notes was read into evidence at the trial. The existence of the magnetic tape transcription was never revealed to anyone outside the Bergen County Prosecutor's office until about a month before the instant hearing. It comprises exhibits R-23, 24 and 25 in this proceeding, and was played in open court. At several points in the transcription, especially those parts coinciding with pages 24, 28, 29, 31 and 32 of the transcript, Exhibit R-26, Smith's voice shows evidence of considerable tension. At pages 40 and 41 of exhibit R-26, and in the equivalent part of the magnetic tape transcription, Galda attempted to obtain an elaboration of the altercation, and admissions of sexual advances, but Smith, obviously tense, retreated to lack of recollection. Pressed to recall his blood stained clothing, he became evasive and equivocal. (Ex. R-26, p. 42). At this point Galda suggested a recess. The magnetic transcription discloses that Smith used the toilet in a small adjoining lavatory. Calissi joined the group. Galda resumed interrogation at 2:13 p.m. At page 43 of Ex. R-26 and in the corresponding part of the magnetic transcription appears:

> "Q. What we are going to do now, on the places you indicated to us, we are going to go to the area. It will be with the same people in this room and we are going in two cars and you can point out those things you mention on the spot. Is that agreeable to you?
> A. Yes.
> Q. And while you were in the custody of the policemen and up at the Mahwah Police Headquarters, did anybody mistreat you or anything?
> A. No, sir.
> Q. Everybody treat you all right?
> A. Better than I expected."

Galda then elicited an admission that Smith was sober on the evening of March 4. Smith was not told that arrangements had been made for the proposed re-enactment trip as early as 11:30 a.m. The Ehrenbeck transcript of proceedings at the Prosecutor's office ends at this point, at 2:15. The magnetic transcription continues, however, beyond the time covered by R-26.

At 2:15 the corridor and rotunda of the Bergen County Court House contained a large crowd of newspaper reporters and spectators. Smith was told there was a big crowd out there and he would have to go through the crowd because there was no other way to get out. He was not told of the rear entrance used by Mrs. Smith and by the priest. Galda said, "You follow me and we'll go right through." Calissi said there was no way of sneaking out of the place and that the crowds could not be kept out because it was a public building. Galda said, "Eddie we're not going to put handcuffs on you or anything." He also said, "I think you ought to shave." He gave Smith an electric razor and instructed him to shave, which Smith did.

Numerous photographs taken of Smith after he left the Prosecutor's office on March 5, 1957, show him clean shaven and in clothing other than the prison coveralls which he wore while being interrogated by Spahr. Thus at some point before he was exposed to the press Smith's prison coveralls were removed and his own or some other outerclothing substituted.

Smith was taken out through the rotunda and main entrance of the Bergen County Court House, where he was photographed by press photographers. Exhibit P-4, a United Press International Photograph, shows Smith entering a car outside the Bergen County Court House. He appears fatigued. He was placed in a car in the company of several detectives, Galda, Kalstad, and the court reporter Ehrenbeck, who continued to record the ongoing inter- rogation. Galda caused Smith to identify landmarks in the vicinity of the sand pit, such as the place where he picked up Victoria Zielinski and the place where he drove Gilroy's car into the drive- way of the sand pit. That the purpose of the interrogation was to obtain evidence which would sustain a first degree murder charge is clear. For example:

"Q. Did you pull in on your own accord without any suggestion?
A. I did." (Ex. R-26 p. 47)

Smith was subjected to a rather rigorous examination with respect to his story of the altercation, the questions seeking to establish the possibility of premeditation. He was asked to identify property of the victim found at locations which he pointed out. He admitted having returned to the sand pit with a searchlight. Smith was photographed in the vicinity of the murder scene by press photog- raphers and by Ridgeway's motion picture camera.[8]

Smith was then taken to the trailer camp where he lived. The party arrived at the trailer at 3:32 p.m.

The party then returned to the sand pit at 3:40 p.m. At 3:42 p.m. they returned to the trailer and obtained the five gallon kero- sene can which Smith said he used on March 4. There was no search warrant. There were no warnings. The party concluded its business at the trailer at 3:45 p.m. and proceeded to the Mahwah Police headquarters. At Mahwah Smith was again photographed by the press.

At Mahwah a complaint charging Smith with the murder of Victoria Zielinski was drawn. Thereafter at about 5:00 p.m. he was brought before Magistrate Young of the Mahwah Municipal Court, the charge was read, and the warnings which N.J.R.R. 3:2-3(b) required were given. Smith asked for and was denied bail. At the rear of the courtroom after his appearance before the magistrate he was posed for news photographs.

---

[8] See note 7 supra.

Smith was next taken by several detectives to dinner at a Hackensack restaurant. The prosecutor joined the dinner party. A reporter was permitted to be near enough to the party to overhear the conversation and observe Smith's demeanor. After dinner Smith was remanded to the Bergen County jail.

Upon instructions of the Prosecutor's office Ehrenbeck forthwith prepared a transcript of his notes of Smith's interrogation. Based on information obtained from the Prosecutor's staff he captioned the transcript:

> STATE OF NEW JERSEY :
> v.   : Charge: Murder
> EDGAR H. SMITH   :
> Defendant[9]

He delivered the ribbon and three carbon copies to the Prosecutor's office on or about March 8, 1957.

The Prosecutor was aware that Smith's family had retained Joseph Gaudielle on March 7, 1957. Gaudielle informed the Prosecutor that he had given Smith instructions not to sign any statement. Nevertheless, on March 11, 1957, Captain DeMarco instructed Detective DeLisle to take the Ehrenbeck transcript to the Bergen County Jail for the purpose of having it signed. DeLisle handed Smith a copy and told him "I want you to read it, make any errors or corrections or additions to it you might want to, and sign it." (Tr. at 782). Smith read the statement. He was again asked to sign it, but refused because his lawyer had advised him not to do so. In DeLisle's words:

> "It was then that he said to me that he was amazed at the ability of the Court reporters to be able to catch everything that was said, and he just thought it was a wonderful thing that they could [sic] this ability." (Tr. at 783).

This version is slightly at variance with that to which DeLisle testified at the trial. There he said:

> "I asked him if the statement was accurate and he said 'Yes, it was accurate.'
>
> He commented upon how accurate it was and it was amazing that the court stenographer could take down with such accuracy such a statement." (Trial tr. at 521).

---

[9] At one point at least in the magnetic transcription the Prosecutor referred to Smith as the defendant.

The difference between the two versions is significant, for the State trial testimony was elicited for the purpose of complying with the rule of *State v. Cleveland*, 6 N.J. 316, 78 A.2d 560 (1951)[10] and thereby making the Ehrenbeck transcript (Ex P-84 in the trial record) admissible in evidence as a confession. The state trial court, on the basis of DeLisle's testimony, admitted this transcript in evidence. The less precise version testified to before this court might have produced a different ruling.[11]

On March 8, 9, and 11, 1957, Smith was transferred temporarily from the Bergen County jail to the Prosecutor's office. In each instance the transfer was accomplished by virtue of a written request from the Prosecutor addressed to Hon. Arthur J. O'Dea, Presiding Judge of the Bergen County Court. Each requisition was approved in writing by Judge O'Dea. (Exhibits P-7, -8, -9, -10). The purpose of these transfers was to have Smith examined by three state appointed psychiatrists for the purpose of determining his sanity. The Prosecutor discussed these examinations with Frank Boggia, assistant to Mr. Gaudielle, who consented. Dr. Collins, who conducted the first examination on March 8, 1957, also spoke to and obtained consent from Mr. Gaudielle,[12] who remained present while Collins spoke to Smith. With respect to the three examinations Mr. Calissi was asked:

"Q. Was there any agreement between you and Mr. Gaudielle as to the use to which the reports of these examinations, or the content of these examinations would be put?

A. No, sir. This was a kind of a routine matter in a case of this kind. First, it was my impression that it was necessary to find out what the mental status of an accused was at the time of the commission, in order that I discharge my duties properly in determining the degree. And, as I said, Mr. Gaudielle had absolutely no objection to—in fact, I believe he was at one of them, he was there. And, of course, we left before the examination took place. And I don't remember which it

[10] This rule governs the admissibility of written confessions and provides that "until the statement is signed or its correctness acknowledged in some fashion by the defendant, it constitutes merely a memorandum of what was said and is inadmissible in evidence." 6 N.J. at 329, 78 A.2d at 567.

[11] There can be no doubt that the admission of Ex. P-74 in evidence had a prejudicial effect beyond the oral testimony of Ehrenbeck as to the same admissions. "A thing in writing carries, particularly with laymen, a weight of its own." *Springer v. Labow*, 108 N.J.L. 68, 70, 155 A.476, 477 (S. Ct. 1931).

[12] Mr. Gaudielle is deceased and thus his version of this consent could not be adduced in the instant proceeding.

was, but it was the first one. And he knew there were going
to be two others after that." (Tr. at 1026).

During the three examinations Smith was asked about his claimed
loss of memory as to some events of March 4, and while sticking to
that version, repeated some of the incriminating statements he had
theretofore made. The incriminating admissions to the psychiatrists
were elicited from Smith when he took the stand at his trial and
were referred to in the Prosecutor's closing address as corrobora-
tive of his confession.

Gaudielle did not represent Smith at the trial. John E. Selser, the
attorney who did represent him, testified in these proceedings. In
1957 he was an experienced criminal defense attorney in Bergen
County, a former First Assistant Prosecutor of that county and a
former Deputy Attorney General. He testified that in 1957 it was
the common practice ". . . to anticipate the possible defense of
insanity and in every such case Dr. Collins or other competent
psychiatrists were called by the Prosecutor to make an appraisal
as to the psychotic health of the accused." (Tr. at 1255). He
testified:

> "Q. What was the purpose of these examinations, sir?
> A. Appraisal of the psychotic status of the accused.
> Q. Was there any other purpose?
> A. No.
> Q. Was that purpose understood by the Bar?
> A. Yes.
>   * * * *
> Q. What was the understanding of the Bar as to that use?
> A. The understanding of the Bar was very definitely a program
>   to arm the prosecution as against the possible defense of
>   insanity, and for no other purpose."

There is no direct conflict between Mr. Calissi's testimony that
"[t]his was a kind of routine matter in a case of this kind" and
Mr. Selser's testimony as to the understanding of the Bar. Moreover only such an understanding as that to which Mr. Selser testified would explain Mr. Gaudielle's willingness to permit his client
to make incriminating statements to the psychiatrists after advising
him not to sign a statement and informing the Prosecutor that he
had so advised him. Judge O'Dea's signature on the requisition
orders is also consistent with such an understanding, for it is incon-
ceivable that the court would order the production of a represented
defendant for interrogation for purposes of incrimination beyond
the issues of criminal responsibility and present sanity. This under-

standing is consistent with N.J.S. 2A:163-2 and the procedure under that statute later formally elaborated in *State v. Whitlow*, 45 N.J. 3, 210 A.2d 763 (1965).[13] The statements made to the three psychiatrists Drs. Collins, Spradley and Zigarelli, in March of 1957 were made pursuant to such an understanding.

The foregoing recital, then, sets forth the historical facts from which must be determined the ultimate issue of voluntariness for federal constitutional purposes. The November 30, 1970, opinion of this court, referred to earlier, requires that this opinion discuss the evidentiary standard applied in making findings both of historical facts and of the ultimate issue. That opinion held that the respondent would in this hearing have the burden of proving voluntariness.[14] It did not, however, decide which evidentiary burden respondent must meet. Three alternatives are possible. Respondent (nominally the Warden of the State prison but actually the State) might be required to prove voluntariness beyond a reasonable doubt. This would be its burden in a criminal trial in New Jersey. *State v. Franklin*, 52 N.J. 386, 245 A.2d 356 (1968);

---

[13] "If an adequate opinion cannot be formed without inquiry into the circumstances attending the alleged crime, the inquiry should be made. The defendant should cooperate therein fairly, unless he lacks mental capacity to do so. The evidentiary character of any inculpatory statements shall be limited expressly to the issue of insanity, and shall not be admissible on the issue of guilt." 45 N.J. at 26, 210 A.2d at 775.

[14] This ruling was an interpretation of 28 U.S.C. §2254(d). That subsection states that factual determinations made by a state court shall be presumed to be correct unless the applicant shall establish one of eight enumerated circumstances or such shall otherwise appear. One of these circumstances is

"(3) that the material facts were not adequately developed in the State court hearing."

The November 30, 1970 ruling of this court held that material facts were not adequately developed in the state court record. Section 2254(d) goes on to say:

"And in an evidentiary hearing in the proceeding in the Federal Court . . . unless the existence of one or more of the circumstances set forth in paragraphs 1 to 7, inclusive, is shown by the applicant . . . the burden shall rest upon the applicant to establish by convincing evidence that the factual determination by the State Court was erroneous."

The opinion reasoned that only in the absence of all the listed instances did the presumption and burden of proof specified in §2254(d) apply, and that where one of the listed criteria appeared the respondent had the burden of proof.

State v. Yough, 49 N.J. 587, 231 A.2d 598 (1967).[15] Respondent might be required to meet the standard of "convincing evidence." This standard applies to a habeas corpus petitioner in those cases in which, because none of the eight criteria specified in 28 U.S.C. §2254(d) have been met, the burden rests upon him to show that the state court factual determination was erroneous. Finally respondent might be entitled to prevail on no more than a preponderance of the evidence. Research has disclosed no case deciding the point. It is discussed but not reached by Judge Mansfield in *United States ex rel. Castro v. LaValle,* 282 F. Supp. 718, 723 (S.D.N.Y. 1968).

The question arises, of course, because of this court's prior ruling, which is law of the case, that when the petitioner establishes by reference to the state court record one of the criteria of 28 U.S.C. §2254(d), the respondent must bear the burden of proof. Perhaps one could distinguish between the burden of going forward (risk of failure to produce evidence) and the burden of persuasion (risk of failure to persuade by the applicable evidentiary standard) and hold that the later burden remained on petitioner. We conclude, however, that Judge Barlow's prior ruling for this court rejected such an approach, and placed on the State both the burden of going forward and the burden of persuasion.

That ruling should not, however, in this collateral attack on a judgment of conviction, have the additional effect of imposing on the State the same burden it had to meet to obtain the judgment in the first instance. Petitioner's contention that the State must prove voluntariness beyond a reasonable doubt is therefore rejected. If none of the criteria listed in 28 U.S.C. §2254(d) applied, the habeas corpus petitioner would have had to meet the evidentiary standard of convincing evidence. Because of deficiencies in the record developed in the state court on the critical issue of voluntariness the petitioner has been relieved of that burden. A persuasive case can be made for requiring the State, in these circumstances, to meet the same convincing evidence test. In the absence of a binding precedent, however, this fact finder has assumed that

[15] See also *Pea v. United States,* 397 F.2d 627 (D.C. Cir. 1968) and the cases therein cited, which discuss whether the government must show the voluntariness of a confession beyond a reasonable doubt before it may be admitted in evidence. These cases were all direct reviews of convictions and are not authority for the proposition that a habeas corpus court should impose the same burden on the State as it would have to meet in a criminal trial.

the State need only persuade by a preponderance of the evidence. The factual findings set forth hereinabove were made pursuant to that standard. Few of these facts are seriously disputed in any event. The real dispute is the ultimate conclusion to be drawn from such facts. Substantially the same factual findings and certainly the same ultimate conclusion would be reached if the burden of persuasion rested on the petitioner.

If *Miranda v. Arizona*, 384 U.S. 436 (1966) were applicable to this case the violation of each of the prophylactic rules for custodial interrogation laid down in that case would require issuance of the writ. *Miranda* is not retroactive. *Johnson v. New Jersey*, 384 U.S. 719 (1966). However a pre-*Miranda* confession is judged by whether, considering the totality of the circumstances, it was voluntarily given or was the result of overbearing by the police. See, e.g., *Clewis v. Texas*, 386 U.S. 707, 708 (1967); *Davis v. North Carolina*, 384 U.S. 737, 739 (1966); *Fikes v. Alabama*, 352 U.S. 191, 197-98 (1957). Since it became clear in *Brown v. Mississippi*, 297 U.S. 278 (1936), that admission of a coerced confession violated the due process clause of the Fourteenth Amendment, the substantive test of voluntariness has become increasingly meticulous. Physical brutality was the first type of coercion to which the federal courts gave attention. See *Brown v. Mississippi, supra*; cf. *Brooks v. Florida*, 384 U.S. 413 (1967). But "[s]ince *Chambers v. Florida*, 309 U.S. 227, [the Supreme] Court has recognized that coercion can be mental as well as physical, that the blood of the accused is not the only hallmark of an unconstitutional inquisition." *Blackburn v. Alabama*, 361 U.S. 199, 206 (1960). "When a strong suspect speaks because he is overborne, it is immaterial whether he has been subjected to a physical or mental ordeal." *Watts v. Indiana*, 338 U.S. 49, 53 (1949). The decision to confess must be freely as well as rationally made. *Lynumn v. Illinois*, 372 U.S. 528 (1962).

> "[A] confession is [not] 'voluntary' simply because the confession is the product of a sentient choice. 'Conduct under duress involves a choice,' and conduct . . . not leaving a free exercise of choice is the product of duress as much so as choice reflecting physical constraint." *Haley v. Ohio*, 332 U.S. 596, 606 (1948).

The choice must be the voluntary product of a free and unconstrained will. *Haynes v. Washington*, 373 U.S. 503, 514 (1963).

It is true that in each case in which the Supreme Court has held that the totality of circumstances disclosed a confession to be the product of coercion[16] the presence or absence of some single fact may serve to distinguish petitioner's precise situation. The assessment of voluntariness, however, "requires more than a mere color-matching of cases." *Reck v. Pate,* 367 U.S. 433, 442 (1961). Reference to factual configurations in similar Supreme Court cases reveals what must be considered impermissible coercive as a matter of law. Guided by those factual configurations this court must determine in the first instance whether the will of Edgar Smith was overborne by the acts of the various law enforcement officials. This determination must look to the totality of circumstances as well as to the established legal significance of each individual circumstance.

The crucial interrogation in this case was that conducted by Spahr and DeLisle beginning at about 10:00 a.m. on March 6, 1957. No case has come to our attention in which since *Chambers v. Florida, supra,* any federal appellate court, on a record disclosing the totality of circumstances surrounding that interrogation, approved of the use of the resulting admissions. Those circumstances include the absence of *Miranda*-type warnings; the knowledge on the part of the prosecuting authorities that Smith wanted counsel and Smith's knowledge that his effort to reach an attorney had been frustrated;[17] the fact of continuous custody from 11:30 p.m. on March 5, 1957; the fact of intermittent but substantially uninterrupted, incommunicado interrogation for most of the intervening time; the submission to a naked physical examination; the taking of hair samples, fingernail pairings and fingerprints; the removal of his clothing and the substitution of prison garb; the forcible physical reaction to Smith's one effort to leave; the confrontation with the bloody pants; the continuation of interrogation after Smith's wife identified the pants as his; the substitution of a new relay of interrogators; Smith's gradual deteri-

---

[16] See *Darwin v. Connecticut,* 391 U.S. 346 (1968); *Greenwald v. Wisconsin,* 390 U.S. 519 (1968); *Brooks v. Florida, supra; Clewis v. Texas, supra; Davis v. North Carolina, supra; Haynes v. Washington, supra; Lynumn v. Illinois,* 372 U.S. 528 (1962); *Culombe v. Connecticut,* 367 U.S. 568 (1961); *Reck v. Pate,* 367 U.S. 433 (1961); *Blackburn v. Alabama,* 361 U.S. 199 (1960); *Spano v. New York,* 360 U.S. 315 (1959); *Payne v. Arkansas,* 356 U.S. 560 (1958); *Fikes v. Alabama, supra; Leyra v. Denno,* 347 U.S. 556 (1954); *Harris v. South Carolina,* 338 U.S. 68 (1949); *Turner v. Pennsylvania,* 338 U.S. 62 (1949); *Watts v. Indiana, supra; Haley v. Ohio, supra; Malinski v. New York,* 324 U.S. 401 (1945); *Ashcraft v. Tennessee,* 322 U.S. 143 (1944); *Ward v. Texas,* 316 U.S. 547 (1942); *White v. Texas,* 310 U.S. 530 (1940); *Chambers v. Florida,* 309 U.S. 227 (1940).

[17] Cf. *Escobedo v. Illinois,* 378 U.S. 478 (1964).

oration of spirit from cocky and confident at 11:30 p.m. on March 5, to subdued at 2:30 a.m. on March 6, to very restless and apprehensive and markedly agitated at 7:55 a.m. on March 6, to broken and crying when finally trapped into an incriminating admission after 10:00 a.m.; the interrogators' preconceived scheme for trapping Smith into a damaging admission, including their appeal to religion, their indication of the certainty of scientific detection; and the suggestion of leniency implicit in the reference to the Ledwin case.

Shedding light on the essentially coercive nature of the Spahr-DeLisle interrogation is the subsequent conduct of the Prosecutor who, instead of taking Smith before a magistrate at a time when under the applicable state court rule this was clearly required, continued the incommunicado interrogation for an additional six hours for the purpose of obtaining additional incriminatory statements.

The admissions made to Detectives Spahr and DeLisle on the morning of March 6, 1957, were the results of a cumulation of coercive circumstances which made those admissions involuntary under federal constitutional standards. Moreover, the totality of circumstances, beyond the sum of component facts, compels me to find that these admissions were involuntary. The admission of the testimony of Spahr and DeLisle at Smith's trial violated the due process clause of the Fourteenth Amendment.

The Ehrenbeck transcript (Ex. R-26 (Ex. 3-84 in the trial record)) stands on no better footing. The coercive circumstances increased by the time the interrogation reflected therein commenced. Adding to circumstances already alluded to was the presence of a juror and an official court reporter both so identified to Smith. Smith must have been left with the quite correct impression that even the judicial machinery was allied with the Prosecutor in his ongoing interrogation. The calculated steps taken to give an appearance of voluntariness during this interrogation are not convincing. They tend as much to shed light on the essentially coercive atmosphere as to show that Smith was acting voluntarily. The admissions made by Smith on the afternoon of March 6, 1957, at the Prosecutor's office, at the murder scene, and at the trailer, were all the result of coercion, and their admission at the trial violated the due process clause of the Fourteenth Amendment.

Independent of the coercive circumstances surrounding the interrogation reflected in the Ehrenbeck transcript, there was no break in the chain of events between that interrogation and the admissions made to Spahr and DeLisle. This alone is enough to make the later confession inadmissible. *Darwin v. Connecticut,* 391 U.S. 346, 349, 351 (1968); *Leyra v. Denno,* 347 U.S. 556 (1954).

The "acknowledgement" admission made to DeLisle in the Bergen County jail on March 11, 1957, must next be considered. That incident falls squarely within the holding of *Massiah v. United States,* 377 U.S. 201 (1964). Were I free to do so I would apply *Massiah* retroactively to this case. That course is ruled out by *United States ex rel. Allison v. New Jersey,* 418 F.2d 332 (3 Cir. 1969), cert. denied, 39 U.S.L.W. 3149 (Oct. 12, 1970), holding *Massiah* to be non-retroactive, although it could have been decided on the ground that it involved the equivalent of a guilty plea. See *McMann v. Richardson,* 397 U.S. 759 (1970); *Parker v. North Carolina,* 397 U.S. 790 (1970); cf. *Brady v. United States,* 397 U.S. 472 (1970).

But in this case, in any event, the "acknowledgement" obtained so as to make the Ehrenbeck transcript admissible in evidence was the fruit of the prior coercive questioning, and the prior illegality was not attenuated by intervening events. To the contrary, this was a clear case of an attempt to exploit the illegally obtained transcript. Cf. *Wong Sun v. United States,* 371 U.S. 471, 488 (1963). Use of the verbal acknowledgement in order to qualify the Ehrenbeck transcript for admission in evidence as a written confession violated the due process clause of the Fourteenth Amendment.

Finally there is the use made at trial of the admissions made to the psychiatrists. These, too, were so directly related to the admissions elicited on March 6 that they could not properly have been availed of. The fact that they were brought out at the trial on cross-examination of Smith puts them in no better footing. They resulted from the chain of coercive events. *Harrison v. United States,* 392 U.S. 219 (1968). Moreover, as found hereinabove, the examination by the psychiatrists took place pursuant to an understanding of the Bar that amounted to informal compliance with N.J.S. 2A:163-2. The examinations were facilitated by court orders transferring the prisoner from the jail to the Prosecutor's office. They could have been ordered. *State v. Whitlow, supra.* Use of incriminating statements obtained in such circumstances is impermissible. Cf. *Murphy v. Waterfront Commission,* 378 U.S. 52 (1964). The actual use of compelled incriminatory statements was never permitted, even under *Twiping v. New Jersey,* 211 U.S. 78 (1908) and *Adamson v. California,* 332 U.S. 46 (1947). The use made in Smith's trial was far more than mere prosecutorial comment. The admissions to the psychiatrists were used to authenticate the truthfulness and voluntariness of other statements improperly admitted.

The respondent presented the testimony of the same three psychiatrists in this hearing. Each stated his expert opinion that the admissions made by Smith on March 6 were the result of his free will and rational choice. I have taken this testimony into account despite the fact that it was strenuously objected to on most of the usual grounds advanced in opposition to the use of expert testimony. On all the evidence I have reached a conclusion different from that proposed by these experts. Expert opinion evidence is valuable on the ultimate issue to be decided only to the extent that the expert can by reasoned exposition demonstrate to the trier of fact the factual basis for his opinion. The testimony of the psychiatrists, rested upon an examination of Smith held for a different purpose over thirteen years ago, and on inferences to be drawn from written materials only some of which are in evidence. No convincing demonstration of the likely truth of their conclusions was made. Indeed in some instances their testimony acknowledged the presence of coercive factors during Smith's interrogation. Thus, while giving due regard to their testimony I have rejected their proposed conclusions on the ultimate issues decided in this proceeding.

The writ of habeas corpus will issue unless within sixty days of the date hereof the State of New Jersey shall grant to the petitioner Edgar Smith a new trial on the indictment charging him with the murder of Victoria Zielinski, at which none of the admissions made by him on the morning of March 6, 1957, to Detectives Spahr and DeLisle, the admissions in the Ehrenbeck transcript, the "acknowledgement" of that transcript made to Detective DeLisle on March 11, 1957, or the admissions made to Drs. Collins, Spradley and Zigarelli in March of 1957 shall be admitted in evidence.

It is so Ordered.

JOHN J. GIBBONS
Circuit Judge Sitting by
Designation

Appendix II

OPINION OF THE COURT OF APPEALS

(Filed—August 2, 1971)

UNITED STATES COURT OF APPEALS

FOR THE THIRD CIRCUIT
No. 71-1490
UNITED STATES OF AMERICA
ex rel. EDGAR H. SMITH,
vs.
HOWARD YEAGER, Warden, New Jersey
State Prison, Trenton,

Appellant.

(D. C. Civil Action No. 766-65)
APPEAL FROM THE UNITED STATES DISTRICT COURT
FOR THE DISTRICT OF NEW JERSEY
Argued July 14, 1971
Before GANEY, VAN DUSEN and ALDISERT,
Circuit Judges

PER CURIAM:

This appeal by the state of New Jersey from the grant of a writ of habeas corpus presents a pre-*Miranda* question whether inculpatory statements of Edgar H. Smith were the voluntary product of a free and unconstrained will.

Following an evidentiary hearing after remand by the United States Supreme Court,[1] the district court concluded that the "ad-

---

[1] Smith v. Yeager, 393 U. S. 122 (1968). See also United States ex rel. Smith v. Yeager, 395 F. 2d 245 (3rd Cir. 1968); 322 F. 2d 810 (3rd Cir. 1963); State v. Smith, 27 N. J. 433, 142 A. 2d 890 (1958); State v. Smith, 29 N. J. 561, 150 A. 2d 769, *cert. denied* 361 U. S. 861 (1959); United States ex rel. Smith v. New Jersey, 201 F. Supp. 72 (D. N. J.), *affirmed* 322 F. 2d 810 (3rd Cir. 1962), *cert. denied* 376 U. S. 928 (1964); State v. Smith, 443 N. J. 67, 202 A. 2d 69 (1964), *cert. denied* 379 U. S. 1005, *rehearing denied* 380 U. S. 938 (1965).

missions made to detectives Spahr and DeLisle on the morning of March 6, 1957, were the result of a culmination of coercive circumstances which made those admissions involuntary under federal constitutional standards. . . . The Ehrenbeck transcript . . . [and] [t]he admissions made by Smith on the afternoon of March 6, 1957, at the Prosecutor's office, at the murder scene, and at the trailer, were all the results of coercion, and their admission at the trial violated the due process clause of the Fourteenth Amendment." —— F. Supp. ——, —— (D. N. J. 1971) (slip opinion at 38-39). We agree.

We hold that there was sufficient evidence adduced at the hearing to support the district court's ultimate findings, considering "the totality of circumstances" under the contemporary case law of 1957 elaborating the due process standard of voluntariness. *Fikes* v. *Alabama*, 352 U. S. 191 (1957); *Turner* v. *Pennsylvania*, 338 U. S. 62 (1949); *Haley* v. *Ohio*, 332 U. S. 596 (1948); *Malinski* v. *New York*, 324 U. S. 401 (1945).

Additionally, upon review of the record, including the testimony of the psychiatrists, referred to in the district court's opinion, —— F. Supp. at ——, —— (slip opinion at 28-31, 40-41), we have concluded that the court did not err in ruling that relator's statements to these physicians were inadmissible as substantive evidence of guilt.

We have considered all of the contentions presented by able counsel for appellant by brief and oral argument. Our own independent review of the evidence does not persuade us that the district court made findings of historical facts which were clearly erroneous or erred in its ultimate conclusions.

For the foregoing reasons, and for the reasons set forth by the district court supporting its conclusion of coercion, —— F. Supp. at ——, —— (slip opinion at 1-28, 34-39), the judgment of the district court[2] will be affirmed, subject however to the previous

---

[2] The original order of May 13, 1971, directed that the writ of habeas corpus would issue unless the state

shall grant to the petitioner Edgar Smith a new trial on the indictment charging him with the murder of Victoria Zielinski, at which none of the admissions made by him on the morning of March 6, 1957, to Detectives Spahr and DeLisle, the admissions in the Ehrenbeck transcript, the "acknowledgement" of that transcript made to Detective DeLisle on March 11, 1957, or the admissions made to Drs. Collins, Spradley and Zigarelli in March of 1957 shall be admitted in evidence.

The amended order of June 8, 1971, provides, inter alia:

The order of this court filed May 13, 1971, hereby is amended to order of this Court, filed June 9, 1971, which vacated paragraphs 2 through 5 inclusive of the June 8, 1971 District Court order. This action is without prejudice to relator's right to apply for release on bail to the state judiciary under appropriate New Jersey law, N.J.S.A. Const. Art. 1, §11. The mandate shall issue in one week.

A True Copy:
Teste:

Clerk of the United States Court
of Appeals for the Third Circuit.

---

provide that the writ of habeas corpus will issue unless within sixty days of the date of final disposition of the appeal of this matter the State of New Jersey shall grant to the petitioner a new trial on the indictment.

Appendix III

On Tuesday, October 12, 1971, New Jersey's last attempt to have Judge Gibbons' ruling overturned failed when the United States Supreme Court, in a unanimous ruling, refused to hear the state's appeal.